D0536505

An Imprint of Sterling Publishing
387 Park Avenue South
New York, NY 10016

This 2013 edition published by Sandy Creek.

Original text: Simona Cervetto, Gaia Giuffredi, Michela Pistidda, Marco Scuderi, Lucio Di Carlo, Marco Scuderi
Illustrations: Marco Ferraris, Leonardo Meschini, Stefano Scagni, Studio Caba & Chesi
Translation: Bronia Fuchs-Willig

ISBN 978-1-4351-5076-8

Manufactured in China

Lot #:
2 4 6 8 10 9 7 5 3 1
06/13

Did You Know?

With **Questions** & **Answers**

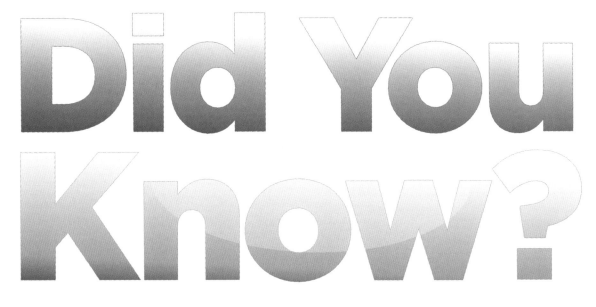

Contents

THE WORLD AROUND US

THE UNIVERSE

The Universe, which is also called the cosmos, includes everything that surrounds us in space – the galaxies, planets, stars, nebulae, black holes, etc. However, according to scientists, we really only know one-tenth of its contents. Even though we do not know whether or not the Universe is finite, 90% of it remains totally unknown! Are there other forms of life out there besides human life?

How was the Universe born?

There are a number of different theories as to how the Universe was created, the most plausible being the Big Bang. About 15 billion years ago, there was a colossal explosion which generated gases and dust. These produced the various galaxies with their stars and planets!

Some scientists believe that the Universe was born 15 billion years ago with the Big Bang; others think that it is infinite and has always existed.

What does a galaxy consist of?

It consists of gas, interstellar dust, and several billion heavenly bodies (planets, comets, stars, asteroids, etc.). They form a group called a cluster which revolves around the center of the galaxy. There are billions of galaxies in the Universe, all with different shapes: elliptical, spiral, and irregular.

How is the Universe expanding?

When astronomers observe the galaxies, they can see that they are moving away from our own galaxy. The further away they are, the faster they move away. This is what is meant by the expansion of the Universe. If this phenomenon continues, several billion years later the old stars will gradually die and the Universe will become black and cold.

What is the "Milky Way"?

This is the galaxy that we live in; it contains almost 140 billion stars, including the Sun. It is a spiral-shaped galaxy, 100,000 light years in diameter. The Milky Way can be seen from Earth with the naked eye. It was discovered by the Italian astronomer Galileo in 1610. In the night sky, it can be seen as a long cloud of white gas. Its milky color gave it its name!

Andromeda is one of the three galaxies that are closest to the Milky Way. It is also the farthest that can be seen with the naked eye.

DID YOU KNOW?

THE SPEED OF LIGHT
Light travels in a vacuum at a speed of roughly 185,000 miles per second. The light year is a unit used to calculate distance in space. It is the distance which a ray of light travels in a vacuum for one year. Its symbol is "ly."

WEIGHTLESSNESS
When a spacecraft leaves Earth to go into orbit, the astronauts and objects inside it became weightless. Whether they were originally as light as feathers or as heavy as lead, they weigh nothing here. They are said to be weightless and float around the cabin, moving slowly.

ASTRONAUTS
The first human to visit outer space was Yuri Gagarin. He rocketed into space on April 12th, 1961 and remained in orbit for 1 hour 48 minutes! The first woman in space was the Russian Valentina Tereshkova in June 1963 on board *Vostok 6*. Since then, many astronauts have traveled into space.

STARS

Stars are heavenly bodies which create their own light. Because they are so far away from Earth, they look like pinpoints of light in the sky, even when observed through powerful telescopes. By studying them regularly over a number of years, their movements can be calculated. The Sun is the closest star to Earth.

A group of stars which appear to form a particular picture is called a constellation. Orion is one of the brightest constellations that can be observed from Earth.

What are stars made of?

A star is a gigantic ball of gases which become incandescent through nuclear fusion reactions produced inside it. Our star, the Sun, is made almost entirely of hydrogen and helium. Its inner temperature is about 28 million degrees, whereas it is only about 10,832°F on its surface.

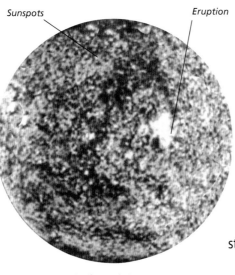

Sunspots   Eruption

Surface of the Sun

How is a star born?

In galaxies, stars are born from very cold clouds consisting basically of hydrogen and helium. As they collide with each other, the atoms of gas set off a chemical reaction which creates heat. A hot, gaseous ball forms – a star!

How long does a star live?

To humans, a star may seem eternal, yet this is not the case. Stars are born and die. The most massive stars quickly burn up the gases of which they are made and only live for hundreds of thousands of years. But the smallest ones have far longer lifetimes – millions or even billions of years!

Nebulae are clusters of stars and interstellar matter.

What is a comet made of?

It consists of a solid nucleus made of rock, dust and ice. As it nears the Sun, this nucleus heats up and the ice suddenly evaporates. The gases, along with the dust and rocky lumps, form a fuzzy head (a halo surrounding a nucleus) and a long luminous tail, which is the only part that can be seen from Earth with the naked eye.

Every year, around the middle of August, watching shooting stars is a fabulous experience. On a dark night, you can see dozens of them. Find out on the internet or in science journals the exact dates when these showers of shooting stars are due to occur.

DID YOU KNOW?

PULSARS
First observed in 1967, pulsars are stars made up of neutrons. As they spin very rapidly on their axes (6 million times faster than Earth), they emit electromagnetic waves which can be seen with the naked eye because they flash at regular intervals.

SUPERNOVAE
A supernova is a massive star which is dying. As it explodes, it produces an exceptional amount of light. The death of this heavenly body can give birth to many new stars! The largest ever observed is the Supernova 1987 A, which, as its name indicates, was discovered in 1987!

BLACK HOLES
These are areas in space with such an enormous gravitational pull that they drag in any nearby particles. Spherical in shape, they are called "black holes" because even rays of light are captured by them and can no longer be seen!

THE SOLAR SYSTEM

Situated in the Milky Way, this is the planetary system to which Earth belongs. In its center is our star, the Sun, around which orbit a large number of heavenly bodies, such as the planets and their satellites, asteroids, comets, and meteorites.

All the planets in the Solar System spin on their own axes as well as orbiting the Sun.

Which planet is furthest from the Sun?

It is Neptune. Invisible from Earth, it was discovered by the German Johann Galle in 1846, thanks to the work of the Frenchman Urbain Le Verrier and the Englishman John Adams. Its diameter is 4 times that of the Earth but its mass is 17 times smaller! It was named after the sea god of Roman mythology, who was represented by a trident.

What are the planets in the Solar System?

There are eight of them. Four are close to the Sun and called rocky planets, because they are solid, consisting of rock. These are Mercury, Venus, Earth, and Mars. The other four are gigantic gas planets, a long way from the Sun: Jupiter, Saturn, Uranus, and Neptune. Apart from Mercury and Venus, they all have bodies orbiting around them. These bodies are called natural satellites or moons.

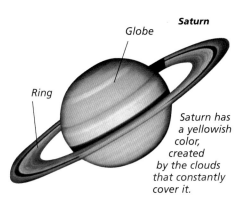

Saturn

Globe

Ring

Saturn has a yellowish color, created by the clouds that constantly cover it.

What is Saturn?

Saturn is the 6th planet in our Solar System. A thousand times larger than Earth, it has a number of small concentric rings around it. These rings are made of pieces of icy rock. Seen from Earth, Saturn has a flat coloured band orbiting around it. It takes more than 29 years for this planet to revolve around the Sun! Earth does it in one year!

Pluto

Rocky globe

Icy surface

Pluto was originally thought to be a planet in the Solar System in its own right, but this is no longer the case.

DID YOU KNOW?

ARTIFICIAL SATELLITES
Any object set in orbit around Earth or any other planet for scientific or technological reasons is an artificial satellite. The first artificial satellite, *Sputnik 1*, was launched on October 4th 1957.

METEORITES
These are heavenly bodies which fall onto Earth's surface. As they travel through the atmosphere they disintegrate, but some may still weigh several tons when they smash into Earth! The largest shower of meteorites took place in Namibia in 1836.

Meteorite fragment

COMETS
Comets were originally thought to be atmospheric phenomena. In 1577, the astronomer Tycho Brahe proved that they were heavenly bodies. However, in the following century, Newton proved that comets were subject to the same laws of movement as the planets.

THE MOON

This is Earth's only natural satellite. Roughly 400 times smaller than our star (the Sun), the Moon is 400 times closer to Earth. This is why it is visible from here with the naked eye. Its temperatures are extreme, going from -274°F on the side not exposed to the Sun to over 248°F on the other side.

The first man to walk on the surface of the Moon was Neil Armstrong, the American commander of Apollo 11. He and his team landed on July 21st, 1969.

What is a sidereal month?

This is the time it takes for the Moon to orbit the Earth completely. This period, called a revolution, lasts approximately 29 days. The Moon also spins on its own axis; this is called a period of rotation.

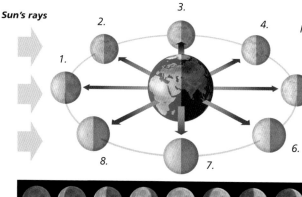

Sun's rays

1.   2.   3.   4.   5.   6.   7.   8.

As the Moon travels around the Earth, varying amounts of its surface are exposed to the Sun. This creates different phases: 1. New Moon; 2. Waxing Crescent Moon; 3. First quarter; 4. Waxing Gibbous Moon; 5. Full Moon; 6.Waning Gibbous Moon; 7. Last quarter; 8.Waning Crescent Moon.

What would you weigh on the Moon?

You would weigh about one-sixth what you do on Earth. Since the Moon has a smaller mass than Earth, its gravitational force on humans and objects is lower than on our planet. In 1969, when Neil Armstrong became the first man to walk on the Moon, he moved forward in great bounds with no effort at all.

In 1959, the Soviet space probe Lunik was able to observe the hidden face of the Moon for the first time.

Why do we always see the same face of the Moon?

Because the Moon spins on its axis at the same speed as it orbits our planet, the same side is always turned toward Earth.

Does the Moon produce light?

No, only stars can do this. We can only see the Moon from our planet because the Sun's light is reflected on its surface.

Moon's surface

DID YOU KNOW?

THE MOON AND TIDES

Tides are alternating movements of the sea's level (low tide and high tide). They are caused by the pull of the Moon and Sun on the mass of water in the oceans.

LUNAR CRATERS

These are holes visible on the surface of the Moon. Scientists have two theories as to their origins: some think that craters are volcanic, while others believe that they were produced by the impact of asteroids and meteorites. Bailly, the largest crater, has a diameter of almost 177 miles.

WEREWOLVES

Popular belief in the existence of werewolves was particularly widespread in the 19th century and later appeared in horror stories. Also called lycanthropes, they were men who would change into monsters at the full Moon. Half man and half wolf, they would turn into men again at dawn.

CLIMATES

There are four zones in various parts of the globe: the equatorial, which is the hottest zone; the tropical, which is very wet with high temperatures; the temperate zone, where it is neither too hot nor too cold; and, finally, the polar zone, which is very cold.

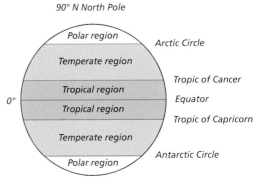

90° N North Pole

Polar region — Arctic Circle

Temperate region

Tropical region — Tropic of Cancer

0° — Equator

Tropical region — Tropic of Capricorn

Temperate region — Antarctic Circle

Polar region

90° S South Pole

Each climatic zone has its own type of vegetation: tundra, savannah, etc.

What is the difference between climate and meteorology?

Meteorology forecasts the weather at a particular place and a given time. On the other hand, climate collects all the meteorological data over many decades for a well-defined zone. In this way, a region can be said to be arid, rainy, icy, etc.

In the tropical region, there are huge rain forests because it is very hot with abundant rainfall.

The Earth seen from outer space

What factors determine climate?

These are of the utmost importance, because they are responsible for the main climate changes. They include geographical position of the region (its latitude on our planet), its pollution (the greenhouse effect can play a very important part in climate change), and its surroundings (whether or not it is close to rivers, oceans, or mountains).

How is climate measured?

By taking into account a great many elements: temperature, humidity, atmospheric pressure, winds, sun, and precipitation. By gathering all this data over a long period, scientists are able to determine the climate of a region. Scientists observe different climatic factors which influence the large plant formations on Earth.

A temperate climate has clearly defined seasons: summers are fairly hot and winters are cold and wet.

A mountain landscape typically has forests, snow, and glaciers at a high altitude.

DID YOU KNOW?

SNOWFLAKES
Each snowflake has a unique shape: created by tiny needles of ice which become stuck together in random fashion; its structure may seem identical to that of all the other snowflakes, but this is not at all the case.

THE COLDEST INHABITED PLACE
Oymyakon, a town in Siberia, northern Russia, holds the record for the coldest temperature; it fell to -90°F in February 1933.

THE HOTTEST INHABITED PLACE
The highest temperature ever recorded in the shade was 136°F. The Libyan town of Al'aziziyah in the Sahara desert has held this record since September 13th, 1922. However, in this region, the temperature can drop below freezing at night!

METEOROLOGY

This is the science that studies the atmosphere: that is, its temperature, pressure, rainfall, the direction and speed of winds, etc. The ancient Greeks were the first to study the atmosphere, but it was not until the 19th century that their fundamental theories could be seriously tested, by means of new discoveries in thermodynamics and fluid mechanics.

Why does it rain?

Clouds consist of ice crystals which become heavier when the temperature drops. These crystals then fall to the ground in the form of rain, snow, or hail. For this to occur, the temperature inside the cloud has to drop to at least -40°F.

"Water cycle" is the name given to the different states through which water passes on our planet: liquid, solid or gas. It can undergo a great many transformations: it may evaporate, condense, fall as rain and fill the oceans or freeze and become ice.

Clouds

Glacier

Air currents

Evaporation

Sea

Lake

Outlet

Subterranean infiltration

Tributary

Water cycle

Mouth of a river

What is meant by atmosphere?

It is a layer of gas and dust surrounding the planets, stars, and some satellites. The Earth's atmosphere consists of nitrogen, oxygen, argon, and minute quantities of other gases.

Where does the wind come from?

It is produced by the difference in atmospheric pressure between two geographical regions. Winds are said to be dominant, seasonal, local, or cyclonic.

Why does it snow?

When the air temperature is low close to the Earth's surface, in the troposphere, ice crystals stick to dust particles and form flakes. Snow will remain on the ground only if the temperature is 0°C or less.

When snow has a soft structure, skiers call it "powdery."

DID YOU KNOW?

CYCLONES
Also called hurricanes or typhoons, they form over the seas in low-pressure areas. The warm air close to the water is blocked by the mass of colder air higher up and can only escape toward the sky by forming a whirlwind inside a column. A cyclone can be over 300 miles in diameter.

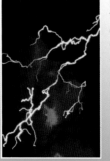

LIGHTNING
This is an electrical discharge between two clouds or between a cloud and the Earth's surface. It can be several miles long and can often be seen (flashes) or heard (thunder).

HAIL
This is a solid form of precipitation. The drops of rain inside clouds freeze and stick together, turning into seeds of ice, called hailstones. When they become too heavy, they fall to the Earth's surface. The largest hailstone to have fallen in the United States was over 6 inches in diameter, the size of a melon.

ECOLOGY

This is the study of the interaction between living beings (animals, humans, and plants) and their environment. For example, this science enables us to understand the negative ways in which humans affect their planet!

Satellite picture of cloud formations over the Pacific Ocean and the American continent

What is an ecosystem?

It is a group of animals and plants (called biocoenosis) living in the same surroundings (the biotope). The biocoenosis and biotope depend on each other in order to co-exist in a sustainable way. For this reason, it is vital to preserve the fragile balance of an ecosystem.

Greenhouse gas emissions are one of the principal sources of pollution on our planet. They are generated by fossil fuel combustion (oil, coal, natural gas) used in industry and transport.

Forest habitats are being threatened by acid rain, fires, and destruction by man.

How can we preserve our environment?

Everyone can play a part by throwing waste into suitable containers for recycling (paper, glass, plastic, cans, etc.), saving water and electricity, using renewable energy, riding a bicycle instead of taking the car to school or the local bakery, etc.

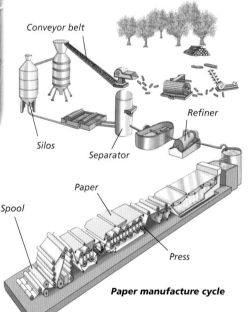

Conveyor belt

Silos

Separator

Refiner

Paper

Spool

Press

Paper manufacture cycle

How does pollution affect our planet?

Carbon dioxide (CO_2) pollution produced by industrial smoke and exhaust from vehicles (like planes and cars) is the main cause of the greenhouse effect. This is causing the planet to become hotter and hotter, so that polar glaciers and ice on high mountains melt, the sea level rises, drought or flooding increases, and so on.

DID YOU KNOW?

NUCLEAR REACTORS
These huge generators produce electricity and the smoke which comes out is only steam. So, one could think that they are ecological, but this is not so! On the contrary, they are very dangerous for humans and the planet, as they generate radioactive nuclear waste which they cannot dispose of.

RECYCLING
We can all play our part in saving our planet. When you throw waste into the correct container, it can then be recycled. For example, instead of cutting down a tree to make paper, the newspapers you throw away can be used to make others. This goes for glass, hard plastic, tin cans, etc.

WIND TURBINES
Wind turbines have large blades which turn at varying speeds, according to the strength of the wind. These generators turn mechanical energy into electricity, which is then stored in accumulators for use when needed. There are enormous wind turbines out in fields, but also small ones on the roofs of houses.

SEAS AND OCEANS

Seas and oceans cover around 71% of the Earth's surface and play a large part in determining the climate of our planet. They also supply humans with enormous resources: food (fish, shellfish, and algae), mining (metals), and energy (oil, gas, etc.).

Waves are masses of water which rise and fall on the surface of the sea.

Why is the sea salty?

As river water travels down from its source, it erodes the surrounding rocks and becomes rich in minerals (mineral salts) before flowing into the sea. In addition, the sun's rays evaporate seawater but not the salt particles it contains. Salinity can be quite different from one sea to another. This depends on how powerfully the river flows into its waters, as well as on the climate. The average salt content is about 4.7 oz of salt per gallon of water.

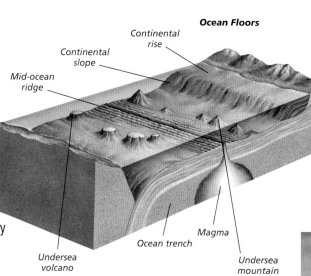

Ocean Floors

Continental rise
Continental slope
Mid-ocean ridge
Undersea volcano
Ocean trench
Magma
Undersea mountain

How were oceans formed?

As our planet evolved, its surface cooled down and solidified. This meant that water no longer evaporated as soon as it reached the ground. After a great many rainfalls, the water was able to flow across the Earth's crust, creating rivers and oceans.

Mont-Saint-Michel is famous for its huge tides.

What is a coral reef?

It is an underwater rock formation produced by the gradual build-up of calcium coral and polyp skeletons. Also called a barrier reef, it is found only near the coastline of warm seas. The largest of these, the Great Barrier Reef, is in Australia and is over 1,200 miles long.

The Great Barrier Reef contains a multi-coloured undersea world, incredibly rich in animal and plant species.

What is a tide?

This is the back-and-forth movement caused by the gravitational pull of the Sun and Moon on the Earth. There are two kinds of tides: high (called "flux") and low ("reflux"). These different tides can be used to make electricity, in a process called tidal generation.

DID YOU KNOW?

THE SALTIEST SEA
The salt content of the Dead Sea is about 6 times greater than that of other seas and oceans. This is due to the high degree of evaporation of its water. Also, it is in a region with very little rain. It is called the Dead Sea because no form of life is possible in it. This sea serves as the border between Israel and Jordan.

THE LARGEST OCEAN
The Pacific Ocean covers over one third of the Earth's surface. It is the deepest and oldest of all the oceans: some of its rocks are about 200 million years old! Magellan gave it its name in 1520 during his first crossing, because its waters seemed very calm.

TSUNAMIS
This Japanese word means "port wave." A tsunami is a succession of huge waves which move through the sea at great speed and crash onto the shore. They can reach a speed of 500mph, the speed of a passenger plane. Tsunamis are caused by earthquakes, volcanic eruptions, or undersea landslides.

RIVERS AND LAKES

River water generally comes from mountains, where glaciers melt, or, at lower altitudes, when snow turns into water. However, some rivers are filled with water from underground springs, in regions with a high rainfall.

This is a volcanic lake. The crater of the extinct volcano is filled with spring or rainwater.

Where do rivers flow?

They flow into seas and oceans or into interior lakes. The former are called exoreic and the latter endoreic. Some sections of a river can flow underground. The mouth of a river can form a delta (channels spread out in the shape of a triangle) or an estuary (channel shaped like a wide funnel).

A mountain torrent, with its characteristic pebbly bank, large rocks, and waterfalls.

Many animals and plants live in lakes and rivers and on their shores. They play an essential part in the ecology.

How are waterfalls formed?

They are generally created by the erosion of a river bed, which then creates a drop in level so that the water falls from a certain height to the level below. They can also be formed by the creation of a dam of rocks which prevents the water from flowing along its normal course. Some waterfalls can be artificially created.

What is a lake?

A lake is a basin, generally containing fresh water, which is not directly connected to a sea or ocean. Its water supply comes from rain but also from rivers and other watercourses called tributaries. When the water in a lake runs into a river, this watercourse is called an estuary or outlet. Lakes seem to dry up and disappear in a relatively short time: it is thought that those we know today are no more than 100,000 years old. On the other hand, the great rivers, like the Colorado in the United States, have been flowing for millions of years.

Where do lakes come from?

Lakes can be formed in a number of ways: their origins can be glacial, if they are created by glaciers; tectonic, if they come from a drop in the level of the ground; volcanic, if they flow into the craters of extinct volcanoes; or coastal, if they are an arm of the sea which has become isolated and closed off.

DID YOU KNOW?

LAKE BAIKAL
This lake in Siberia is the oldest and deepest in the world. It also contains the largest amount of fresh water, with almost 1,200 species of fauna, some of which can be found nowhere else in the world. In 1996, Unesco declared it a World Heritage site.

THE NILE DELTA
The mouth of the Nile is one of the world's largest deltas (9,200 sq miles). When it floods, the river deposits sediment on the surrounding land, which in turn acts as a fertilizer. This is why it is called the cradle of Egyptian civilization. The Nile divides into two branches when it flows into the Mediterranean.

THE AMAZON
This is the longest river in South America, covering over more than 2 million sq miles. More than 3,500 miles long, the Amazon runs through 6 countries: Brazil, Bolivia, Peru, Colombia, Ecuador, and Venezuela.

TEMPERATE FORESTS

They make up nearly half of the planet's forests. As their name suggests, they grow in regions where the climate is temperate, that is, neither too hot in summer nor too cold in winter. These forests are found mainly in Europe, North America, Japan, and parts of China.

Which animals live there?

A temperate climate, abundant food, and dense vegetation are the three conditions required for these forests to exist. This is why they are home to a large variety of fauna, from the smallest (insects, rodents, and birds, etc.) to the largest (deer, wild boar, and others).

From earliest times, temperate forests have been exploited by man: the wood from trees has been used as fuel or to build homes, furniture, etc. After years of uncontrolled deforestation, this destruction is being increasingly regulated.

Like all forests, the temperate forest is an ecosystem where all living beings form a food chain, that is, animals and birds live off each other.

What trees grow in temperate forests?

Apart from certain pines, most of their trees are deciduous, that is, their leaves fall in fall. Depending on whether these forests are in regions near the ocean or inland, they are composed of beech, oak, ash, elm, or hazel trees.

Why do leaves turn yellow?

In order to live and grow, a tree needs sunlight to produce chlorophyll and other substances. This is what gives leaves their green color. In fall, however, the hours of sunshine are fewer and the weather is colder. So, to save energy, the tree stops producing chlorophyll and the leaves change color and fall. As they decompose, they fertilize the ground.

An oak in fall

What threatens temperate forests?

Apart from deforestation by humans (even though this is subject to increasing controls), the main threats to these forests are air pollution, fires (whether lit deliberately or not), and acid rain.

DID YOU KNOW?

HIBERNATION
In winter, the vital functions of some animals (among invertebrates and mammals) slow down: they hibernate underground or in holes in trees and cease all outside activity. Many birds, on the other hand, migrate to warmer climates.

MUSHROOMS
These plants grow very rapidly in warm areas. They are often found near deciduous trees for two reasons: the trees' leaves protect the mushrooms from the sun's rays, and when the leaves fall, they decompose to form food for the mushrooms.

THE SEASONS
Temperate forests are found in regions with a four-season cycle: summer, when everything is green; fall, when plants and animals prepare to face the cold; winter, when all living creatures seem to be asleep; and, finally, spring, when mammals reproduce and buds appear on the trees.

TROPICAL FORESTS

Also called rain forests, they are found at latitudes situated between the Tropics of Cancer and Capricorn. They are very wet, with an average temperature of 77°F and abundant rainfall. The largest of these forests are to be found in Latin America, Africa, Australia, Malaysia, and India.

Leaf from a tropical plant

In these forests, the leaves are often long and their tips point downward so that rainwater can run off.

What lives in these forests?

Tropical forests are believed to contain about half of Earth's animal and vegetable species! Some members of the animal world are insects, parrots, hummingbirds, snakes, iguanas, geckos, chameleons, frogs, and monkeys. Most animals in tropical forests do not live in groups but alone or in pairs.

In tropical forests, most animal activity takes place at dawn, dusk, or night.

A night hunter, the red-eyed tree frog is an excellent acrobat.

What plants grow there?

The tropical forest contains several layers of plants: undergrowth (consisting mainly of ferns), trees of medium height and, finally, huge trees whose tops form a thick vault through which the sun's rays can barely filter. This upper section is called the canopy.

A Macaw

What part do these forests play on our planet?

They are considered the "lungs of the world," because their many trees absorb carbon dioxide (CO_2) and turn it into oxygen. As our industries and vehicles produce more and more CO_2, these forests play an essential role in preserving our planet.

Are we a threat to tropical forests?

Yes, because the trade in wood, especially in extremely rare species of tree, has led to intensive exploitation of the forests. We have endangered a great many species of plants and animals!

DID YOU KNOW?

ORANGUTANS
This Malay term means "man of the woods." These animals are so called because they bear a slight resemblance to humans and, during the day, swing through the forest from tree to tree on their long arms. This is called "brachiation." They feed chiefly on fruit, leaves and insects.

BUTTERFLIES
Hundreds of species of mainly multi-coloured butterflies live in the tropical forests. The cobra butterfly is a nocturnal variety and one of the largest in the world. Its wing span can reach a foot long.

TOUCANS
These birds can be recognized by their long, thick beaks, which are quite light despite their size. These beaks are used for gathering fruit, defending themselves and, in the case of males, fighting during the mating period. Some varieties, like rainbow toucans, exist in all colours.

GRASSLANDS

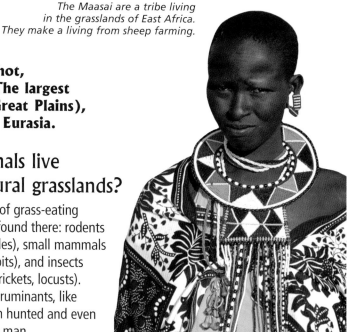

The Maasai are a tribe living in the grasslands of East Africa. They make a living from sheep farming.

These are areas in which very few trees grow. They are found in climates with cold winters and hot, dry summers. Rainfall there is low and irregular. The largest of these are found in North America (called the Great Plains), South America (pampas), Africa (savannahs), and Eurasia.

Prairie dogs

Prairie dogs are little American rodents.

What animals live in the natural grasslands?

A large number of grass-eating animals can be found there: rodents (prairie dogs, voles), small mammals (hares, wild rabbits), and insects (grasshoppers, crickets, locusts). Most large wild ruminants, like bison, have been hunted and even exterminated by man.

How important are grasslands for humans?

The ground in grasslands is fertile. For this reason, humans have been using them to raise cattle and grow crops. In temperate regions cultivated grasslands become fields of oats, alfalfa, or clover on which sheep, cows, or goats graze.

Grasses are the most widespread plants on the prairies, along with other herbaceous plants. Trees and bushes can be found growing on river banks.

Typical pampas vegetation

What kinds of grasslands are there?

They can be either natural or artificial. Once very extensive, natural grasslands were used as pastures for wild animals, but today some of these have been turned into wheat or cornfields. Artificial grasslands, on the other hand, have been planted by humans to feed their cattle.

DID YOU KNOW?

THE ARGENTINE PAMPA
The pampas are immense grasslands in Argentina where large herds of horses roam. The herdsmen are called "gauchos." This word dates from the 18th century and probably comes from the Arabic word meaning "man on horseback" or the Quechua Indian word for "motherless."

THE STEPPE
This is an entirely treeless plain; its vegetation consists only of short grass. These austere landscapes are found in regions with insufficient rainfall for plants to flourish. Summers are hot here and winters very cold.

THE AMERICAN PRAIRIE
This immense stretch of land is a typical American prairie. Its short vegetation, herds of bison and horses, and its lonely ranches have been the backdrop for many famous Westerns.

MOUNTAINS

Rhododendrons, snowdrops, gentian, edelweiss, and daffodils are just some of the flowers that grow at high altitudes.

This is the name given to reliefs which are at least 195 feet higher than the surrounding land. They form either massifs or a chain. Some are said to be young (like the Andes in South America or the European Alps) because they were formed only several million years ago. Others, like the Massif Central in France, go back at least 200 million years!

How are mountains formed?

They are created by tectonic plates: the Earth's surface consists of about a dozen plates which move an inch each year. They can either move apart or closer together. When they collide, this creates mountains over millions of years.

This illustration shows some of the animal species that live in the mountains: birds like the golden eagle and mammals like the gray wolf, brown bear, puma, chamois, and ibex, for example. Despite extreme temperatures, a wide variety of fauna and flora live in the mountains.

What is a glacier?

It is an enormous block of ice formed by the accumulation of compacted snow. Glaciers are found in polar regions or on mountains, at high altitudes.

What trees grow on mountains?

When one looks at a mountain from afar, one can see different levels of vegetation. On the lowest level are trees with deciduous leaves (which fall in autumn), while evergreen pines (with leaves in the shape of needles) grow on the upper levels. The higher one looks, the sparser the vegetation.

How are animals protected from the cold?

Some have a thick furry coat so that they can survive at extremely low temperatures. Others pass into a lethargic state in their dens, feeding from time to time on food they have collected during the fall.

DID YOU KNOW?

MONT-BLANC
This is the highest mountain in Western Europe, with a height of 13,700 ft. Situated on the border between France and Italy, it forms part of the Alps. Two French mountain-climbers, Jacques Balmat and Michel Paccard, were the first to climb it in 1786.

MOUNT EVEREST
Part of the Himalayas, on the border between Nepal and Tibet, Everest is the world's highest peak, 29,000 ft high. The first to reach the summit were Edmund Hillary and Tenzing Norgay, his Nepalese sherpa, in 1953.

MACHU PICCHU
This is a former citadel built in Peru by the Incas at a height of 6,700 ft. Its name means "old mountain." It is thought to have been built in the 15th century. Discovered in 1911, this town lies in a landscape of almost inaccessible mountains.

DESERTS

These are hostile regions where little or no vegetation can grow. Hot climates have mainly sand deserts, but in cold deserts the ground is frozen and icy. The largest hot desert is the Sahara in North Africa.

Dunes have different shapes: they can be crescent-shaped, elongated, or hills.

What is an oasis?

This is an area near a spring, in the middle of a hot desert. For thousands of years, oases have been indispensable for the humans and animals which cross these hostile regions. The vegetation and water found there provide shade for them to rest in and water to drink.

Today, many oases are artificial and are used for the cultivation of citrus fruits, dates, figs, olives, and apricots, as well as for raising cattle.

Where are the arid deserts found?

Some lie in the tropics (windy regions which are extremely hot during the day), others are in the middle of a continent where the clouds which form over the sea are so far away that they cannot approach them. Finally, there are the deserts near mountain chains which create a barrier to clouds and rain.

What are the different types of desert?

They can be classified in five groups: subtropical, coastal, continental, cold, and sheltered (those close to mountain chains which block cloud formation).

Needle rocks are created by wind or sand erosion.

Arizona desert

Sahara dune

The Sahara is a subtropical desert with an area of 3.5 million sq miles!

What are sand dunes?

They are hills of sand shaped by the winds. Their appearance is continually changing because of the force and direction of these winds. They are to be found chiefly in subtropical and continental deserts.

DID YOU KNOW?

CAMELS
Like dromedaries, camels are desert animals used by the local population. Their hoofs are flat to prevent them from sinking into the sand, and the two humps of fat on their backs enable them to remain without food and drink for several days at a time.

THE TUAREGS
These nomads of the Sahara live in small groups of 30 or 40. Their main activities are raising sheep and crops in the oases. They are also called "blue men" because of the color of their turbans.

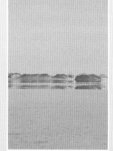

MIRAGES
These are natural optical illusions created when the sun's rays fall on layers of air of varying temperatures. These luminous rays are deflected, giving rise to images of men or objects on the ground that appear to be real.

POLAR REGIONS

These are the coldest areas of our planet. They lie at both poles of the Earth: the Arctic, in the north, an ocean surrounded by land, and, in the south, the Antarctic, a continent surrounded by seas and oceans.

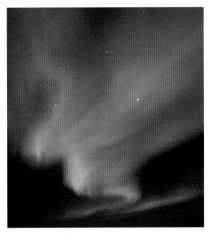

The luminous bands of the aurora borealis are green, red, or blue.

What is an iceberg?

An iceberg is an enormous block of ice which has become detached from an ice sheet or glacier. It floats along with the sea currents in the polar regions. As it consists of fresh water, it is less dense than seawater and is therefore able to float, even though 90% of it remains below water level. The "mountains of ice" are a source of danger for ships.

The largest iceberg ever seen had an area of 4,200 sq miles. The most famous iceberg in history is the one which caused the sinking of the Titanic on April 14th, 1912.

What is a polar aurora?

This is a light display which occurs in the upper atmosphere. Auroras can be coloured or black-and-white streams, columns, or spots. They can be admired both in the Arctic region (aurora borealis) or in the Antarctic (aurora australis).

Polar bear

Here we can see how blocks of snow are put together to form an igloo.

Who lives at the Poles?

The Antarctic has no inhabitants, apart from scientists who stay less than a year to undertake research. However, in the Arctic, things are different. During the Paleolithic era, around 10,000 BC, it is thought to have been inhabited by humans: the Inuit (or Eskimos) are believed to have come from Greenland via the Atlantic Ocean, and the Lapps are said to have come from Norway.

DID YOU KNOW?

THE INUIT
"Inuit" in Eskimo means "men." These skilful hunters and fishermen live in small communities. In former times, the Inuit spent their winters in snow houses, called "igloos." Today, they live in wooden or stone houses but still build igloos as shelters when they are out hunting.

TEMPERATURES
They are very cold. In summer, they rarely rise above 50°F, while in winter they are always below 32°F. The Antarctic has the world's lowest temperatures: in 1960, the thermometer fell to -126°F.

MINERAL RESOURCES
The Arctic has not only huge sources of gold, diamonds, uranium, and nickel but also oil and natural gas. In contrast, little is known of the underground mineral resources of the Antarctic.

ROCKS AND MINERALS

Rocks are hard matter formed by the accumulation of minerals found on the Earth's surface or deep below ground. The study of rocks and minerals is extremely important, as it enables us to understand the structure and composition of the Earth and make use of its resources. This science is called geology.

Mines are underground or open deposits from which minerals are extracted.

What are minerals?

They are solid substances which are found in their natural state in the Earth's crust. They can be either simple, consisting of a single chemical element, or compound, made up of several elements. The fragility or hardness and color of each mineral are determined by the way its atoms are distributed and linked together.

What do rocks consist of?

In general, rocks consist of a large number of minerals, but the one that is found in the largest quantities determines the type of rock it is. Granite, for example, is composed of a variety of minerals but mainly of quartz. There are three categories of rock: sedimentary (composed of layers of compressed sand, mud, and rock), igneous (made of cooled lava), and metamorphic (sedimentary and igneous rock altered by heat and pressure).

Geode

To find gold, rocks are excavated to reveal the gold-bearing veins, or sieves are dipped into rivers to find flakes and nuggets.

How many kinds of minerals are there?

Minerals are classified according to their chemical composition. There are eight categories: silicates (asbestos, quartz), carbonates (calcite, dolomite), sulfates (gypsum, barite), sulfosalts (argentopyrite, bornite), sulfides (pyrite), oxides and hydroxides (hematite, limonite), halides (halite), and native elements.

Block of calcite

What are native elements?

Gold, silver, and copper are said to be native minerals because they consist of only a single element. Diamonds and graphite also belong to this class because, while both are made up of carbon, they are not identical, as their atoms are assembled differently.

DID YOU KNOW?

TABLE SALT
This is a chemical compound called rock salt or halite which has cube-shaped crystals. It can either be mined or extracted from sea-salt by evaporation. Salt marshes are shallow pools whose water evaporates.

HARDNESS
The hardness of minerals, that is, their resistance to scratches, is an important quality. It is measured in numbers from 1 to 10 on the Mohs hardness scale. A fingernail can scratch talc and gypsum, whereas diamond is the hardest mineral of all.

GRAPHITE
Like diamond, it consists only of carbon atoms in horizontal layers, which makes graphite a brittle mineral. When mixed with pure clay, it is used as lead in our pencils.

VOLCANOES

A volcano begins in a hole in the Earth's crust from which lava, gases, and ashes escape when it erupts. Some volcanoes are considered to be extinct, while others are dormant and could erupt again. A volcanic eruption is most spectacular but also very dangerous for anyone living close by! The word "volcano" comes from the Latin "Vulcanus," meaning "Vulcan," the god of fire in Roman mythology.

Gases, ash, stone and magma come out of the volcano's main crater.

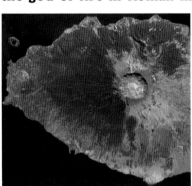
Tambora (9,350 ft), an active volcano on the island of Sumbawa (Indonesia) seen from a satellite. Over 60,000 people are said to have died when it erupted in 1815.

How are volcanoes formed?

By the action of the tectonic plates which form the Earth's surface. When they collide or move apart, these plates leave an opening for the magma far below, which is pushed to the surface by the pressure of the hot gases. At the fault lines at the edge of the plates, the magma gushes out, creating one or more volcanoes. Sometimes, the magma reaches a simple crack in the tectonic plate and pierces the Earth's crust, making a volcano.

What is magma?

It is melted, incandescent rock mixed with gases inside the depths of the Earth. As it is closer to the core with temperatures as high as 9,000°F, the magma is extremely hot. It rises to the Earth's crust through the pressure of the heat and gases.

Are there deep-sea volcanoes?

Yes, and there are far more than on the Earth's surface. They are mainly found along ocean ridges (mountain chains of tectonic origin which rise up from the ocean floor).

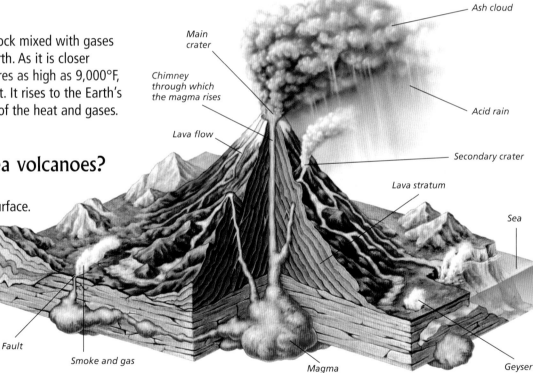

Ash cloud

Main crater

Chimney through which the magma rises

Acid rain

Lava flow

Secondary crater

Lava stratum

Sea

Fault

Smoke and gas

Magma

Geyser

DID YOU KNOW?

SANTORINI
On the Greek island of Thera, the volcano Santorini erupted around the middle of the 18th century BC. This was certainly one of the most gigantic volcanic eruptions in history. It is thought to have caused the disappearance of the Minoan civilization.

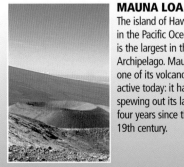

MAUNA LOA
The island of Hawaii in the Pacific Ocean is the largest in the Hawaiian Archipelago. Mauna Loa, one of its volcanoes, is still active today: it has been spewing out its lava every four years since the early 19th century.

ETNA
This active volcano in eastern Sicily is the highest in Europe (11,000 ft). Its most dramatic eruptions were those of 1169 (which destroyed the city of Catania) and 1928, when two villages were buried. Despite this, many people still live on its slopes today, even though it is still active!

ANIMALS

DINOSAURS

Oviraptor was a small fast-moving dinosaur from the end of the Cretaceous age. Its name means "egg stealer."

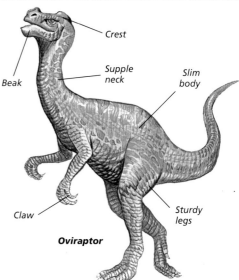

Crest

Beak

Supple neck

Slim body

Claw

Sturdy legs

Oviraptor

These reptiles appeared 230 million years ago and disappeared from the Earth's surface 65 million years ago. How do we know that they really existed? By the fossils that paleontologists discovered in the Earth's surface. Bones, teeth, and horns, for example, have been discovered on every continent, including the Antarctic.

Long jaw   **Compsognathus**

Sharp teeth

Short front legs

Did they live in herds?

It is thought that most herbivores did so in order to protect each other from predators. Some carnivorous animals also gathered together to hunt their prey.

Long tail   **Plateosaurus**

Plateosaurus was a 20-foot-long herbivore weighing nearly 4 tonnes!

Were all dinosaurs alike?

Apart from the fact that they were all reptiles, they were very different from each other. Diplodocus, for example, was as long as a tennis-court, while Compsognathus was the size of a chicken! Some moved on their hind legs (bipeds), others on all four legs (quadrupeds).

How can you recognize carnivores?

Generally by their pointed teeth, sharp claws, their relatively small or medium size, and their hind legs, which are far bigger than their front legs, allowing them to chase after their prey at great speed.

Small skull

Tail

Hollow vertebrae

Coelurus

Long hind legs

Very muscular tail

Tyrannosaurus Rex

How did dinosaurs vanish?

No one really knows! The cause could have been volcanic eruptions or an asteroid falling onto our planet. In both cases, which scientists believe quite possible, the sky would have been full of dust, preventing any sunlight from getting through. First plants, then herbivores, and finally carnivores would have died of cold or hunger!

Triceratops

DID YOU KNOW?

Fossil of a tridactyl (three-toed) foot

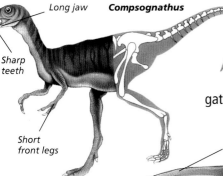

FOSSILS

By studying a dinosaur's remains, paleontologists can determine its size, shape, or behavior. Just a fossilised footprint can tell us if the animal was a quadruped or not. Fossilised excrement can inform scientists whether it was a vegetarian or carnivore.

TYRANNOSAURUS REX

This dinosaur, 16ft high, 45ft long and weighing 5 tonnes, was one of the most terrifying of all carnivores. Its 4-foot-long head had powerful jaws with about sixty pointed teeth, some measuring 6 inches.

IGUANODON

Its name means "iguana tooth," because its teeth were like that of present-day iguanas, even though it was 20 times as big! On each of its front toes, this herbivore had a bony spur which it used as a dagger to defend itself.

REPTILES

These are cold-blooded animals; that is, their body temperature depends on the surrounding temperature. This means that they cannot live in cold regions and when it is too hot, they retreat to take shelter under leaves or in water; otherwise, they will die.

The chameleon thrusts out its long sticky tongue onto its prey in a fraction of a second!

Land tortoise

What do they eat?

Different species have different diets. Some are herbivores (like many turtles), while others (lizards and chameleons) feed on insects. Crocodiles eat mammals; snakes prey on insects, eggs, small mammals, or other reptiles.

What is mimicry?

This is the ability of animals to camouflage themselves in their surroundings. Some reptiles do this very well: the vine snake is as green as the leaves of the trees in which it lives. When it is angry or feels endangered, the chameleon changes the color of its skin.

This snake kills its victims by injecting them with venom.

King cobra

Powerful tail   *Alligator*

Coral snake

This extremely venomous snake is no more than 35 inches long!

Where do they live?

They inhabit every continent except Antarctica. They are found on the ground, in trees, but also in water. Water-dwelling reptiles, like some snakes and turtles, can stay underwater for a long time without coming up for breath!

How do they reproduce?

By internal fertilization: that is, the male introduces its sperm into the body of the female. Most reptiles are oviparous: they lay their eggs in the ground, where the young hatch on their own.

Long snout with pointed teeth

Sturdy legs

This reptile lives mainly in water.

DID YOU KNOW?

SKIN
The skin of snakes is entirely covered with small side-by-side scales, like fish. Other reptiles (such as crocodiles) have huge scales on their backs or stomachs, while their legs are covered with very thick, grainy skin.

LIZARDS
There are about 3,800 species. Most have four legs, but some, like the glass-lizard and slow worm or blindworm, have no legs and look like snakes! Members of the saurian sub-family, lizards come in various sizes, from 5 inches to 10 feet long!

THE KOMODO DRAGON
This enormous lizard is the biggest of all, growing to a length of up to 10 feet and weighing more than 285 lbs. It is found on a number of Indonesian islands. When it bites, it inoculates its prey with a bacterium which can be deadly, making it a ferocious predator.

SNAKES

Members of the reptile family, they are easy to recognize by their long, scaly, legless bodies. There are about 3,000 species of snake. They are carnivorous animals, but each has its own way of killing its prey. Some inflict a deadly, venomous bite, others prefer to constrict or strangle the prey with their bodies.

Like many snakes, the boa can open its mouth very wide and so eat prey far larger than itself!

Slim neck

Triangular head

Muscular body

Red-tailed boa

Why are they called cold-blooded?

Because the temperature of their bodies depends on that of their surroundings. When it is too hot, they take shelter under leaves or in trees, and when it is too cold, they try to find sunshine.

Forked tongue

Snakes have protractile tongues (which can be stretched forward); they are forked (split in two).

How do they move around?

Ground snakes can move in many ways, the most common being a lateral undulating motion: with their supple spine and muscles, they use the irregularities on the ground (stones, earth, etc.) to lean on their sides and push themselves forward.

Hood

How do snakes smell odours?

They use their nostrils but mainly their tongues! By flicking it out at regular intervals, snakes gather microscopic particles of odours which are then transmitted to a part of their mouths near their palate called the Jacobson's organ. This is why they have such a highly developed sense of smell!

Over 16ft in length, the king cobra is the world's largest venomous snake.

King cobra

What is moulting?

This process occurs when a snake sheds its skin. As it grows in length, it has to do this, because its skin cannot keep stretching. To shed its skin, the snake rubs its muzzle against a rock to detach the old skin (called exuvia) from around its mouth. Then it simply crawls out of it, leaving the entire shed skin behind in one piece.

The emerald boa is common in the tropical forests of South America.

DID YOU KNOW?

RATTLESNAKES
Also called rattlers, these highly venomous snakes are found in North America. When it feels threatened, the snake vibrates the end of its tail, made of horny segments (the rattle), to produce a strident rattling sound.

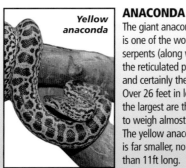
Yellow anaconda

ANACONDA
The giant anaconda is one of the world's largest serpents (along with the reticulated python) and certainly the heaviest. Over 26 feet in length, the largest are thought to weigh almost 440 lbs! The yellow anaconda is far smaller, no more than 11ft long.

MAMBAS
Closely related to the cobra family, there are four species of mambas. These agile and extremely venomous snakes are found in tropical Africa. They generally live in trees. Some can eat prey as large as mongooses or eagles!

AMPHIBIANS

These vertebrates spend part of their life in the water and the rest on land. Their lungs are not highly developed and some amphibians only breathe through the pores in their skin! There are three kinds: anurans (frogs, toads, and tree frogs), urodeles (salamanders and newts), and apoda (caecilians).

What do they feed on?

Although the tadpoles of some anurans are vegetarians, amphibians are carnivores. The largest ones can eat small rodents and fish, but most live on insects, slugs, and larvae. Many frogs and toads, as well as some salamanders, have a sticky tongue that they project outward at lightning speed to catch an insect in flight!

Easily recognised by its bright-red belly with black spots, this Oriental fire-bellied toad is an Asian toad.

The color of some toads and frogs is a camouflage, allowing them to hide in their natural surroundings.

Alpine newt

Spotted back

Belly free of spots

How do they walk?

Urodeles push themselves forward on their legs, while undulating their bodies and tails. Anurans walk on four legs and some even leap!

Where do they live?

They are found in water or near river banks. However, there are land species which return to the water only when reproducing.

How do they reproduce?

Once fertilised, the eggs, covered by a jelly-like membrane, are placed in the water or humid surroundings (in this case, an adult carries them into the water before they hatch). Out of the egg comes a sort of long, legless larva with gills for breathing. It undergoes a series of changes (metamorphoses) until it becomes an adult.

Two species of salamander

There are salamanders with no lungs which breathe through the pores in their skin!

DID YOU KNOW?

THE GECKO
This lizard has legs with suction pads under its feet, making it a very good climber. In Asia, they can even be found on walls or ceilings of houses!

THE RED SALAMANDER
Although it is found in great numbers in its natural habitat, it is difficult to see, because it comes out only at night and remains hidden during the day. It avoids exposing itself to sunlight because it becomes dehydrated very quickly and can die in minutes!

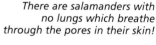

THE RED-EYED TREE FROG
Found in the tropical forests of South America, this amphibian is brightly coloured with red eyes, which are a sign to any predator that it is toxic when eaten!

ARACHNIDS

They belong to the class of chelicerate arthropods. Unlike insects, they have neither wings nor antennae and consist of two segments: the cephalothorax (head and thorax, which are fused) and the abdomen. In addition, they have eight legs. Members of this class include spiders, daddy-long-legs, scorpions, and acarina (ticks and mites).

The scorpion is a night hunter whose sting can be painful to humans but is rarely fatal.

Long, curved tail

Sting

Pedipalp

Leg for locomotion

The female scorpion gives birth to fully-formed young and always carries them with her on her back!

Are they oviparous?

Some are oviparous, others are not. After being fertilised, female ovipare lay her eggs in the ground or wrap them up in cocoons, whereas the eggs of ovovivipares develop inside the female's body and the young are born fully formed.

Are they venomous?

Yes, but not many of them. Some spiders have hooks on their mouths (chelicerae) containing venomous glands. Scorpions have a poisonous sting in their tails with which they attack their prey and inject their poison into them.

What do they eat?

They are mainly insectivores. Some species cover their prey in secretions from their mouth and digestive juices, which turn them into liquid. Then they simply suck them in to eat them! Other species are detritivores, which feed on decomposing organic matter.

Hairy legs

Tarantula

Pedipalp

Black and red tarantula

How do they hunt?

Each species has its own strategy for finding food. Scorpions use a poisonous sting to kill their prey; most spiders make a web and others hide in a hole and pounce on their victims.

The hairs on a spider's leg are sensory organs.

DID YOU KNOW?

SPIDER WEBS
The spider spins threads of silk secreted by its abdomen. When an insect is caught in the web, the spider pounces on its prey and paralyzes it with its venom. Sometimes it does not eat it all and envelops the remains in a cocoon which it uses as a larder!

ACARINA
There are about 7,000 species throughout the world. Many are so tiny that they are invisible to the naked eye, for their average length is 0.01 inch. One of the largest is the tick.

TICKS
A parasite living off a large number of animal species (bovines, dogs, cats, birds, humans, etc.), the tick is an acarina. It attaches to its victim's skin and sucks its blood. Its bite can transmit serious diseases.

INSECTS

Like the honeybee, the bumblebee is a pollinator, which enables flowers to reproduce.

There are nearly one million species of insects, recognizable according to two criteria: they have six legs and consist of three sections: the head, thorax, and abdomen. Some scientists (called entomologists) think that there are really 10 million species, because large numbers live in tropical forests and have not all been cataloged.

What do they eat?

They are basically vegetarians (eating flowers, plants, and berries), but some feed on other insects or their own larvae.

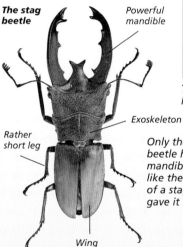

The stag beetle

Powerful mandible

Exoskeleton

Rather short leg

Wing

Only the male stag beetle has long mandibles shaped like the antlers of a stag (which gave it its name).

The grand monarch butterfly lives in North America but flies long distances to migrate to warmer countries in winter.

How do they reproduce?

They lay eggs, often in large quantities. To meet and reproduce, insects of both sexes use different methods: auditory, visual, or sensory signals.

Do they use mimicry?

Yes, many make use of it as a defense against predators. Some insects are shaped like twigs or leaves, others are the same color as the trees or plants on which they live.

Phasmid

Fine antenna

Elongated thorax

Leaf-shaped wing

Praying mantis

Once she has mated with the male, the female frequently eats him!

What is metamorphosis?

This refers to the different stages in an insect's development until it reaches adulthood. The butterfly, for example, begins as an egg (embryo). When it hatches, the insect becomes a larva (caterpillar) which spins a cocoon around itself. It then becomes a pupa (or chrysalis), the last stage before turning into a butterfly.

DID YOU KNOW?

THE FIREBUG
Easily recognizable by its red body with various black geometric patterns, this insect belongs to the bug family. It is called the firebug because its colours are reminiscent of the red and black uniforms once worn by firemen!

THE CRICKET
Unable to fly, this insect hops about. It is very well known for singing at sunset. Only the male sings, however. This sound is called stridulation and is made by rubbing its hard outer wings against each other.

INSECT SOCIETIES
Some insects, like bees, live in organized, hierarchical societies. An anthill contains the queen, the reproducing males and sterile individuals who are divided into two groups: the workers fetch food and take care of the nest, the soldiers protect the whole community.

INVERTEBRATES

These animals have no backbone and there are a great many of them! Invertebrates include worms, mollusks, echinoderms, and coelenterates or cnidarians. The French zoologist Jean-Baptiste Lamarck coined the term "invertebrate" in 1801. In 1815, he wrote a huge work of seven volumes on the subject, "The Natural History of Animals without Vertebrae"!

Starfish

A member of the echinoderm family, the starfish usually has five arms with suckers which enable it to move over rocks with no difficulty.

What are annelids?

These are a large group of invertebrates which include all worm-shaped animals, consisting of a series of identical rings (called metameres). There are about 8,600 different species living on land or in the sea.

Millipede

In spite of its name, the millipede does not have a thousand legs! Even the longest millipedes (iules) have only 240 pairs, that is, 480 legs!

Sponges live without moving, stuck to a rock. They can be shaped like a ball, a branch, or a string and are therefore called spherical, branched, or filiform.

Are invertebrates really a group?

Not anymore. At the time of Jean-Baptiste Lamarck this was the case, but today, the term "invertebrate" has no real scientific meaning, although it is still in use for practical reasons. Some invertebrates are very simple organisms (jellyfish, sponges) and others far more complex (cuttlefish, octopuses, etc.). It therefore became impossible to include all these animals scientifically in the same group!

What are coelentarata?

They are mostly sea animals, with a cylindrical body, no mouth, and tentacles. Jellyfish and corals are members of this family.

Medusa

Osculum

Sack

Pores

Sea sponge

What is an echinoderm?

These are animals with a symmetrical skeleton (and, of course, no backbone!). Among these are sea urchins, for example, whose skeleton, called a test, is rounded and slightly flat but perfectly symmetrical. Sea cucumbers belong to this group, despite their elongated bodies which make them an exception. However, they move around slowly like all echinoderms on tube-shaped feet with suckers.

DID YOU KNOW?

STARFISH
At first sight, they seem harmless, but they are, in fact, great predators. As they move around on rocks or the seabed, they feed essentially on shellfish which they can open with their muscular arms to stick their stomachs inside.

CORAL
Although it looks like a plant, the coral is actually an animal (called a polyp). It consists basically of calcium carbonate, which makes up its skeleton, and has tentacles which capture plankton at night and place it in its mouth to eat!

SEA URCHINS
There are about 700 species in existence. Round in shape, a sea urchin moves by means of mobile spines of different lengths. It feeds on organic matter (animal or vegetable) and its mouth is at one end of its body, with the anus (where its excrements are released) at the opposite end.

MOLLUSKS

These invertebrates have soft bodies, which in some cases are protected by a hard shell. Most are aquatic but some species, like snails and slugs, live on land! During their research, archaeologists have found mollusk fossils dating back 600 million years!

A cephalopod, the cuttlefish has a slim fin all around its body which it undulates to move through the water. It has 10 tentacles around its mouth; 8 fairly short ones and another 2 longer ones which allow it to feed, defend itself and reproduce.

Many gastropods have shells, all shaped like spirals.

How do mollusks defend themselves?

Some do so with their shells, others by mimicry: their color enables them to hide on the ground, or they cover themselves with algae so as not to be seen.

The snail moves along on its foot by means of mucus which enables it to slide along the ground.

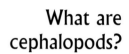

Shell

Antenna with the eye at its end

Foot

What is a bivalve?

This is a mollusk whose shell separates into two parts (called valves) joined by a hinge. They live on rocks or beneath the sand under the seabed. Bivalves feed on particles of plankton which they filter through their gills. Mussels, the giant clam, and the razor clam belong to this group.

What are cephalopods?

Sea creatures, these mollusks have tentacles near their head through which they feed. Octopuses have eight, squids and cuttlefish have ten, and the nautilus has close to 90! The nautilus is the only one with an external shell; the others have only an internal one or none at all. "Cephalopod" in Greek means "foot-like head." There are almost 600 species in existence.

The octopus squirts ink from its body when it feels threatened, so that it can take flight very quickly.

What are gastropods?

There are nearly 50,000 species! Except for slugs, gastropods have visible shells shaped like a spiral. Most live in water. Land snails and slugs have lungs for breathing, but almost all marine species have gills.

DID YOU KNOW?

THE GIANT SQUID
It lives in the depths of the sea and is the largest existing invertebrate. Although the maximum length of the giant squid is not known, some have been found measuring close to 60ft (including their tentacles) with a weight of roughly 2 tonnes!

THE NAUTILUS
An inhabitant of tropical seas, this strange cephalopod is a primitive life form, as fossils have been found dating back 450 million years. The inside of its shell is made of mother-of-pearl and consists of several chambers, creating a spacious living-area for the animal.

SLUGS
These are land gastropods with no shell. Yet, some species, like the gray slug, do have a tiny one inside their body. Herbivores, they come out at night or after heavy rain.

CRUSTACEANS

These are arthropods, invertebrates with an outside skeleton (called an exoskeleton) protected by a hard carapace. Most crustaceans have antennae and claws so that they know what is going on around them and can catch their prey.

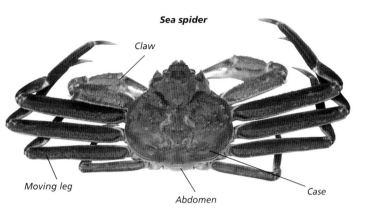

Sea spider

Claw

Moving leg

Abdomen

Case

What are the claws for?

The large claws found on a great many species are often used for defense but also for eating. They use them to break the shells of other crustaceans or to pick up bits of food from the sea depths and carry them to their mouths. Some types of male crabs use them to parade in front of the females.

A hermit crab

Do crustaceans moult?

Yes, because their carapaces do not expand as they grow. They have to moult regularly to change carapaces.

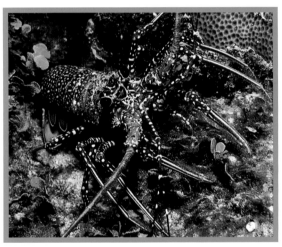

Crayfish explore the ocean depths looking for dead or living animals.

Do they all have carapaces?

Yes, but unlike crabs, which are entirely protected, some species have a soft abdomen. One such animal is the hermit crab. It finds refuge in a shell into which it withdraws at the slightest hint of a threat. Without this shelter, the animal would be exposed to a great many dangers.

Why do crayfish have such long antennae?

In order to explore their habitat better. They use their antennae to inspect the territory, find food, and sense the presence of a predator so that they can flee in time! These antennae therefore play a fundamental part in the life of these crustaceans.

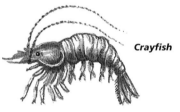

Crayfish

Like the lobster or langouste, the crayfish moves backward on its fan-shaped tail.

DID YOU KNOW?

WOODLICE
Found only on land, the woodlouse loves humid spots, under stones or dead leaves. It is a detritivore, feeding on decomposing animal and vegetable matter. When it feels threatened, it rolls itself into a ball to protect its soft abdomen.

Leg

Case

Large claw

SAND FIDDLER CRABS
Living partly on land, it gets its name from its large claw (4 times as large as the others) with which it makes grand movements. Only males have this claw, which they use to intimidate an adversary or parade in front of a female.

KRILL
This is plankton consisting of tiny crustaceans, most of which belong to the family of euphausiacia. There are nearly 90 species, with lengths measuring from 0.3 to 3 inches. They travel in swarms and play a vital part in the lives of certain cetaceans which feed only on krill.

CETACEANS

Despite their appearance, they are mammals, not fish! As they have lungs, they have to rise to the water's surface in order to breathe. Some cetaceans are gigantic: the blue whale, 100ft in length and weighing 150 tons, is the Earth's largest animal.

Dolphin bodies are hydrodynamically shaped, making them champion swimmers!

How do they know where they are?

By echolocation, a kind of natural radar: cetaceans emit high-frequency sounds which bounce off all surrounding obstacles and echo back to them. They receive these echoes by means of an organ (called a melon) on their heads. With this system, they can tell the distance, size, and even the speed of living beings or objects around them.

How do they reproduce?

Like all mammals. The sexually mature animals court and mate. After a gestation period which varies from 9 to 16 months depending on the species, the females give birth underwater to a single calf. Able to swim from birth, the calf is nourished by its mother's milk.

The killer whale can weigh as much as 5 tonnes and swim faster than 30mph.

What do they eat?

Cetaceans are divided into two groups, according to their dentition. The odonteceti are carnivores with teeth, which eat fish, squid, and crustaceans. The killer whale, a fearsome predator, also feeds on birds and marine mammals. Mysticeti, on the other hand, have baleen (horny plates attached to the upper jaw) with which they filter the water. They feed on phytoplankton and krill.

What is a blowhole?

This is an orifice on the heads of cetaceans through which they breathe. Before diving, they inhale air and close the blowhole so that no water can enter. Then, when they surface, they expel the air violently from their lungs, creating an impressive column of jetting steam.

Baleen whales have no teeth but long plates called baleen.

To move through the water, cetaceans move their wide, flat tails up and down.

DID YOU KNOW?

NARWHALS
The male is distinguished by a long spiral tusk at the end of its muzzle. Sometimes over 7ft long, this is, in fact, an enormous tooth which it uses to fight other males in order to win the female. This characteristic has earned it the name "sea unicorn."

BELUGAS
This amusing-looking cetacean is completely white, hence its name "white dolphin." However, baby belugas are brown or black at birth and change color only when they reach the age of 5 or 6 years. The beluga lives mainly in the Arctic Ocean in large groups, although today it is an endangered species.

THE COMMON BOTTLENOSE DOLPHIN
Research on this species led to the discovery of how some dolphins sleep. Like all animals, they need rest and therefore sleep. When they are asleep, only one hemisphere of their brains is at rest, while the other remains awake all the time!

FISH

The clownfish lives in symbiosis with the sea anemone.

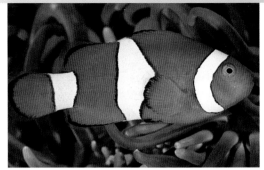

Fossils of fishes' ancestors have been found dating back 500 million years. They were tiny (only an inch long) and had no jaws! The first fish with jaws only appeared 100 million years later. Today, there are about 28,500 classified species, both freshwater and living in seas and oceans.

The strange-looking scorpionfish hides its poisonous glands at the base of its fins.

How large are they?

Their size can vary – the smallest known fish is the pygmy goby from the Philippines, around 0.4 inch long! The largest, on the other hand, is the whale shark: it weighs more than 18 tonnes and can measure up to 50 feet in length!

Yellow surgeonfish

Pectoral fin

Morays, similar to eels, have fins on both back and abdomen.

How do they move around?

With a spine and a skeleton made of bone or cartilage, most move around by undulating their supple bodies. Many species have mucus on their scales, which enables them to move more quickly.

The yellow surgeonfish has a sharp "blade" near its tail (which gave it its name).

How do they breathe?

Through fine strips of tissue (called gills) on either side of their head. As the dissolved oxygen from water passes through them, it is filtered into the animal's blood and expelled through these gills as carbon dioxide.

Tubular mouth

How do they reproduce?

Generally speaking, the female is fertilised after a courtship dance by the male. She lays her eggs in clusters on algae or hides them away in nests in the ocean depths. Some fish abandon them to their fate, but others are good parents, ventilating the nests with their fins until the young are born!

Rays are cartilaginous fish with flat round bodies who live in warm and temperate seas.

DID YOU KNOW?

PORCUPINE FISH
Weighing between 4 and 6 lbs, it seems a friendly fish when calm. However, as soon as it senses danger, it fills itself with water and turns into a ball covered with venomous spines – so watch out, predators!

SEAHORSES
Called seahorse because of its resemblance to a horse, it has a unique way of reproducing. The female lays its eggs in the abdomen of the male, who looks after them until they hatch. Then he gives birth to fully formed young!

SHARKS
These are predators whose ancestors appeared on Earth very early in its history. They belong to the same group as rays (selachians), because their skeletons are made of cartilage instead of bone.

SHARKS

Unlike bony fish, sharks are cartilaginous fish, and can be extremely aggressive. Apart from their highly developed sense of smell and taste, they have organs on their sides and noses that transmit to their skin the vibrations made by the muscular contractions of their prey.

A shark's teeth are arranged in rows on both jaws. The outermost ones are used to tear the flesh of its prey. When a tooth is worn down or damaged, it falls out and is quickly replaced by another from the row behind.

What do sharks eat?

Most are carnivorous and feed on wounded fish or decomposing animals, squid, turtles, and seals. Only the largest sharks – the whale shark and basking shark – eat plankton, which they filter through their mouths and gills.

Great white shark

Pointed nose

Huge mouth

Sharp teeth

Hammerhead shark

The hammerhead shark is easily distinguished by its flat, T-shaped head with eyes and nostrils on either side.

How many species are there?

About 350 species exist. Their size varies: while most are no more than 3ft long, the largest, the whale shark, measures nearly 60ft, making it the world's biggest fish.

What shark is most dangerous to man?

The great white shark, with its large, pointed teeth, is fearsome. It can swim either at the surface of the water or in its depths, covering long distances in very little time. It can smell blood from a great distance. When it reaches its prey, it swallows it without chewing. However, sharks very rarely attack humans, especially if they are not wounded.

Most sharks found in the high seas have fine, streamlined bodies and powerful tails which allow them to swim very quickly.

DID YOU KNOW?

SMELL

Sharks have a very acute sense of smell. This allows them to smell proteins, the females' hormones, the blood of wounded animals, etc., even though these odours have been diluted in thousands of gallons of water.

SKIN

While shark skin may appear smooth, it is covered with tiny scales like miniature teeth (called denticles). These point backwards, so that the water can flow readily past the shark's body, allowing it to swim faster.

FINS

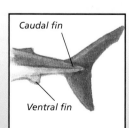

Caudal fin

Ventral fin

Sharks' fins are rigid, unlike the flexible ones of bony fish. To propel itself forward, it energetically undulates its body with its very flexible spine and slides through the water.

BIRDS

These feathered vertebrates have two wings, two scaly legs, and a beaked head. All birds are oviparous, that is, they lay eggs in nests and incubate them until the young are born.

Curved beak

Pink feathers

The flamingo uses its curved beak like a sieve to filter muddy water for food.

Red stripes

How do they communicate?

The best time to watch how they communicate is during their reproductive period: many birds sing and some can be very talkative! Others parade about in a dance or display fine plumage. A good example is the male peacock, which unfolds its huge, brightly coloured tail.

A peacock couple

Why do some birds migrate?

Migrating birds go on long, tiring journeys to escape from cold climates. Not only are the temperatures too low there, but food becomes scarce. The Arctic tern holds the record: it lives near the North Pole but migrates to the Antarctic in summer, traveling almost 18,500 miles every year!

Webbed feet

The owl has large eyes which face forward, but its neck can revolve 270°, which gives it a wide range of vision.

Wings with indented edges

Large eyes

Talons

Do all birds fly?

No. The penguin and ostrich, for example, are called flightless birds, although they cannot fly for different reasons. The penguin uses its wings as fins for swimming, whereas those of the ostrich, the largest bird on Earth, are too small to bear the weight of its body.

Although it cannot fly, the ostrich can run at nearly 40mph!

How do birds fly?

Each has its particular technique. Small birds alternately flap their wings and make short pauses to save energy. The largest ones also flap their wings but some also glide on rising air currents. Birds have different types of feathers. The longest (called remiges) are on their wings, and their tailfeathers (rectrices) are used for flying and steering. The down allows them to maintain their body temperature.

DID YOU KNOW?

TOUCANS
These colourful birds found in tropical regions have beaks which can measure half their body length in some species. Toucans generally live in small colonies or in couples.

THE EMPEROR PENGUIN
Its habitat is the Antarctic and it is an excellent swimmer. When the female lays an egg, she places it at the feet of the male, who hatches it by covering it with the skin of his abdomen so that it will not freeze!

Bony crest

THE SOUTHERN CASSOWARY
Like the ostrich, this large bird does not fly. It lives in Australia and New Guinea. Its head has a bony crest which, among other things, protects it when it runs into the bush. Unfortunately, it is threatened with extinction.

Long feathers

BIRDS OF PREY

These are carnivorous birds, recognizable by their hooked beaks and the sharp claws on their feet, called talons. Their sight is highly developed, allowing them to hunt small animals! The peregrine falcon, for example, can detect an animal the size of a pigeon almost 5 miles away!

The gyrfalcon lives in the northernmost regions of Europe.

Are they predators?

Yes, and they are at the top of the food chain in the ecosystem of their habitat. They hunt herbivores and rodents as well as other small mammals and reptiles. Their beaks have a curved, pointed upper jaw shaped like a hook.

Golden feathers on its head

Hooked beak

Wings with wide span

Feathered feet

Golden eagle

Long tail

The extremely sharp vision of the golden eagle is six times as powerful as ours. This bird is a fearsome predator: it can attack prey as large as small deer!

How do they hunt?

Whether diurnal or nocturnal, these birds of prey have sharp vision which allows them to detect a moving animal, no matter how small. As soon as they see it, they pounce on their prey at great speed, catching it in their claws to carry it off to a quiet spot. Then they eat it by tearing it into pieces with their hooked beaks.

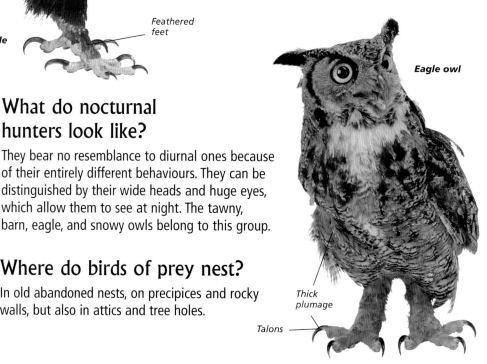

Eagle owl

Thick plumage

Talons

What do nocturnal hunters look like?

They bear no resemblance to diurnal ones because of their entirely different behaviours. They can be distinguished by their wide heads and huge eyes, which allow them to see at night. The tawny, barn, eagle, and snowy owls belong to this group.

Where do birds of prey nest?

In old abandoned nests, on precipices and rocky walls, but also in attics and tree holes.

The barn owl may be distinguished from the horned owl by its large, flat head, with no tufts of feathers on its ears.

DID YOU KNOW?

CALIFORNIA CONDORS
They have long wings so that they can glide for long distances. They can travel almost 100 miles in a day at a top speed of 50mph! Like its cousin, the Andean condor, it is a scavenger, feeding on carrion.

FALCONRY
This is the art of breeding and training certain species of birds of prey for hunting. Already practised in ancient China and Mesopotamia, this art was introduced into Europe by the Romans and became very popular with knights in mediaeval times. Emperor Frederick II (1194-1250) wrote a book on falconry.

THE BALD EAGLE
The symbol of the United States, this eagle is monogamous, i.e., it has only one mate for life! A clumsy predator, it feeds mainly on carrion. The couples build their nests raised above the ground; they are the biggest nests in the world, weighing as much as 2 tons.

MAMMALS

They appeared on Earth during the Mesozoic Era, 220 million years ago. It is thought that around 5,400 species exist today. Found all over the planet, this is the best-known and most-studied group in the animal kingdom. Humans belong to this group.

Primates are mammals.

What are the features of mammals?

Except for cetaceans, they are covered with hair which keeps their bodies warm. Warm-blooded animals, they have a more complex brain and nervous system than other living beings. In addition, the females have mammary glands which they use to nurse their young. The majority of mammals are ground-dwelling animals which live in a variety of habitats: from deserts to tundra and from mountains to tropical forests.

White mouse

What do they eat?

They belong to three groups according to what they eat: carnivores, which eat meat; herbivores, which feed on leaves, berries, fruit, and seeds; and omnivores, which eat both plants and animals.

Mobile ear

Tawny coat

The leopard is a mammal belonging to the feline (cat) family.

Raccoon

Pouch

How are they born?

In three different ways, depending on the species. In the case of placental animals, the young develop in the mother's womb in a pouch supplied with blood vessels (called the placenta) which provides its food. Baby marsupials are born in the embryonic stage and finish their growth in a pouch of skin on the mother's stomach (called a marsupium). Lastly, there are monotremes which lay eggs but suckle their young.

Very long hind leg

Long tail

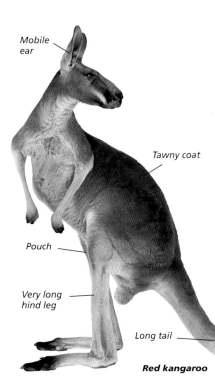

Red kangaroo

DID YOU KNOW?

BATS
This is the only mammal that can fly by flapping its wings. Bats have poor eyesight but steer at night by echolocation: they emit ultrasounds (very high-pitched sounds) which bounce off objects as echoes. These are then sent back to the animal, giving it precise information about its surroundings.

CETACEANS
These are placental, aquatic mammals, like whales or dolphins. They breathe through their lungs, and so have to surface regularly to inhale oxygen and exhale carbon dioxide.

MONOTREMES
Found in Australia, the platypus and echidna reproduce by laying and hatching eggs. However, the mouths of the newly hatched young are not equipped to suck their mother's milk. In fact, the females have no teats, but produce milk which the young lick from the mother's fur.

ENDANGERED ANIMALS

A large number of animal species on our planet are in danger of extinction. Some wild animals have already disappeared. Unfortunately, the list is growing over time. The main causes are due to humans: pollution, hunting, domestication of animals, deforestation, etc.

The giant panda, highly threatened with extinction, is the WWF's symbol.

Only a few hundred mountain gorillas remain.

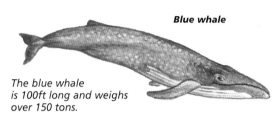

Blue whale

The blue whale is 100ft long and weighs over 150 tons.

Why do they die?

Many animals die because of a missing link in their ecosystem. For example, when a forest is destroyed, herbivores that live there have no food and die. And carnivores that live off these herbivores have no food either.

Why are humans to blame?

Apart from hunting protected species, humans also destroy forests for agriculture or farming and pollute the air with industry and cars. All of this annihilates entire ecosystems, bringing about the extinction of a great many species.

What is poaching?

This is illegal hunting of animals, including fishing. Even today, people still engage in this illegal practice for money. For example, the elephant is hunted for its ivory tusks, which are made into decorative objects, the seal is hunted for its fur and fat, and the rhinoceros for its horn, which is supposed to have medicinal properties.

White abdomen

Longer hind legs

Three species of tiger are already extinct and two others highly endangered.

Who protects animals?

The International Union for Conservation of Nature (IUCN), a world organisation with 141 member states, as well as other associations, is taking action so that certain animal species will not vanish. However, this is a difficult and costly undertaking. The WWF (World Wildlife Fund) is the best-known benevolent organization for the protection of the environment. Created in 1961, it now has 5 million members. It carries out campaigns to raise awareness and intervenes in practical ways to save the Earth's biodiversity.

DID YOU KNOW?

SNOW LEOPARDS
This is a highly endangered species which is on the IUCN's "red list." It was so widely hunted for its fur that only a few thousand still exist in the wild, in the mountains of Central Asia.

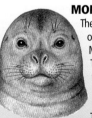

MONK SEALS
There are three species of monk seals: the Caribbean, Mediterranean, and Hawaiian. These are the only seals which live in warm seas. The Caribbean monk seal is thought to be totally extinct. The other two species are in serious trouble and are among the most endangered mammals in the world!

THE GIANT GALÁPAGOS TORTOISE
Although it is able to live over 100 years, it is nonetheless endangered, due to the recent introduction of other animals into its habitat. Goats and donkeys eat its food, while dogs, rats, and pigs destroy its eggs and kill its young!

HERBIVORES

These are animals which feed on plants. Zoologists distinguish between frugivores, which eat mainly fruit and seeds, and folivores, which feed essentially on leaves. They also make a distinction between monogastric herbivores (with a single stomach, like the horse) and polygastric animals (with several stomachs, like ruminants).

What are their digestive systems like?

They can be monogastric or polygastric. The former system has a single-chambered stomach where digestion takes place, whereas the latter, found in ruminants, consists of four gastric compartments.

What is the abomasum?

This is the fourth of the chambers which make up the stomachs of ruminants. The others are called the rumen, reticulum, and omasum. Each chamber plays a different part in the process of digestion.

Thanks to its long neck and prehensile tongue, the giraffe feeds on leaves growing very high up in trees. The giraffe eats nearly 130 lbs of leaves per day.

The red deer is one of Europe's largest herbivores.

Are all herbivores mammals?

No, many insects eat only plants. Grasshoppers, for example, are formidable plant eaters: when clouds of them arrive in a field, it can be totally stripped of vegetation in a matter of minutes!

Zebra

Cows need to give birth to calves in order to provide milk.

Which animals are ruminants?

Ruminants include ovines (sheep, llamas, etc.), bovines (oxen, buffalo, etc.) and other animals like camels or giraffes. The stomachs of these herbivores have several chambers: once the food has been chewed and swallowed, it passes into the first chamber, the rumen. Then it is regurgitated and passes into the second, the reticulum, and so on. This is why digestion takes so long in a ruminant!

DID YOU KNOW?

KOALAS
This Australian marsupial, 2 feet tall, spends its life in trees. In fact, it never comes down to the ground unless it needs to change trees because it has eaten all the eucalyptus leaves in its present tree.

CATERPILLARS
Most caterpillars feed on plants. This is why they are considered pests, because they attack plants in gardens or vegetable patches. However, when the caterpillar changes into a butterfly, it gathers nectar from flowers and helps them pollinate.

SHEEP
These ovine mammals are among the most widespread on our planet. They were domesticated nearly 9,000 years ago and are raised almost everywhere in the world for their milk (in the case of ewes), meat, skin and, above all, their soft wool!

HORSES

Members of the equidae family (like the donkey and zebra), horses are hoofed mammals. The word "horse" is a generic term, because an adult female is referred to as a mare and an adult male as a stallion; a young male is called a colt and a young female a filly.

Horseshoe

What is a thoroughbred?

This is a race of horses bred in the 18th century from the siring of Arab stallions with English mares. Since then it has never been crossed with other breeds, and only reproduces with other thoroughbreds.

How many strains are there?

There are a great many breeds.
They are divided into three large categories: saddle-horses (with slender bodies suited for racing), draft horses (short and heavy, formerly used for pulling heavy loads), and ponies. Although there are few of them, wild horses are classed as a separate category.

When were they domesticated?

Horses are thought to have been domesticated 6,000 years ago, but some doubt remains. What is certain, however, is that, by 2,000 BC, they were being used in the fields but also for transportation (drawing carts or carrying men on their backs). In Europe, the horse became a prestigious animal in the Middle Ages, the era of knights!

Mane

Nostril

The many equine strains include the Arab thoroughbred, the English thoroughbred, the Lipizzan, the Andalusian, and the Appaloosa.

There is only one remaining wild breed which has never been domesticated: the Prjevalski horse, which lives in Mongolia.

What are the origins of the horse?

The ancestor of the horse, Eohippus, appeared around 50 million years ago. From fossils that have been found, paleontologists estimate its size at roughly a foot at its withers, no taller than a medium-sized poodle! Its forelegs had four toes in place of a hoof. Studies of its teeth have shown that it fed on leaves, which it found in abundance in forests.

DID YOU KNOW?

CONQUESTS
Thanks to horses, the settlers were able to explore the United States. America is a huge continent. Without horses and mules, the European settlers would never have been able to cross it and establish new cities. They also used their mounts to guard their cattle and guide them to pasturelands.

HIPPOTHERAPY
This therapy involves healing humans through contact with horses. People with physical or serious mental handicaps look after horses or even ride them. This restores their self-confidence, allowing their condition to improve!

CALIGULA
Around 40 AD, this Roman emperor became famous for his eccentricity and bloodthirsty insanity. He proclaimed his favorite horse a consul (a magistrate with great authority) in front of the members of the Senate. Caligula was assassinated shortly afterward by his guards.

PACHYDERMS

There are only two species of hippopotamus, both found in sub-Saharan Africa.

These massive animals were once (mistakenly) thought to be related, and, because they all have very thick skin, they were called "pachyderms." The term was applied to elephants, hippopotamuses, and rhinoceroses. They have huge toes instead of hooves and are found only in Africa and Asia. When they feel safe from danger, they stroll nonchalantly and very slowly. Their eyes are small in proportion to their heads; in fact, their vision is not very well developed.

What do they eat?

Pachyderms are herbivores which spend almost all their time in search of food. They have enormous appetites. An adult African elephant, for example, can take in over 485 lbs of plants daily.

Whole populations of rhinoceroses and elephants have been wiped out by poachers for their horns or tusks.

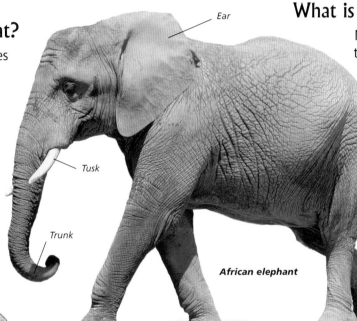

Ear

Tusk

Trunk

African elephant

What is the largest pachyderm?

Measuring almost 13ft at its withers, the African elephant of the savannah is not only the largest pachyderm but also the biggest mammal living on earth. There are three species of elephant: two live in Africa (one in the savannah and the other in the forest) and are distinguished by their large ears and trunk ending in two finger-like points. The third species is found in Asia; it is not as tall as the African ones, it has smaller ears and its trunk has only one "finger"!

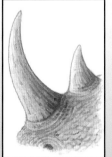

Elephant calf

Where do they prefer to live?

Even though their skin is thick, it is also very fragile and easily burnt by the sun. For this reason, pachyderms are often found in water or taking mud baths.

Do they live in groups?

Not all of them. Nevertheless, elephants are social creatures that live in large herds of up to 80 animals.

The Indian rhinoceros

There are three species of rhinoceros: two African (white and black) with two horns, and one Indian, with a single horn.

DID YOU KNOW?

TICK BIRDS

These little birds spend their time on the backs of pachyderms, especially hippopotamuses and rhinoceroses. Rhinos let them stay there because they are very useful for getting rid of parasites (insects, mites, and ticks), something pachyderms cannot do for themselves.

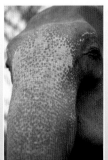

RHINOCEROS HORNS

The animal uses it to unearth the bulbs of plants it feeds on or to defend itself against predators. In Asia, the Indian rhinoceros is hunted for its horn because it is thought in traditional medicine to have healing properties. Today the species is protected.

ELEPHANTS' MEMORY

Research has shown that elephants can remember for many years the trumpeting of fellow elephants that they come across regularly. This means that an old animal can recognize nearly 150 elephants by the sounds they emit.

PRIMATES

This is a group of mammals, many of which live in trees. They can vary greatly in appearance, behavior, and size. For example, one of the smallest is the mouse lemur, scarcely larger than a mouse and weighing only 1.4 oz. The gorilla, on the other hand, can be up to 6ft tall with a weight of 400 lbs!

A small macaque

What are their characteristics?

Most have prehensile hands and feet with thumbs placed opposite the other fingers. Some even have flat nails, like us, instead of claws! In addition, primates are well known for their intelligence, as their brains are more highly developed than those of other mammals!

Long, supple arm

Very maternal, female gorillas carry their young on their backs. In the wild, gorillas have very few enemies. They use their impressive strength to fight almost any predator, including the most ferocious big cats.

What do they eat?

They are vegetarians, their daily diet consisting of fruit and leaves. Some primates add insects to complete their meals!

What exactly are primates?

They are an order that consists of two main groups: prosimians (or lemurs) and simians (monkeys and anthropoids). There are nearly 190 species of primates, including humans.

Prehensile fingers

Baboons live in very large colonies.

Baboon

Orangutans are intelligent and use tools which they have made. When it rains, for example, the orangutan covers its head with a large leaf, using it as a hat to protect it from the rain!

How do they communicate?

In a number of ways: cries to recognize each other or warn of danger, movements and mimicry to show if they are pleased or not. In social groups, simians delouse each other to show their pleasure and love for each other!

DID YOU KNOW?

GORILLAS
When an intruder enters the territory of a dominant gorilla, it becomes very aggressive. It stands up and utters cries while showing its teeth and beating its chest violently. Needless to say, intruders beat a hasty retreat!

CHIMPANZEES
This anthropoid is highly intelligent. Scientists believe that it can use about forty different tools, as needed. For example, it uses a large stone as a hammer to hit a nut placed on another stone, in order to break it open and eat its kernel.

GIBBONS
These are surprising simians! They have no tails, but have very long arms and swing in trees from branch to branch with great agility, using their hands as hooks. They are the best acrobats in the forest! They are also the only anthropoid simians able to walk on their hind legs for long periods, while raising their arms to keep their balance.

BEARS

There are three sub-species of brown bear, varying by location: the grizzly, found in North America, the Kodiak of Alaska, and the Eurasian, which (as its name suggests) lives in Europe and Asia.

Huge, powerful animals, bears are plantigrades, that is, they walk on the soles of their feet. Their paws have little pads underneath to protect them as they walk on different types of terrain. These are very useful for the brown bear, which lives in the mountains, and the polar bear on the frozen ground of the polar regions.

What do they eat?

Their diet varies according to the species and behavior. The brown bear rounds off its meat meals with plants, making it an omnivore, while the polar bear is exclusively carnivorous, because no plants grow in its habitat.

The brown bear is excellent at fishing.

Do they live in groups?

No, they are solitary by nature and each bear marks its territory to prevent intruders from entering. Bears only come together to reproduce. In fact, a male often has to fight another male to win the female.

How do they spend the winter?

Bears that live in cold regions go into a deep sleep, called hibernation. During this period, their body processes slow down, that is, their breathing and heartbeats are weaker and slower. They do not die of hunger because of the reserves of fat they have built up beneath their skin in fall. These are gradually depleted during the course of their hibernation.

As it lives in the Arctic, the polar bear has white fur which allows it to hide in the snow.

Why do they have thick fur?

This is to protect them from extreme cold. Their fur is impermeable, that is, it allows them to dive into freezing water without getting wet.

DID YOU KNOW?

BLACK BEARS
Also called the baribal, it is common in the forests of North America. It can be found in Alaska and Canada but also in the mountains of northern Mexico. This is a very special bear, because when humans destroyed its habitat, it was able to adapt and can even live in the suburbs of some cities!

GIANT PANDAS
The giant panda looks like a bear but is not one. The largest can be up to 5 ft tall and weigh more than 220 lbs. They live only in central China, in bamboo forests which provide most of their food.

GRIZZLIES
Why was this American brown bear given this name, which means "greying"? Simply because its brown fur can take on a dark gray tint and sometimes has blond tips. Although it is very good at fishing, its diet is 80% vegetarian.

RODENTS

These are small to average size mammals whose distinctive feature is their teeth. They have a pair of long, sharp incisors on each jaw. Rodents are found on every continent but the Antarctic. There are about 2,000 species in existence, living on the ground, in trees or in water.

Sharp, beveled incisors

Five clawed fingers

The beaver is a semi-aquatic rodent; it lives in the water but builds its nest on riverbanks.

Waterproof fur

Webbed hind leg

Scaly spade-shaped tail

How do they make their nests?

Arboricoles (tree-dwelling rodents) make their nests in tree trunks or underneath trees near their roots. On the other hand, ground-dwelling and semi-aquatic rodents build far more complicated nests: they are dug underground and consist of several tunnels which lead to chambers used for sleeping, pantries for the winter, etc. These nests have several exits, allowing the rodents to flee when hunted by predators.

The dormouse feeds on grasses, buds and roots, fruit, flowers and bulbs.

What do they eat?

They are vegetarians, feeding on fruit, nuts, almonds, and hazelnuts as well as plants like carrots, tomatoes, or lettuce. Some rodents round off their meals with small insects.

What kind of teeth do they have?

Rodents have four long, beveled teeth (incisors) which grow continuously. Gnawing on tough plants not only prevents rodents from dying of hunger but also wears down the teeth, which would otherwise keep growing and make the rodents unable to eat!

The gray squirrel can be distinguished from the red one because it has no long hairs on its ears.

Do they breed rapidly?

Yes. A female gives birth to as many as 6 to 12 young in each litter and many species have 3 or 4 litters a year. This means that she can give birth to 48 babies each year!

A prairie dog watching over its territory

DID YOU KNOW?

CABIAI
Also called capybaras, they are the world's largest rodents, measuring up to 4 ft long with a weight of 110 lbs. They live in South America, near the banks of watercourses that they can jump into and swim away at the slightest hint of danger.

Membrane of skin

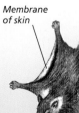

FLYING SQUIRRELS
This strange type of squirrel has a wide membrane on its sides, from its wrists to its ankles. This does not allow it to fly like a bird, but it can glide from tree to tree.

GUINEA PIGS
Introduced into Europe in the 16th century, this small rodent has become a much-loved companion for humans. But how did it get its name "guinea pig"? "Pig" comes from the fact that its cries resemble those of a pig. There are many theories as to where "guinea" came from, none of them conclusive. It might be a corruption of "Guyana."

FELINES

The cheetah is the fastest land animal. It can reach a top speed of 65 mph over a short distance.

Carnivorous mammals, felines have supple bodies with fur that can be all one color, spotted, or striped. They have powerful jaws with large canines which allow them to hunt and tear flesh. The only domesticated feline species is the household cat!

How do they see in the dark?

By using their senses of smell, sight, and touch. The pupils of their eyes are reduced to vertical slits when there is a great deal of light. But as soon as it gets dark, the pupils become round in order to let in as much light as possible, allowing them to see in the half-light. In addition, they use their whiskers (called vibrissae) to detect obstacles around them.

Mane

Tawny coat

Long tail

Hairy tuft

Long hairs

Lion

What kind of claws do they have?

The claws are retractile, that is, they are drawn in when the animal is walking. However, when it hunts or climbs a tree, for example, it extends them. Only the cheetah does not have retractile claws: they are always extended, allowing it to run very fast because they sink into the ground, ensuring that it will not slip.

A small feline related to the lynx, the caracal lives in the savannahs and dry hills of Africa and south-west Asia.

How do they hunt?

Apart from cheetahs, which chase after their prey, felines hunt by lying in wait. Alone or in groups, they crouch in the grass or on the branch of a tree and wait for the prey to come close before attacking. Sometimes, they hunt in groups (like lions), surrounding their victims and harassing them until they drop from exhaustion.

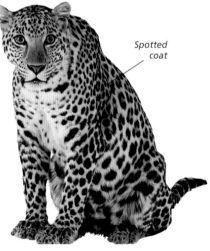

Spotted coat

Leopard

DID YOU KNOW?

PUMAS
Also called cougar and mountain lion, the puma can be found anywhere from marshlands to mountains. It is widespread all over America and is the largest feline on this continent: it can be nearly 6ft long and weigh over 220 lbs.

BLACK PANTHERS
The black panther is not a species as such but a dark-pigmented variety of spotted panther (which is also called a leopard). This means that when the female panther gives birth, there can be both spotted and black young in the same litter.

ROARING
Like most large felines, lions roar instead of purring. This characteristic sound is produced by a flexible cartilage in their throat. Their roar can be heard as far away as 5 miles.

Lion cub

DOMESTIC CATS

Members of the feline family, these small animals have become favorite household pets for humans. Very good hunters, they were domesticated around 3,500 BC by the Egyptians to rid their fields of rodents. Some scientists believe that they were actually tamed far earlier, at least 9,500 years ago in the Middle East, but this remains uncertain.

Today, there are around 60 breeds of cat.

Why do cats purr?

They begin purring as soon as they are born, while nursing. This tells the mother that all is going well. Once it has become an adult, the cat also purrs to show its owners affection and tell them it is feeling fine. But how is this sound produced? By a cartilage in its throat that the cat vibrates.

How do they behave?

Even though they are now domesticated, cats have kept their hunter's instincts. This can be seen by watching them at play: they run after a ball with claws extended, and catch flying insects or rodents in the garden.

Cats walk on tiptoe (they are digitigrades), not on the soles of their feet.

Cats have two weapons for hunting: their long canines and their retractile claws, which are curved and always well sharpened!

Can cats be trained?

Only to a small extent, for they are very independent creatures! They can be taught not to climb on tables and not to sharpen their claws on carpets or furniture, but this will not stop them from doing so when the owner's back is turned. The cat decides whom it will allow to pat it, and it makes very clear when it wants to be left alone to sleep.

Gentle and calm, Persian cats have to be brushed daily so that their silky fur does not get knotted.

What are whiskers?

These are long hairs on the cheeks and around the eyes. They are very sensitive and most useful in exploring the cat's surroundings. In addition, whiskers enable the cat to tell where it is going in the dark.

DID YOU KNOW?

VISION
Their vision is excellent in dim light, allowing cats to hunt at night. In daylight, however, cats have poorer sight than humans; they can make out movements but not sharp details or colours.

PLAY
Cats play at different games from the time they are very young: exploring, investigating, and imitating hunting and fighting. These instincts are innate. The games teach kittens how to defend themselves and find food if they should have to live in the wild.

FOOD
Cats are strictly carnivorous: in the wild, they eat small rodents, baby birds, lizards, and insects. The household cat is often fed ready-made meals (kibble). They must absolutely never be given bones, fish-bones, and candy (especially chocolate, which is poisonous to them).

DOGS

*Puppies are born blind and deaf.
It is only two weeks later that their eyes open
and they can begin hearing sounds around them.*

Dogs are thought to be the first animals domesticated by humans, around 11,000 BC. Today, there are almost 400 different breeds which vary greatly in size, coats, and behavior, etc. The smallest dog is the Chihuahua, the smallest of which measures only 6 inches long and weighs 2 lbs!

How are they trained?

They are trained from a very young age. Pets are taught not to bark without a reason, to wait patiently when its owners are having a meal, as it will be fed when it is over, etc. Other dogs, however, are trained specially for work: thanks to their exceptional sense of smell, they can find people buried in snow or in rubble after an earthquake, detect drugs in vehicles or suitcases, guide the blind, etc.

Pit bull

What different types of dogs are there?

There are five types: companion dogs (Chihuahuas, Maltese), guard dogs (German shepherds, boxers), sheep dogs (Briard, Pyrenean shepherd), hunting dogs (Brittany spaniel, setter), and finally, working dogs (St. Bernard, husky, Newfoundland).

Dalmatian

What are their origins?

It is believed that all dogs are descended from wolves. A very long time ago, humans and wolves hunted on the same territories. It is thought that through this constant contact, the wolf let humans approach it and even helped them hunt as well as protecting them from predators. This is how they became domesticated.

Labarador retriever

Why are dogs called "man's best friend"?

Because they are faithful companions, always close to their masters: they obey orders (when well trained), are joyful, and love having fun with adults or children. They also love being patted and return affection a hundredfold!

Thanks to their movable ears (amongst other things), dogs have a particularly sharp sense of hearing; they can even hear high frequencies that we humans are incapable of hearing.

DID YOU KNOW?

MOLOSSERS
This word refers not to a breed but to dogs of a particular physique and character. Large and robust, molossers can be quite aggressive toward humans – other than their master, of course. Pit bulls, mastiffs, Neapolitan mastiffs, etc. are all molossers.

HUSKIES
Originally from north-east Siberia, these dogs were used to pull the sleighs of the inhabitants. Robust and very muscular, they need to go for a daily run. Their characteristic feature is their blue eyes, even though some can have one black eye and one blue.

SCOTTISH TERRIERS
These terriers are believed to have originated in Scotland around 1700. For a long time, they have helped humans get rid of pests because, as their name suggests, they are able to make their way into burrows and flush out rodents or rabbits.

GEOGRAPHY

EUROPE

Europe is a continent consisting of 47 countries, some of which were created by recent divisions. It is surrounded by the Arctic Ocean to the north, the Mediterranean to the south, the Atlantic Ocean and North Sea to the west, and the continent of Asia to the east.

In both Greek and Roman mythology, Europa was a young girl who was taken by the God of the heavens. This is why it was decided to name the continent after her many years ago.

The waters of the Volga run into the Caspian Sea through a large delta.

Which is Europe's longest river?

It is the Volga, 2,300 miles long. With its source in a small lake north-west of Moscow, it flows into the Caspian Sea. Its immense basin is over 800,000 sq miles in area.

Flag of the European Union

Member countries in 2009: Germany, Austria, Cyprus, Denmark, Spain, Estonia, Finland, France, Greece, Hungary, Ireland, Italy, Latvia, Lithuania, Luxembourg, Malta, Netherlands, Poland, Czech Republic, Romania, United Kingdom, Slovakia, Slovenia, and Sweden. However, other countries have applied for membership.

What is the EU?

Created on February 7th, 1992 by the treaty of Maastricht, the European Union (EU) is an economic and political organization of independent, democratic member countries. As its name suggests, it enables the various States to agree on economic and social progress by means of a common policy, as well as not going to war with each other.

Which mountain range separates Europe from Asia?

It is the Urals, part of one of the world's oldest ranges, 1,500 miles long. The Urals begin at the Arctic Ocean and end near the Caspian Sea.

Which is Europe's largest island?

The largest island is Great Britain, to the north-west of continental Europe. It consists of three countries – England, Scotland, and Wales – and is surrounded by the Atlantic Ocean, the North Sea, the English Channel, and the Irish Sea.

The Urals were formed about 250 million years ago, when two tectonic plates collided.

Which capital was called Lutetia?

It is Paris. In Gallo-Roman times, it was built at a bend in the Seine. Since then, Paris has grown. It is full of history and many kings, presidents, and architects have left their mark on the city. It has been called the "City of Light" for centuries and is a very important cultural, political, and economic centre.

DID YOU KNOW?

LONDON
The capital of the United Kingdom and England, London is at the south-east end of Great Britain. It is a cosmopolitan metropolis with immense cultural, political, economic, and artistic influence.

MADRID
Situated in the center of Spain, Madrid is on a plateau at an altitude of 2,188ft above sea level, making it one of the highest capitals in Europe. Madrid is not only a metropolis containing the main head offices of businesses but also a highly important cultural and university center.

BERLIN
The television tower is Berlin's tallest monument: it dominates the city from a height of 368m. Built between 1965 and 1969 by the architects Fritz Dieter and Günter Franke, it was the pride of the East German regime.

FRANCE

Almost 340,000 sq miles in area, France has 64.3 million inhabitants, including those in its overseas departments and territories (called D.O.M and T.O.M.). These are distant islands or land which belong to the country. On the European continent, France is called the "hexagon" because of its shape!

Loire Valley, Château of Azay-le-Rideau. Built on an island on the Indre River, it is surrounded by a small lake.

What is its capital?

The Eiffel Tower (1889)

Paris. Its name comes from the Parisii, a Celtic tribe which settled on the Ile de la Cité in the 3rd century BC. At the time, it was called Lutetia. It was only named Paris in 52 BC, when the city fell into the hands of the Romans. Roman remains that can still be seen today are the Thermes de Cluny (baths) and the Arènes de Lutèce (amphitheater).

The Louvre Palace, a museum since 1793

What can one admire in the Loire Valley?

Over 300 châteaux built by kings and noblemen as their main or summer residences. One of the best-known is the Château of Amboise, where Leonardo da Vinci lived. In 2000, the valley was listed as a World Heritage site by Unesco.

Which are its largest cities?

Apart from Paris with its Eiffel Tower, the symbol of the country, Marseille, Lyons, Toulouse, Bordeaux, Nantes, Lille, Strasbourg, and Rennes are France's largest cities. Spread around the whole country, they are very important economic and cultural centres.

What is the Camargue?

This is a region in the south-east of France, triangular in shape and created by sedimentary deposits from the Rhône river. A huge plain with ponds, marshes, and reeds, the Camargue regional park became a natural reserve in 1972.

Camargue, Daudet's Mill at Fontvieille (1815)

DID YOU KNOW?

CORSICA
It belongs to France and is the fourth-largest island in the Mediterranean. It is separated from Sardinia by the Strait of Bonifacio. Many of its fortifications go back to Genoese rule, which also left its mark on the Corsican language.

PRINCIPALITY OF MONACO
This is an enclave within France but does not belong to it. With an area of only 1,2 sq miles, Monaco is the second-smallest country in the world after the Vatican. Its territory is entirely urban.

PRINCIPALITY OF ANDORRA
It is situated between France and Spain. An independent European country, its 292 sq miles are almost entirely mountainous territory. Its population consists largely of Spaniards, but includes Portuguese and French minorities.

SWITZERLAND

The Swiss flag has a distinctive feature: it is square, like that of the Vatican.

Switzerland has common borders with France, Germany, Austria, and Italy. This country has an area of around 25,662 sq miles and is different from most because, depending on the region, the population speaks German, French, Italian, or Romansh (a language peculiar to a particular region of Switzerland).

The Swiss flag has a distinctive feature: it is square, like that of the Vatican.

What is the capital of Switzerland?

It is Bern. The city was founded in the 12th century on a peninsula formed by a bend in the Aar river. The symbol of Bern is the bear. The old ramparts of the city, today transformed into walkways, provide inhabitants and tourists alike with a fantastic view of the Alpine landscape.

Construction of the Gothic cathedral in Bern began in the 15th century. Its spire was added 400 years later.

How many cantons make up Switzerland?

It is composed of 20 cantons and 6 half cantons, which are like 26 small States. Each has its own government and parliament. Together they make up the Swiss confederation. Grisons is the largest of these and three languages are spoken there: German, Italian, and Romansh.

Fountain on Lake Geneva

What are the principal Swiss lakes?

Switzerland's lakes, over 1,500 in number, represent 6% of Europe's freshwater reserves. The largest of these are Lake Geneva and Lake Constance. The former lake forms the border with France, the latter with Germany and Austria. Also called Lake Léman, Lake Geneva is the biggest freshwater basin in Western Europe.

Lucerne, capital of the canton of the same name

DID YOU KNOW?

THE GLACIER EXPRESS
This scenic railroad runs across the Swiss Alps, passing magnificent valleys and breathtaking viaducts. Its route takes it over 291 bridges, through 91 tunnels and across the Overalp Pass, at an altitude of more than 6,500ft .

THE JUNGFRAU
The 13,600-ft-high Jungfrau (the Virgin) is a mountain in the Bernese Alps. Europe's highest cog railroad climbs to a height of 11,340ft. Together with the Mönch and Eiger mountains, the Jungfrau is a site of exceptional beauty.

ZURICH
This is the capital of the canton of the same name. Situated on the banks of the Limmat river at the northern tip of Lake Zurich, it is one of Switzerland's largest cities (with Bern and Geneva). It is also one of the most important financial and economic centers in the country.

SPAIN

Located on the Iberian Peninsula, Spain is a country of high plateaus and mountain ranges (the Pyrenees and the Sierra Nevada). Running from these heights are several of its major rivers: the Ebro, Duero, Tagus, and Guadalquivir. The Balearic Islands, an archipelago in the Mediterranean opposite Morocco, are an autonomous community (or province) of Spain.

The Aneto is one of the highest peaks in the Pyrenees.

The Plaza Mayor in Madrid. Designed in 1620, it is rectangular in shape and completely surrounded by similar buildings.

What is its capital?

Madrid. The city is built around a Moorish fortress called Magerit which dates from the 10th century. Its remains can still be seen in the city. Madrid has a great many architectural monuments of all styles, such as the Prado, one of the largest museums, where one can gaze at nearly 18,000 masterpieces of Flemish, Italian, and Spanish art.

The Sagrada Familia Church in Barcelona

What separates Spain from France?

The Pyrenees, a mountain range which begins at the Pacific Ocean and extends as far as the Mediterranean Sea. This natural border, 267 miles long, has two high summits on the Spanish side: Aneto (11,150ft) and the Posets peak (11,055ft).

Which are its principal cities?

Madrid, Barcelona (the second-largest city and capital of Catalonia), Seville (capital of Andalusia), Saragossa (capital of Aragon), and Bilbao (capital of Biscay and Spain's second-largest port).

Green rolling landscape in the Meseta

The Guggenheim Museum in Bilbao

What is the Meseta Central?

This is an immense plateau in the center of the Iberian Peninsula. It covers nearly half the surface of the country. The Meseta includes a long, fairly low mountain range (called the Sierra Morena). Despite the quite harsh winters and dry summers, this region is largely agricultural.

DID YOU KNOW?

FLAMENCO
This is a rhythmical, sensual dance form accompanied by music (mostly guitars), song, and hand-clapping. Flamenco is thought to have been born in a quarter of Seville where poets and musicians found refuge. It is a mixture of Islamic, Jewish, and Andalusian elements.

THE CORRIDA (BULLFIGHT)
This is a popular tradition in many regions of Spain: a man (torero) confronts a bull in an arena. As he waves a red cape – called a muleta – he has to avoid the animal as it charges him before he moves in for the kill.

THE ALHAMBRA
This is a fortress in Granada which was built by the Arab rulers in the 13th century. It is surrounded by walls enclosing places, gardens, fountains, a mosque, a citadel (the Alcazaba), and magnificent courtyards decorated with mosaics.

PORTUGAL

This is the westernmost country in Europe. It borders the Atlantic Ocean and has 520 miles of coastline with its archipelagos. This is why the Portuguese are excellent sailors: over the centuries, they founded a colonial empire throughout the world. Portugal has only one land border, which it shares with Spain.

Lisbon, built on the northern bank of the Tagus, extends over seven hills.

Designed by Francisco Arruda, the Belem Tower is an example of the Manueline style of architecture.

What is the Belem tower?

It is a citadel built between 1515 and 1521 to celebrate the discovery of a sea route to India by the navigator Vasco da Gama. It was also erected to guard the entrance to the port of Lisbon. Initially it stood in the middle of the Tagus. However, after a terrible earthquake, the waters of the river were diverted and the Belem Tower ended up on one of its banks!

What is its capital?

Lisbon. It is thought to have been founded by the Phoenicians and then occupied by the Romans. Then it was invaded by the Visigoths, but later conquered by the Moors. Over the centuries, its long history has left Lisbon with a rich heritage of historical monuments from very different periods.

Where is the Azores archipelago?

Volcanic in origin, it lies in the Atlantic Ocean to the west of the Portuguese mainland. It consists of nine islands and several islets. Its climate is temperate: 57°F in winter and around 77°F in summer.

The Lisbon earthquake of 1755

The Algarve, a region in southern Portugal

What happened on November 1st, 1755?

A terrible earthquake, followed by a huge tsunami and fire, destroyed a large part of Lisbon. This is why some quarters of the city have no remains from before this date. Reconstruction work was carried out by the Marquis of Pombal, who had the lower part of the city (the worst hit) restored in what was a very modern style for the time.

DID YOU KNOW?

FADO
The Fado is a traditional and popular musical genre. Accompanied by guitars, the singer expresses deep feelings, such as nostalgia, sadness, love, and passion through his songs.

PORTO
Situated in the north-west of Portugal, this is one of the country's most dynamic cities. It is here that the wine of the same name (port) is produced by being aged in a storehouse. Served as an aperitif, nearly 90% of port is exported abroad.

THE TAGUS
This 620-mile-long river begins in Spain and drains into the Atlantic Ocean at Lisbon. A huge bridge was built at its mouth: 7 miles long, the Vasco da Gama bridge is the longest in Europe! It was constructed when Lisbon was renovated for the Universal Exhibition in 1998.

57

ITALY

The Castel Sant'Angelo was originally a mausoleum for Emperor Hadrian. It later became a papal citadel, a prison and, today, a museum.

Italy is the boot-shaped peninsula with a coastline for most of its boundaries, as it lies in the Mediterranean. To the north, it shares borders with France, Switzerland, Austria, and Slovenia. It is a parliamentary republic with close to 60 million inhabitants. The small, independent states of the Vatican and San Marino are enclaves within Italian territory.

Venice

Which is its highest mountain?

Mont Blanc (13,700ft), which straddles the Franco-Italian border, is Italy's highest summit and one of the highest in Europe. It is part of the Mont Blanc Massif and the mountain range of the Alps. The first ascent was carried out by Michel Paccard and Jacques Balmat in 1786.

Summit of Mont Blanc, between the Aosta Valley and Haute-Savoie.

Which are its main cities?

Milan and Turin are the main economic centers, while Venice, Florence, Rome, Naples and Palermo are known throughout the whole world for their artworks.

What is its capital?

It was not until 1870 that Rome was declared the capital of unified Italy and then of the Italian Republic. It was founded on the banks of the Tiber River, in the historical center of the seven hills. It is the country's most populous city: its population has grown from 226,000 in 1870 to over 2.5 million in the middle of the 2000s. Within its walls is the independent state of Vatican City.

What is its longest river?

The Po has its source at the foot of Monte Viso, in the Piedmont region, at an altitude of 6,600 ft. With a length of 405 miles, it is joined by more than 140 tributaries before emptying into the Adriatic Sea through a large delta.

The Po delta is home to over 300 species of birds.

Why does the tower of Pisa lean?

In the past, it was commonly thought the tower leaned because its architect had designed it that way. Not at all! In fact, this bell tower was erected to stand vertically, but began to lean at the outset of construction: the alluvial subsoil made the ground unstable and unable to support the weight of the building. For many years, it was believed that the tower would eventually topple over, but there is no longer any risk, as it has been stabilized. Today it inclines at 5.5 degrees.

DID YOU KNOW?

THE UFFIZI GALLERY
This museum in Florence is the oldest in the world. From 1591 on, anyone who made a request of the owner, the Grand Duke of the Medici family, was permitted to come and admire the works displayed there. Today, the museum has almost 1,700 paintings in 45 rooms.

THE MOLE ANTONELLIANA
The symbol of Turin, this monument was erected by the architect Alessandro Antonelli from 1863 to 1889. With a height of 550ft, the Mole today houses the National Museum of Cinema. A scenic lift takes visitors right to the top of the spire.

VESUVIUS
Vesuvius, 4,200ft high, is a volcano still active today. It lies about 6 miles to the east of Naples (the capital of Campania). Its best-known eruption occurred in August of AD 79, when its ash and lava buried the surrounding cities, including Pompeii. Nearly 2,000 people perished that day!

GREECE

Situated in the south-east of Europe, this country has land borders with Albania, Macedonia, Turkey, and Bulgaria. However, its longest borders are coastlines along the Aegean, Mediterranean, and Ionian Seas. Greece is a rather mountainous country, its highest peak being Mount Olympus, at 9,570ft.

Windmill on the Island of Mykonos in the Cyclades

Monastery at Meteora. Four churches were built at different periods on a rocky outcropping.

What is its capital?

Athens, also its main city. It lies in the heart of a plain surrounded by mountains called Parnes, Hymettus, and Pentelicos. The city has a rich heritage of monuments dating from antiquity. The Parthenon temple, dedicated to Athena, Goddess of Wisdom, can still be admired today, and this is only one example!

The Athens Acropolis was declared a World Heritage site by Unesco in 1987.

What is Meteora?

Situated in Thessaly, the Meteora are tower-like rocks. In the 14th century, monks erected a number of monasteries there in order to retire from the world. They were accessible only by means of long stairways of movable ladders. Of the 24 original monasteries, only 5 remain today, since most of them were destroyed by the Germans during the Second World War. In 1988, Unesco declared Meteora a World Heritage site.

On which island is the palace of Knossos?

On Crete, the fifth-largest island in the Mediterranean. According to Greek mythology, this palace, built by Daedalus, had a labyrinth which concealed a monster called the Minotaur. It is thought to have been constructed around 2,000 BC and was rebuilt four centuries later, following an earthquake.

What are the Cyclades?

This is an archipelago consisting of roughly 220 islands whose chief town is Hermoupolis, on the island of Syros. The best-known other islands are Andros, Delos, Naxos, Paros, Santorini, Melos, and Mykonos. The economy of this archipelago is based on tourism but also on the agricultural production of wine, olive oil, fruit, and tobacco.

This island group, situated in the Aegean Sea south-east of mainland Greece, gets its name (Cyclades) from the circular arrangement of the islands around Delos, which was once sacred.

The Palace of Knossos was discovered in 1900 by the British archaeologist Arthur John Evans, who found a large number of rooms and frescoes.

DID YOU KNOW?

PIRAEUS
This city lies on the Mediterranean coast, in Attica. The port of Athens and the country's principal port, Piraeus is also one of its main industrial centers. In addition to maritime trade and naval construction (connected to the port), its economy is based on the production of textiles, chemicals, and machinery, as well as the milling of grain.

THESSALONIKI
This northern city is the capital of Greek Macedonia. It was founded in 315 BC by Cassander, king of the Macedonians. In the course of its history, it was captured by the Romans, the Saracens, the Crusaders and, finally, the Ottoman Turks, who governed it until 1912, when it was annexed to Greece.

PATRAS
This is the capital of the province of Achaea, in the center of Greece. Its port, on the Gulf of Corinth, is one of the most important in the country, due to its many shipyards and its export industry. Its geographic location makes Patras a transit town for tourists, as well.

🇬🇧 UNITED KINGDOM

This country includes Great Britain (England, Scotland, and Wales) and Northern Ireland. It is surrounded by the Irish Sea and Atlantic Ocean on the west, the North Sea to the east and by the English Channel to the south.

The Highlands have often been used as the setting for films.

What is the capital of the United Kingdom?

London. This large city is cosmopolitan because, in former times, Britain owned a great many colonies whose inhabitants came to the United Kingdom and, in particular, to London in search of a better life. This led to a mix of races and cultures. For example, London has churches, Hindu temples, and synagogues so that all its inhabitants can practice their religion. Also the capital of England, it has a population of over 7.6 million.

Westminster Palace in London has over one thousand rooms and a clock tower which stands nearly 328ft high.

The Custom House in Belfast has undergone many alterations. It was severely damaged in a fire set by Irish nationalists in 1921.

What is the Custom House?

This is one of the most beautiful architectural creations, symbolizing the power of the British Empire and the trading success of Belfast. It was designed by Samuel Ferris Lynn in the Italian Renaissance style and was completed in 1856. Its façades are adorned with a number of carved angels and gods like Neptune and Mercury.

How is the United Kingdom governed?

It is a constitutional monarchy. Parliament consists of two Chambers: the House of Lords, which is non-elective, and the House of Commons, which holds legislative power. The Queen has no power in government.

What are the Highlands?

This is a mountainous region in northern Scotland. Sparsely populated, the Highlands are still wild and have thus inspired many poets and film producers. The inhabitants, called Highlanders, live from fishing and sheep farming.

Why is Cardiff Castle special?

This is one of the finest castles in the United Kingdom. Located in Wales, it was built inside a Roman fortress with a wooden courtyard and walls. Its keep (main tower) dates back to the 12th century. Its rooms were renovated in the 19th century. Each one is sumptuously decorated (marbles, gilding, frescoes) and dedicated to a particular theme: Arab, Greek, or Gothic.

Cardiff Castle

DID YOU KNOW?

THE ISLE OF MAN
Located between the coasts of Ireland and England, this island is part of the United Kingdom and contains many ancient remains: prehistoric stone dwellings, Druid monuments, old roads, forts, castles, and towers. Visiting this island is like going on a wonderful trip back in time!

THE UNION JACK
Dating back to 1801, this is the United Kingdom's flag, symbolizing the union of three countries. It contains the St. George's cross (English flag), the cross of St. Andrew (Scottish flag), and the cross of St. Patrick (Irish flag).

THE SHETLAND ISLANDS
This is an archipelago of around a hundred smallish islands, only twelve of which are inhabited. There are only 25,000 people living on 870 sq miles. The Shetlands are located very far north and can be very cold there. In addition, the land is quite uneven, due to erosion. People live largely from fishing, sheep farming and oil production.

THE REPUBLIC OF IRELAND

This independent republic occupies over 80% of the island of Ireland. To the west lies the Atlantic Ocean and to the east, the Irish Sea and St. George's Channel (which separates it from Great Britain). Under English rule for many years, it proclaimed its independence in 1937 and took the name Eire (an ancient Gaelic name used by the Celts).

Circle of megaliths

The Cliffs of Moher are the habitat for large numbers of puffins, seagulls, and cormorants.

What is the capital of the Republic of Ireland?

Dublin. Founded in the 9th century, it was named "Dubh Linn" by the Vikings. It was only in 1170 that it officially became the capital of Ireland, but fell to the English 43 years later. Located on the eastern side of the island, Dublin has a wealth of historical monuments: its castle, the Four Courts, the National Museum, the terrible Kilmainham Gaol, Trinity College, and the Spire.

The Custom House in Dublin

What are the megaliths?

These are prehistoric monuments consisting of large stones, often standing upright. It is believed that megaliths were set up for ritual ceremonies or used as sanctuaries or tombs. Those at Drombeg are among the best known.

What are the cliffs of Moher?

These are cliffs of sandstone and shale which erode with the passing of time due to the strong winds and waves. They are located on the western edge of the island, rising to a height of over 650ft above the Atlantic Ocean and stretching for almost 5 miles!

Dungarvan Castle

How many provinces make up Ireland?

There are 4 provinces: Leinster, Munster, Connacht, and a small part of Ulster. However, it also has 32 counties (6 of which are in Northern Ireland). The provinces have no political power, although in some cases, counties can have administrative and governmental authority. These counties were created by Great Britain when Ireland was under its rule.

DID YOU KNOW?

WOOL PRODUCTION
Ireland is called the "Emerald Isle" and rightly so. Outside its urban areas, it is a land of huge meadows, where sheep are raised for their wool. This important industry is recognized the world over for the quality of its wool.

SAINT PATRICK
He is the patron saint of Ireland. In the 10th century AD, he was kidnapped by Irish pirates and held in slavery for six years. He then managed to escape to France where he became a priest. Finally, he returned to Ireland, where he was named bishop. On March 17th, the Irish celebrate St. Patrick's Day.

NORTHERN IRELAND
It occupies the greater part of the province of Ulster, in the north-east of the island. Northern Ireland is ruled by the United Kingdom. However, from the early 20th century on, it has shown a strong desire to separate from Britain, through the activities of the IRA, an armed organisation.

AUSTRIA

The Republic of Austria is a federation of nine States (called Bundesländer), governed by a parliamentary democracy. It has been a member of UNO since 1955 and entered the European Union in 1995. The official language, spoken by the population, is German.

The large scenic wheel in the Prater Amusement Park in Vienna

Aerial view of Graz town hall

What are the main cities in Austria?

Vienna, of course, but also a number of capitals of the Bundesländer which make up the country: St. Pölten, Linz, Salzburg, Innsbruck, Bregenz, Klagenfurt, Graz, and Eisenstadt.

The Danube is Europe's longest river, after the Volga (Russia).

Which great river runs across the country?

This is the Danube. With a length of 1,770 miles, it has its source in Germany and empties into the Black Sea. It crosses Austria from west to east and is the longest river in Europe. It is known the world over as the "Blue Danube," after a waltz composed by Johann Strauss.

What is the capital?

This is Vienna. At the end of prehistory, it was occupied by the Celts and then captured by the Romans in the 1st century BC. It lies on the Danube, which makes the city a highly important center of river commerce, particularly since it is located half-way between Germany and the Black Sea.

What is the Austrian landscape like?

More than half the country is mountainous: near the Italian border, the Alps occupy a great part of southern Austria. To the north and east, on the other hand, the landscape consists more of hills, plains and forests.

DID YOU KNOW?

THE HABSBURGS
This important family reigned for several centuries over the Holy Roman Empire, Spain, Hungary, and also Austria. This dynasty took its name from the Castle of Habichtsburg, built in 1020 near the modern city of Zurich (Switzerland).

MOZART
Born in 1756 in Salzburg, Wolfgang Amadeus Mozart was an unusually gifted child prodigy: from the age of six, he gave concerts on the violin and piano. Although he died young (at 35), he left several hundred amazing masterpieces!

HUNDERTWASSER
An artist of the last century, Fritz Hundertwasser was a very famous painter, sculptor, and architect. He is also well known for his activities in promoting ecology and in politics, as well as for his antitotalitarian views.

GERMANY

This is a federal republic in central Europe. It is bordered to the north by the North Sea and Baltic Sea, and has land borders with several countries: France, Belgium, Luxembourg, and the Netherlands to the west, Austria and Switzerland to the south, Poland and the Czech Republic to the east, and Denmark to the north.

The 18th century Brandenburg Gate symbolizes Berlin, which was re-unified in 1990.

What is its capital?

Berlin is not only its capital but also the country's largest and most populous city (nearly 3.5 million inhabitants). It was built on a plain on the Spree River which runs through the city.

The Gendarmenmarkt is one of the finest squares in Berlin.

Where is the Brandenburg Gate?

This neo-classical monument stands on a square called Pariser Platz. This gate, with its 65-ft-high Doric columns, was erected in 1788 at the request of Frederick William II of Prussia and opened to traffic in 1791.

The bridge over the Rhine at Remagen, near Cologne.

How long is the Rhine?

Its length of 820 miles makes it one of Europe's main rivers. It has its source in the Swiss Alps, then it crosses France, Germany, and the Netherlands to empty into the North Sea. For centuries, the Rhine has been of the utmost importance for trade, as it is Europe's largest internal navigable route.

What is the Black Forest?

This is a region of pine forests which cover the mountain slopes. Located in south-west Germany, the Black Forest is almost 100 miles long with an area of 3,231 sq miles.

Building of the Castle of Neuschwanstein was begun by King Ludwig II of Bavaria in 1869 and completed 15 years later.

Erfurt, in the centre of Germany, is the capital of Thuringia.

What are the main cities in Germany?

Along with Berlin, there is Hamburg (with Germany's largest harbor), Bonn (a great university city), and Munich (the country's industrial and manufacturing center).

DID YOU KNOW?

THE OKTOBERFEST
This annual festival is held in Munich (Bavaria) between the second week in September and the first week in October. Since 1801, the residents of Munich and its many tourists drink enormous quantities of beer there – accompanied by music!

LUDWIG VAN BEETHOVEN
Born in Bonn in 1770, he was a musical genius. A highly creative composer, he gained international fame for his remarkable symphonies. At the end of his life, he became deaf, but this did not stop him from writing masterpieces!

THE BERLIN WALL
On October 7th, 1949, Germany was divided into two states: the DDR, to the east, was under the control of the USSR, while the west was controlled by the USA, the United Kingdom, and France. Both countries had Berlin as their capital. It was also split in two by a 10-mile-long concrete wall. Built in 1961, the Berlin Wall was torn down on October 3rd, 1990, when Germany was reunified.

BELGIUM

Bordered to the north-west by the North Sea, to the south-west by France, to the east by Luxembourg and Germany and, finally, to the north by the Netherlands, Belgium is the crossroads of many cultures. This is why the country (which has an area of 19 sq miles) has two quite distinct regions: Flanders to the north (where Dutch is spoken) and francophone Wallonia to the south.

The historical centre of Bruges was listed as a World Heritage site by Unesco in 2000.

Brussels

What is its capital?

It is Brussels. Its geographic location makes it a center of rail, road, and river commerce with all of Western Europe. Not only are the royal residence and the country's government located here, but Brussels is also the seat of the European Union Commission and Nato.

What is Benelux?

This is a union that was created in 1958 by a treaty signed by Belgium, Luxembourg, and the Netherlands. Led by a Council of Ministers, Benelux enables these three small member countries to work together for the economic and social development of each one.

LUXEMBOURG

The Grand Duchy of Luxembourg is a small state with no maritime border. Belgium lies to its north and west, Germany to its east, and France borders it to the south. It is divided into two natural regions: Osling, to the north and Gutland, to the south. Frenchis the official language of the country.

How is Luxembourg governed?

The Grand Duchy of Luxembourg is a hereditary constitutional monarchy. The head of state is the Grand Duke, who holds the executive power. The law also allows him to name or dismiss member of the government.

The capital of Luxembourg is also called Luxembourg. It lies on a plateau at the confluence of two rivers, the Pétrusse and the Alszette.

DID YOU KNOW?

YPRES
Ypres (or Ieper in Flemish) is a little town in western Flanders. It is unfortunately famous for the bloody battles waged there during the First World War, during which the dreadful mustard gas (which creates huge blisters on the skin) was used for the first time by the German army.

BRUGES
A medieval town which rose to artistic and economic prominence between the 11th and 15th centuries, it has a large number of canals running through it. Its architecture of carved façades and mullioned windows attract so many tourists that it is one of Europe's most visited cities!

LUXEMBOURG
This is the last remaining Grand Duchy in the world. In the 19th century, Europe still had others, like Tuscany (Italy) and Baden-Württemberg (Germany).

THE NETHERLANDS

Also called Holland, the Netherlands were under Spanish domination until the revolt by William I of Orange in 1572. In the 18th century, this country was one of the most powerful economic forces in Europe. With an area of 25,800 sq miles and 16.5 million citizens, it is one of the world's most densely populated countries (486 inhabitants per sq mile).

Amsterdam has nearly 160 canals.

Which is the country's largest port?

It is Rotterdam, in the city of the same name in southern Holland. It is not only the largest port in the Netherlands, but also in all of Europe. On one side, it links the Rhine with the Ruhr and, on the other, it is directly connected with the North Sea by a canal.

Aerial view of the port of Rotterdam with its basin extending over more than 2,000ha

What is its capital?

Amsterdam was founded in the 13th century in a fishing village located near a dam on the river Amstel (hence its name). It has 18 quarters and consists of about one hundred islets, all linked by many bridges to form canals. The city is also a large port.

Road built alongside a dike

When were the first windmills built?

In 1407. However, most date from the 18th and 19th centuries. The whole country contains more than 1,000, the majority of which are near the village of Kinderdijk, which has been listed as a World Heritage site by Unesco.

Windmills are used for private housing or are open for guided tours.

What are polders?

Holland is a flat land, with no hills. In addition, 50% of its area is at least 3ft below sea level. Tracts of this land (called polders) are drained for agricultural purposes by artificial dikes. The old windmills were constructed partly to do this job.

DID YOU KNOW?

VINCENT VAN GOGH
Born in 1853, he is one of the most famous Dutch painters. He created over 700 paintings and thousands of drawings and sketches. However, he did not achieve success during his lifetime and lived in poverty. Today, there is a museum dedicated to him in Amsterdam: it contains many of his works.

DIAMONDS
Along with Antwerp (in Belgium), Amsterdam is a city of diamonds. After being imported, the diamonds are cut and polished by professionals to be sold to the world's most gifted jewellers. Each year, over one million tourists come to see the work of the polishers. Quite an art!

TULIPS
This the national flower of Holland. Every year, the country exports them to the entire world. At the end of spring, one can see billions of tulips in huge fields along mile after mile of road in Holland.

 # ICELAND

Iceland has a great many geysers which make a deafening noise as they erupt.

It is an island located between Greenland and Scotland and is surrounded by the Atlantic and Arctic Oceans. Its economy is based mainly on fishing and farming (especially cattle). Under Norwegian and then Danish domination since 1380, it proclaimed itself an independent republic in 1944, following a national referendum.

View of Reykjavik overlooking Faxa Bay and the Atlantic Ocean

What is a geyser?

When a column of underground water reaches boiling point as it passes close to a layer of magma, the pressure is so great that the water bursts through the splits in the rocks. This is why huge jets of water and burning steam are sometimes seen in volcanic regions.

What is the capital?

This is Reykjavik, in the south-west of the island. The name, meaning "bay of smoke" after the many geysers found there, was given it by the first settlers who arrived there in 874 AD.

Typical stone and wood houses covered in grass

What is Iceland's topography?

It consists of plateaus covered by glaciers, volcanoes, almost all of which are still active, thermal springs and geysers. Earthquakes occur there often. Water heated by underground magma is used to provide heating for households.

Large numbers of rivers and streams flow down the glaciers to the ocean, creating about 10,000 waterfalls.

DID YOU KNOW?

VATNAJÖKULL
With an area of over 2,144 miles, this is Europe's largest glacier. Its icecap, 3,900ft thick in some parts, covers several active volcanoes. Like many of Iceland's glaciers, Vatnajökull was formed around 2,500 years ago.

SKOGAFOSS
This enormous waterfall runs down the slopes of a glacier near Skogar, a little village at the southern end of the island. It is 82ft wide and 196ft high. A very popular tourist attraction, its name means "water falling in the forest" in Icelandic.

BJARGTANGAR
This is the westernmost point in Europe, characterized by a long, rocky coastline. Large numbers of birds, like puffins or guillemots, build their nests on these rocks in summer.

NORWAY

A European state, Norway is the westernmost country in Scandinavia, with many sea borders. With its of coastline, its fjords which cut into its geography, and its roughly 1,500 islands, it has the eighth-longest coast in the world.

Oslo is, on the whole, a city of very modern architectural design.

Its abundant forests make Norway one of the countries most famous for traditional wooden buildings.

An aerial view of a fjord. Many of these grandiose natural formations are still wilderness today.

What is a fjord?

During the Ice Ages, glaciers dug valleys into the land at quite a distance from the coast. As the climate grew warmer, the glaciers melted, causing the sea level to rise. Since that time, these flooded valleys have become connected with the sea, creating fjords! They look like narrow bays and inlets, with high steep cliffs covered in forests.

What is the capital?

Oslo, the capital, is located at the mouth of one of Norway's coldest fjords. It is surrounded by a huge forest and the fairly modern city center contains a great many green spaces: the Frogner Park is one of the best known.

What are the Svalbard Islands?

This is an archipelago with a total area of about 38,000 sq miles in the Arctic Ocean between Norway and the North Pole. Most of its islands are covered with ice, hence its name "Svalbard," which means "cold coasts" in Icelandic. Part of the kingdom of Norway, these islands are mined for their rich coal resources.

Lofoten archipelago consists of two groups of rocky islands with fishing providing the principal resource for its inhabitants.

What is the "midnight sun"?

This is a phenomenon created by the inclination of the Earth on its axis. In the northernmost parts of the Northern hemisphere, the sun never sets completely for one month during summer. So, the country is in daylight for almost twenty-four hours! In winter, on the other hand, the sun never rises above the horizon and it is night almost all the time.

DID YOU KNOW?

NORTH CAPE
This is the northernmost point in both Norway and Europe, at a latitude of 71°10. It is not located on mainland Norway but on an island called Mageroy. In summer, the most amazing midnight suns can be admired there!

KARASJOK
Lapland is a region spread across Norway, Sweden, Finland, and Russia. Karasjok is a small Norwegian town where the parliament of Lapland sits. It also contains a museum-park dedicated to the culture of its people.

STOCKFISH
In Norwegian, this means "a fish as hard as a stick." In fact, it is unsalted cod which is dried in the open air. One of the country's most-exported products, it is soaked in water before being eaten and is delicious!

🇩🇰 DENMARK

This is the smallest country in Scandinavia (a region which also includes Norway and Sweden). Denmark is a kingdom which owns the Faroe Islands and Greenland in the North Atlantic. With an area of 26,700 sq miles, it has almost 5.5 million inhabitants. The currency is the crown.

Its windmills (amongst other things) place Denmark at the top of the list in the Aeolian energy sector.

What is its capital?

This is Copenhagen. It is often described as a city of fairy-tales, with its superb Tivoli Gardens, the Amalienborg Palace (the winter home of the Danish Royal Family), and the statue of the Little Mermaid. The architecture of the city is typically Nordic and the city has been rebuilt several times due to fires and bombing during wartime.

Frederiksborg Castle (in Hillrod) is the largest palace not only in Denmark but in all Scandinavia!

What are the main Danish cities?

Aarhus, the capital of Jutland, overlooks the sea and is famous for its university center and cultural life. Odense has a 10th century historical center (St. Canute's Cathedral and the Church of Our Lady) and, finally, Aalborg has a very important port for trade and export.

What does the country look like?

Denmark is one of the flattest countries in Europe: its overall average elevation is scarcely more than 98ft above sea level (the maximum being 558ft). However, its landscapes do include some valleys. For centuries, the economy of the country was based on agriculture, whereas today industry and the tertiary sector (services, banking, etc.) are highly developed.

Façades of houses lining the port of Copenhagen, the largest in Denmark

Denmark has many long stretches of cropland.

DID YOU KNOW?

THE VIKINGS
They arrived in Denmark in around the 6th century AD. Excellent sailors, they were nevertheless often made to retreat from all of Northern Europe's coasts. This is why they went on sailing until they arrived in America five centuries before Christopher Columbus!

HANS CHRISTIAN ANDERSEN
This famous writer, the author of fairy-tales like "The Little Mermaid" and "The Ugly Duckling," was born in Odense on April 2nd, 1805. Some of his works have been translated into 80 languages and, today, 200 years later, they are still classics loved by children the world over!

SKAGEN
This town is situated in the northernmost part of Denmark, overlooking the Kattegat strait. Its lively port, its beaches and sand-dunes have attracted not only many tourists, but also several painters who have come here to take advantage of the exceptional light in this area to record on their canvases the daily life of the inhabitants and the beauty of the landscape.

FINLAND

One third of the territory of this Northern European state lies north of the Arctic Circle. Finland is bordered by Norway to the north, Russia to the east, and Sweden to the north-west. The Baltic Sea forms its southern border.

The most common religion in Finland is Lutheran Protestantism.

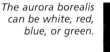

Helsinki Cathedral

What is the Finnish landscape like?

Forests cover almost 74% of the land, making Finland one of Europe's largest forest reserves. Except in the south of the country, it contains only pines or other conifers as well as nearly 1,200 species of plants and ferns.

Typical wooden house

What is the capital?

Helsinki is the capital not only of the country but also of the district of Uusimaa. It is situated in the south of the country, overlooking the Gulf of Finland and the Baltic Sea. Its natural basin is divided into five ports which handle half the national maritime traffic. Although climatic conditions can be difficult, particularly between January and May due to ice, the city's economy is based mainly on shipping exports of ore, cereals, and wood.

How many lakes are there?

The landscape of Finland is mostly flat with a multitude of stretches of water covering more than 18,500 sq miles, or over 10% of the country's area. There are roughly 180,000 of them, including over 40,000 lakes, most in the centre and south of the country. The largest lake is Lake Saimaa, with an area of about 808 sq miles.

The aurora borealis can be white, red, blue, or green.

A species of seal which is almost extinct lives in Lake Saimaa. There are only 260 Saimaa ringed seals left today!

What is the aurora borealis?

This is a phenomenon only seen in polar regions. In the upper layer of the Earth's atmosphere (called the ionosphere), molecules of air collide with a flow of charged particles from the Sun (called solar wind), thus creating a spectacular light effect.

DID YOU KNOW?

ESKERS
These are long pine-covered ridges of sand or gravel which separate Finland's lakes or are scattered among them. Generally, they are formed by sediment which has been deposited and then become stratified, creating these strips of land rising above the water.

THE KANTELE
Also called the Finnish cithara, the kantele is a mediaeval instrument with a triangular, wing-shaped body. It is played by plucking the strings while holding the instrument against one's body or on a table. The oldest existing kanteles were found near Novgorod (in Russia).

THE MIDNIGHT SUN
In regions with a latitude of over 66°33', due to the inclination of the Earth, one can see the sun at midnight, because it does not descend lower than the horizon. So in summer months it is always daylight there, even at midnight, which is how it got its name!

🇸🇪 SWEDEN

With an area of close to 280,000 sq miles, Sweden is the third-largest country in Western Europe. 84% of its 9 million inhabitants are concentrated in cities. The Swedish are well known for their policy of protecting the environment and renewable energy. This is a priority for the majority of the population!

Göteborg harbor is protected from ice, making the city the country's most important port.

What is the capital?

Stockholm, in the south-east of the country, lies at the junction of Lake Mälar and the Baltic Sea. The seat of government and parliament, it is also the home of the head of state, King Carl Gustav XVI. The old medieval part of the city has buildings with remarkable architecture, such as the Royal Palace and St. Nicolas' Church, where the monarchs Òare crowned.

Stockholm is built on a number of little islets linked by bridges. As this creates a great many canals, it has been named the "Venice of the North". It is an important commercial port.

What are its principal cities?

Along with Stockholm, these are: Göteborg, with the country's main port; Malmö, in the south, which belonged to Denmark until 1658 (and was linked with the Danish capital, Copenhagen, by a bridge in 2000, allowing it to increase its economic power); and finally Birka, a city founded in the 8th century AD and rich in Viking archaeological remains.

Who are the Sami?

Better known as Lapps, this is a people from the region of Lapland, which covers the north of Sweden, Norway, Finland, and the Kola Peninsula in Russia. It has one of the lowest populations in the world: in Sweden, there are only 15,000 inhabitants! Their main activities are reindeer farming, fishing, and handcrafts (knives, fabrics, and basket weaving).

A Lapp in traditional costume

Built in 1546, Malmö's town hall has a façade in the Dutch Renaissance style dating from the 19th century.

DID YOU KNOW?

JOKKMOKK

This is a municipality inhabited by the Sami (or Lapps). Exhibits from their civilization are on show in the Ajtte Museum. Since 1605, a huge fair of Sami handicraft has been held at Jokkmokk every first weekend in February.

SAREK NATIONAL PARK

Along with Abisko Park, Sarek is one of the most beautiful national parks in Sweden. Located in Laponia, it has a great many mountains and nearly 100 glaciers. There are large numbers of birds in the lakes scattered throughout the park, as well as reindeer, polar foxes, and wolverines on its plateaus.

ALFRED NOBEL

This Swedish chemist (1833-1896) invented dynamite in 1867 in order to stabilise nitroglycerine, which was so unstable that it would explode at the slightest shock. He created a foundation that supported those involved in research. Since 1901, a prize is awarded each year to a person who has attained distinction in physics, chemistry, medicine, literature, economics, or work for peace.

THE BALTIC STATES

These include three states: Latvia, Lithuania, and Estonia. Located on the Baltic Sea, these countries were members of the former Soviet Union, from which they broke away in 1991, when each was proclaimed a republic.

The Daugava river crosses Russia, Belarus, and Latvia before emptying into the gulf.

Why is the capital of Latvia famous?

Riga was a member of the Hanseatic League, which brought together German merchants in the Netherlands, England, the Baltic Sea, and Northern Germany. In addition, the old town, founded in 1201, is surrounded by a moat and contains a number of mediaeval buildings, such as the 13th century cathedral and several houses dating from the 14th century. A real treasure!

The old-town area of Tallinn, with monuments dating from the 14th to the 16th centuries, overlooks the factories on the harbor.

What is the capital of Lithuania?

Built where two rivers, the Nelvia and the Neris, cross, Vilnius lies in the south-eastern part of the country. In 1323, it was chosen as capital by Prince Gediminas and, in the 16th century, became one of the most important trading cities in Europe. However, in 1795 it was annexed to the Russian Empire. After two World Wars, Vilnius was almost destroyed and its Jewish community, which comprised a large part of the population, was exterminated.

One of the many pedestrian streets in Vilnius

What is the capital of Estonia?

Tallinn is a mediaeval city but also a very important port in the Baltic Sea. Not only does it manufacture ships and have a large number of fish canneries, but it also has metal, textile, and electronic industries.

DID YOU KNOW?

PALANGA
Palanga is a little town on the Lithuanian coast, one of the country's main seaside resorts where the inhabitants and tourists can swim in the Baltic Sea or sunbake on its sandy beaches. The summer season in Palanga ends in an entertaining carnival.

LIEPAJA
This Latvian town on the shores of the Baltic Sea has a number of historical monuments including the market, the synagogue and St. Peter's Church. It became famous because of the mass murder of its Jewish population by the Nazis.

TARTU
Built in 1030, this is one of the most densely populated cities in Estonia. Today, it is an important industrial center. Not only are farming and printing equipment as well as shoes manufactured there, but there is also a great deal of woodworking. Tartu is also known for its old, prestigious university.

POLAND

In Warsaw, the old town (called Stare Miasto) has been almost entirely rebuilt.

A central European country, Poland has an area of over 190,000 sq miles. To the north lie the coastal plains of the Baltic Sea; in its center, the country is flat, but the south is fairly mountainous. This state has always been an important reference for Christianity and today is still the most Catholic country in Europe.

Since December 1997, Malbork Castle has been listed as a World Heritage site by Unesco.

When was Malbork castle built?

In the 13th century. From 1309 to 1457, this huge fortress was the seat of the Teutonic Order of knights (from Germany). Consisting almost entirely of brick, the castle has been restored a number of times since its construction.

Where is the Lake Region?

Masuria is in the north-east of Poland. It has about 400 lakes, connected by a multitude of rivers. A popular tourist area, this is the ideal region to go canoeing! The largest lakes are Sniardwy and Mamry.

One of the Masurian lakes

What is the capital?

It is Warsaw. During the Second World War, the city was not only the center of the Polish resistance but also the headquarters of the Nazis, who created a reign of terror in the city. During this war, Warsaw was almost entirely destroyed and thousands of its inhabitants exterminated. The city was later rebuilt as it had been in former times.

With its many skyscrapers, Warsaw has a modern city center.

The Vistula can be navigated along practically the whole of its length (585 miles) except in winter.

What is the main river?

With a length of 650 miles, the Vistula the longest river in the country. From its source in the Beskid mountains (part of the Carpathians) in the south of Poland, the river crosses the country, passing Krakow and Warsaw until it drains into the Gulf of Gdansk in the Baltic Sea.

DID YOU KNOW?

CHRISTMAS TRADITIONS
Every Christian feast day is celebrated in Poland because its people are very religious. At Christmastime, songs (called koledy) can be heard everywhere in the streets and houses. On Christmas Eve, a banquet is prepared for at least a dozen guests.

KRAKOW
This is certainly one of the oldest cities in Poland. In the 14th century, it was the capital of the country, but in the 16th century, King Sigismund decided that he preferred Warsaw. Nevertheless, for many years monarchs were still crowned here. Today, it is an artistic and cultural center and the country's main tourist destination!

THE TATRA MOUNTAINS
This is a mountainous range on the border between Poland and Slovakia. Its highest peak on Polish territory is Mount Rysy (8,035ft). The Tatras are a very popular tourist destination for winter sports enthusiasts.

THE CZECH REPUBLIC

Historically, the Czech Republic consists of three large regions (Bohemia to the west, Moravia to the east, and Silesia to the south). It is a land rich in history and tradition. Its castles and villages may be old, but so are its lakes and forests.

The Vltava runs its whole course in the Czech Republic.

What is the capital of the Czech Republic?

Prague is the capital, a city fascinating for its wealth of art and culture. Founded at the end of the 9th century, it still has in its historical center an immense heritage: the castle, St. Guy's Cathedral (where the kings of Bohemia are buried), the Clock Tower, and the Charles Bridge.

The Old Town is the heart of Prague.

What is the Vltava?

This is the longest waterway in the Czech Republic. It has its source in the forest of Bohemia and runs north merging with the Elbe at Melnik. With a length of 270 miles, it crosses the whole country, passing through its capital, Prague.

SLOVAKIA

This has been an independent state since 1993, when Czechoslovakia was divided into the Czech Republic and Slovakia. It has borders with Hungary to the south, Ukraine to the east, Poland to the north, and Austria and the Czech Republic to the west.

The Tatra mountains, between Poland and Slovakia, are the highest peaks in the Carpathian ranges.

Built from the 10th century on, Bratislava Castle dominates the capital.

What is the capital of Slovakia?

The capital is Bratislava. Its historical center shows the influence of a variety of architectural styles, bearing witness to different rules, Hungarian, Czech, and Austrian, for example. Its castle is the national emblem and can be seen on all the 10-, 20- and 50-cent coins of the country.

DID YOU KNOW?

FRANZ KAFKA
The writer Franz Kafka was born in Prague, where he spent a large part of his life. To be more precise, he worked for many years in a tiny little room in Alchemist's Street to find the peace and quiet he needed for his writing. This magical place near the castle was the inspiration for a great many of his works.

OLOMOUC
The Czech city of Olomouc has many large squares. The main one is adorned with a Baroque column to the Holy Trinity, a monument listed as a World Heritage edifice by Unesco. It is 115ft tall and dates from the 18th century.

KOSICE
This city in eastern Slovakia has one of the largest churches in the country, the cathedral of St. Elisabeth, a superb Gothic edifice built in the 14th and 15th centuries.

 **HUNGARY**

This central European state is a landlocked country, consisting of mountains to the north and a vast region of plains crossed by the Danube in the centre. Its area is roughly 58,000 sq miles and the population is estimated at almost 10 million, more than 65% of whom live in its cities.

The Danube crosses Hungary from north to south.

What is the capital?

This is Budapest, consisting of two municipalities: Buda, on the right bank of the Danube, and Pest, on the left bank. They are linked by six bridges, including the Chain Bridge. Buda is a residential area with embassies and other official building, while Pest is a commercial center.

A view of Lake Balaton. The south bank of the lake is a plain, but the north bank consists of hills covered in vineyards.

Which river divides Hungary in two?

The Danube, the second-longest river in Europe after the Volga, divides the country in two. About 1,770 miles in length, it has its source in the Black Forest in Germany and drains into the Black Sea through a large delta.

Which is the largest lake?

This is Lake Balaton, with an area of 415 sq miles. While it is not very deep, some 30 waterways flow into it. It lies 430ft above sea level and is a very popular tourist center, as it has beaches and a thermal resort.

The Protestant Reformed Great Church in Debrecen.

Which are the main cities in Hungary?

Debrecen, Mskolc, Szeged, Pécs, Gyöt, Szekesfehérvar, Eger, Esztergom.

The Royal Palace in Budapest

DID YOU KNOW?

GYÖR
Once a province in the Roman Empire, Györ was called Arrabona. Due to its geographic location halfway between Vienna and Budapest, it was and still is a gateway for trade between Eastern and Western Europe.

FERTOD CASTLE
Formerly called Eszterhazy Castle, this monument was nicknamed the "Hungarian Versailles." In the 18th century, it belonged to the Eszterhazy family. For them, art was a reason for living, and one which had to be shared. For example, the composer Joseph Haydn gave many concerts there!

AGGTELEK KARST
The national park of Aggtelek, listed as a World Heritage site by Unesco, contains a large number of caves. They were formed by erosion over thousands of years. As the drops of water infiltrated its walls, in time they created stalactites, long columns which hang down from the ceiling. However, as these drops fall onto the ground of the cave, they also create columns of limestone called stalagmites.

FORMER YUGOSLAVIA

The socialist Federal Republic of Yugoslavia was a large state in the Balkan Peninsula from 1945 to 1992, when it was dissolved. It then became six republics: Slovenia, Croatia, Macedonia, Bosnia and Herzegovina, Serbia, and Montenegro (the last two remained federated until 2006, when they separated).

Sveti Stefan on the coast of Montenegro. An ancient fishing village, it has become a popular tourist destination.

What is the capital of Serbia?

Belgrade, the capital, lies at the confluence of two rivers, the Danube and the Sava. It is the heart of a coal and lead mining region and the economy of the city is based on industry (chemicals, foods, textiles, pharmaceuticals, etc.). The principal economic center in the country, Belgrade has a road and rail network as well as an active river port and a large airport.

St Sava Church in Belgrade. Sava was the founder of the Serbian Orthodox Church.

What is Novi Sad?

It is the capital of the northern Serbian autonomous province of Vojvodina. Its economy is based on trade, thanks to its fertile agricultural lands and its harbor.

Its population makes Novi Sad the second-largest city in Serbia after Belgrade.

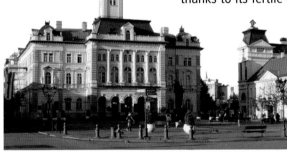

In the 18th and 19th centuries, Novi Sad was the most important cultural centre in Serbia.

What is known as Montenegro?

This small mountainous state became an independent republic on June 3rd, 2006. Its capital, Podgorica, got its name from a hill overlooking the town of Gorica ("little mountain"), because "pod" means "below." In the Middle Ages, it was called Ribnica, and then, between 1945 and 1992, it was named Titograd in honor of the Yugoslav leader, Tito.

What is the capital of Kosovo?

Pristina is the capital of Kosovo, a province of Serbia. With its 200,000 inhabitants, most of whom were Albanian, the city was at the heart of the conflict with the Serbs at the end of the 1980s: the Kosovars wanted to separate from Serbia and become part of Albania. The violence came to a climax in 1999, when Pristina was bombed, destroying much of the city. It has had considerable difficulty in recovering from this war.

The war has left visible marks on Pristina in Kosovo.

DID YOU KNOW?

THE PETRVARADIN FORTRESS
This huge building in Novi Sad lies on the right bank of the Danube. It was built in the 17th century by the Austrians, on a site dating from Roman times, as a strategic military post during the war with the Ottoman Empire. Today it houses a museum.

BELGRADE
The capital of Serbia and its most densely populated city, it was called "home of the holy war" by the Ottoman Turks in the 17th century because it was the scene of many bloody ethnic and religious battles. At this time, Belgrade was full of mosques, nearly all of which are now gone.

STUDENICA MONASTERY
Named a World Heritage centre by Unesco in 1986, this monument was built in the 12th century. It is one of the largest and richest monasteries belonging to the Serbian Orthodox Church. Its walls enclose two white marble churches and it has Byzantine style frescoes dating from the 13th and 14th centuries.

BOSNIA AND HERZEGOVINA

The river Neretva runs through the deep gorges of the Dinaric Alps before emptying into the Adriatic Sea.

Bosnia and Herzegovina is so called because it consists of two historical regions: Bosnia and Herzegovina. On the Balkan Peninsula, the country is bordered by Montenegro, Serbia, and Croatia but has only a very small opening onto the Adriatic Sea (12 miles).

What is its official language?

It is called Serbo-Croatian. This is also the language spoken in Serbia, Croatia and Montenegro. Yet, there are differences depending on the ethnic group, especially concerning the alphabet. The Serbo-Croatian of the Bosnians and Croats is written with the Latin alphabet, while the Serbs use Cyrillic characters.

Sarajevo, with the old town shown above, lies in a valley and is divided in two by the Miljacka.

What is its capital?

Sarajevo lies on the Miljacka river in the south-eastern region of the country. Before the 1992 war, it was one of the principal cultural centers in Yugoslavia. Since then, it has been rebuilt but with great difficulty.

Which mountain chain runs across Bosnia and Herzegovina?

Also called the Dinarides, the Dinaric Alps are a mountain chain which runs through the whole Balkan Peninsula from north to south. Formed largely of limestone, they include many of the deepest grottos in the world, a joy to speleologists!

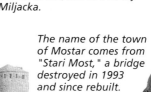

The name of the town of Mostar comes from "Stari Most," a bridge destroyed in 1993 and since rebuilt.

Pasturelands on the high peaks of the Dinaric Alps

Which are the main cities?

Along with Sarajevo, the capital, the country has a number of cities important for trade and tourism: Mostar, Luzla, Bihaca and Zenica and Banja Luka.

DID YOU KNOW?

BIHAC
This little town is known for its beauty and its river Una, which means "unique." It lies in the Federation of Bosnia and Herzegovina, only about 25 miles from a superb site: Plitvice National Park in Croatia.

NEUM
With its 12 miles coastline on the Adriatic Sea, Neum is the only sea town in Bosnia and Herzegovina. With a population of less than 5,000, it is a great tourist resort, due to its Mediterranean climate: long, hot summers and short, mild winters.

ETHNIC GROUPS
With over 4 million inhabitants, Bosnia and Herzegovina comprises several ethnic groups. The majority are Bosnian Muslims, followed by the Serbs, and then the Croats. A tiny minority (less than 1%) are of other origins.

CROATIA

This republic is surrounded by Slovenia, Hungary, Serbia, Bosnia and Herzegovina, and Montenegro. The Adriatic Sea borders the whole coast of the country, with a length of 1,060 miles. In addition, Croatia has islands in the Adriatic called the Dalmatian archipelago. With its coast, airports and motorways, the economy of this state is based on industry and tourism.

In the city of Zagreb, the Croatian National Theater has seen a large number of artists perform: Franz Liszt, Richard Strauss, Jean-Louis Barrault, Gérard Philippe, Sarah Bernhardt, and many others!

What is the capital of Croatia?

It is Zagreb. Founded in the 11th century in the north of the country, it lies near the river Sava at the foot of Medvednica Mountain. It is one of the most important industrial, commercial, and cultural centers in the country, as it acts as a connecting point between central Europe and the Adriatic Sea.

The Croatian Adriatic coast is a tourist paradise.

What is the main river in Slovenia?

The Isonzo has its source in the Julian Alps and runs through Slovenia for a distance of 90 miles. It has been nicknamed "the emerald beauty" because of the intense green of its waters. During the First World War, the Isonzo valley was the scene of many battles between the Austro-Hungarian and Italian forces. At its mouth in the Gulf of Trieste, there is a natural reserve where one can admire over 300 species of bird.

SLOVENIA

A European State, Slovenia is bordered by Austria and Hungary to the north, Italy to the west, Croatia to the east and south, and by the Adriatic to the south-west. With an area of over 12,500 sq miles, it is a particularly mountainous country with a large number of forests.

The architecture of Ljubljana is very heterogeneous, with elements from various periods in its history (Roman, Austrian, etc.).

What is the capital of Slovenia?

Ljubljana, the capital, is believed to have been built on the remains of a Roman site called Aemona, founded in AD 15. Trade is an ancestral tradition in this city but its industry has developed enormously: it includes manufacture of porcelain, paper, furniture, and leatherwork.

DID YOU KNOW?

LJUBLJANA
With a population of some 270,000, the Slovenian capital lies at a strategic spot on the map of Europe. This is why it has been influenced by many several different cultures: Latin, Germanic, and Slavic.

DINOSAURS
In the Croatian region of Istria, dinosaur footprints and bones have been found. These fossils are now in the paleontology reserve of Datula-Barbariga.

ARCHAEOLOGY
Many archaeologists have excavated the Island of Pag, in Croatia, and found a large number of remains: a Roman aqueduct carved into the 1st century rock, the foundations of three basilicas and a reliquary dating from the first centuries of our era.

THE REPUBLIC
OF **MACEDONIA**

A small state on the Balkan Peninsula, with a largely mountainous topography, it was a southern region of the former Yugoslavia before gaining independence. The Republic of Macedonia occupies only part of the whole geographic region of Macedonia: the rest is divided between its neighboring countries, Greece and Bulgaria.

When did the Republic of Macedonia gain independence?

It proclaimed its independence in September 1991 but was not admitted as such by the UN (United Nations) until 1993. It goes by the official name of FYROM (from the English words "Former Yugoslav Republic of Macedonia") to avoid objections from Greece.

After being captured by the Turks in 1392, Skopje was an important city in the Ottoman Empire at the end of the Middle Ages.

What is the capital of FYROM?

With a population of roughly 515,000, Skopje, the capital, is its most densely populated city. It is an important center for trade: cereals, cotton, and tobacco (grown in the neighboring regions). After Skopje, the largest cities are Bitola, Kumanova, Prilep, and Tetova.

The city of Durrës has Albania's largest port.

ALBANIA

Its sea borders are the Adriatic Sea, the Strait of Otranto and the Ionian Sea, in all, a coastline of 160 miles. Most of the country is mountainous and difficult of access. Mount Korab, the highest peak, rises to a height of over.

What is the capital of Albania?

It is Tirana, of the main industrial and cultural centres in the country. The Et'hem Bey Mosque is one of the most remarkable monuments in the city, which also boasts a university, an academy of science, a museum of Albanian folklore, and an archaeology and ethnology museum.

TIRANA

The old buildings in the centre of Tirana were repainted in bright colors by order of the mayor, Edi Rama.

Which are its most important ports?

Durrës, 21 miles from Tirana, is the chief port of Albania and one of the oldest cities in the land. Vlorë is another important port which exports oil, olives, and fruit.

Lake Ohrid was declared a World Heritage site by Unesco in 1979.

DID YOU KNOW?

BERAT
Since 2005, this little town has been listed as a World Heritage site by Unesco. It lies in southern Albania and is one of the few towns whose Ottoman architecture has been preserved. Its impressive castle is evidence of this.

MACEDONIAN FOLKLORE
With their dancing and singing, the men and women, dressed in traditional costumes, carry on a tradition which is several centuries old. They give performances in the big cities but also in concert halls in small municipalities. A splendid show!

BITOLA
Founded on the ruins of a Greek city (Heraclea Lyncestis), traces of which can still be seen today, Bitola is the second-largest urban centre in the Macedonian Republic. It lies in the Pelagonia Valley, where leather and cereals are produced.

THE CAUCASUS

This is a large region spreading over south-eastern Europe and western Asia. It is crossed by the Caucasus mountain range. The northern part of the Caucasus is called Ciscaucasia (comprising various Russian federal republics) while the southern part, known as Transcaucasia, is composed of three countries, Georgia, Armenia, and Azerbaijan.

Scenic panorama of the city of Erevan

What is Greater Ararat?

This is a mountain in Turkey, near the Armenian border, which offers a fine view of it. Over 14,000ft high, it is covered in eternal snows. Greater Ararat is part of a mountain massif called Mount Ararat. According to one interpretation of the Old Testament of the Bible, Noah's Ark is said to have landed here after the deluge!

Mount Ararat behind the Khor Virap monastery in Armenia

What is the capital of Armenia?

Erevan, the capital, was occupied successively by the Romans, Parthians, Arabs, etc. On its strategic site (altitude of 3,280ft on the banks of the river Razcan), Erevan was fought over for many years by Persia (present-day Iran) and the Ottoman Turks. In 1920, it was a very small town of 30,000 inhabitants. Today it has a population of over one million!

When was the Caucasus formed?

This mountain chain is thought to have formed beginning in the Jurassic era, over 100 million years ago. Almost as long and high as the Alps, the Caucasus has several peaks with altitudes of at least 16,400ft.

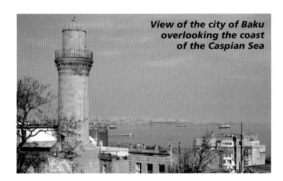

View of the city of Baku overlooking the coast of the Caspian Sea

What is the capital of Georgia?

Although evidence shows that the city was inhabited in 4,000 BC, Tbilisi as such was not mentioned and was apparently not founded until the 4th century AD. Today, its many archaeological remains, museums and its university make it a famous cultural and artistic city.

What is the capital of Azerbaijan?

Located on the eastern coast of the country, the capital, Baku, is a large port city overlooking the Caspian Sea. Almost 80% of industrial manufacturing in Azerbaijan is carried out here: textiles, foods, metallurgy, shipbuilding, and especially petroleum, as its ground is rich in oil deposits.

Metekhi Church and Narikala Fortress bear witness to the long, rich history of Tbilisi.

DID YOU KNOW?

MOUNT ELBRUS
This is the highest peak in the Caucasus. In fact, this extinct volcano is nicknamed "twin peaks," because it has two craters of almost equal altitude: 18,356ft and 18,510ft.

LAKE SEVAN
This mountain lake lies on a high plateau at an altitude of 6,235ft. With an area of 870 sq miles, it is the largest lake in Armenia. It is fed by many tributaries but has only one outlet, the Razdan River, which flows through the capital, Erevan.

GYUMRI
Armenia's second-largest city, it was called Alexandropol under the Russian Empire, then Leninakan during the Soviet era and finally known again as Gyumri in 1991, when the country got its independence. On December 7th, 1988, a terrible earthquake caused enormous damage and over 25,000 deaths.

BULGARIA

Bulgaria is in the eastern region of the Balkan Peninsula. It shares borders with Romania to the north, Serbia and Macedonia (FYROM) to the west and Turkey and Greece to the south. It is crossed from east to west, by two mountain ranges: to the north, the Balkan Mountains and to the south, the Rhodope Mountains. Between them lie the plains.

Bulgarian women wearing dazzling traditional costumes

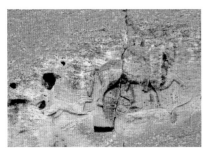

The Madara Rider

What is the Madara Rider?

This is a sculpture carved in bas-relief on a rocky wall depicting a horseman killing a lion with a spear and a dog running after him. The Madara Rider is carved into a 330-ft-high cliff 75ft from the ground!

What is its capital?

Located at the foot of the Balkan mountain range, Sofia is the capital. It is an important rail and river center which links the country with Athens (Greece), Belgrade (Serbia), Bucharest (Romania), and Istanbul (Turkey).

Formerly known as Philippopolis, Plovdiv is one of the oldest cities in Europe.

The Alexander Nevsky Orthodox Cathedral lies in the heart of Sofia.

What is its sea border?

It is the Black Sea. This inland sea is about 750 miles long with a width of 380 miles. In ancient times, it was a rich source of fish for the surrounding countries and still remains an essential crossroads leading to the East.

The coast of Varna on the Black Sea

What are its main cities?

Along with the capital, Sofia, these are Plovdiv (home to many industries), Varna (important seaport), Burgas (with its fishing industry), and Ruse (important river port).

DID YOU KNOW?

PIRIN NATIONAL PARK
Listed as a World Heritage centre by Unesco since 1993, it has an area of 27,000ha and is therefore the largest national park in Bulgaria. Located in the Prin Mountains, it boasts huge forests, torrents, waterfalls, grottos, and chasms. It is the habitat for many animal species, many of which are under threat of extinction.

NESEBAR
Built on a peninsula in the Black Sea, this city was invaded by different peoples throughout its history: the Thracians, Greeks, Romans and, finally, the Turks. Today, many remains and monuments recall all these periods: they include an acropolis, a temple, an agora, and several churches. In 1983, it became a Unesco World Heritage site.

PLOVDIV
This is the second-largest city in Bulgaria, located in an agricultural region where tobacco is grown and cattle are raised. It is also an industrial center with tobacco, food, and textile factories and carpentry businesses, etc. Many monuments from its past are still in existence: gates and thermal baths dating from antiquity, walls, churches, mosques, and even the ruins of a Turkish market!

ROMANIA

In 107 AD, Romania was a province in the Roman Empire called Dacia. It was subjected to many invasions throughout its history: the Goths, Gepids, Huns, Avars, Bulgarians, Mongols, etc. In 1881, Romania became a kingdom and then a democratic state in around 1920. However, in 1965, Nicolae Ceausescu made it a dictatorship, which was overthrown by the people in 1989.

Coast on the Black Sea

What is its capital?

Bucharest is the capital. In the 1930s, it was known as the "Paris of the Balkans" because of its great boulevards and its architecture. However, it was greatly altered during the regime of Nicolae Ceausescu, who had its historical heritage destroyed to make way for enormous new buildings, like the Casa Poporului (House of the People), a huge building with 11,000 rooms, which today houses the Chamber of Deputies and the Senate.

What is the sea border of Romania?

This is the Black Sea, a large inland sea between Eastern Europe and the Middle East. Constanta is the main Romanian city on the coast, a port from which cereals and petroleum are exported and also an industrial center.

Built in the early 19th century, the Romanian Athenaeum in Bucharest is a theatre and concert hall.

The tower of the Orthodox Cathedral in Chisinau

MOLDAVIA

This is a small European state between Romania and Ukraine. Two rivers, the Dniester and the Prut, form part of its border. Moldavia was once a republic of the former Soviet Union and acquired its independence in 1991.

What is the capital of Moldavia?

Chisinau, the capital, is one of the greenest cities in Europe. Built on the river Bic (a tributary of the river Dniester), it lies in the center of the country. Its economy is based essentially on farming products, wine, and tobacco. The architecture of its many monuments is varied because of the different ethnic groups who ruled Chisinau in the course of its history.

Desolate landscape in the steppes found mainly in central Moldavia

What is the topography of Moldavia like?

Its territory covers the historical region of Bessarabia, where the landscape of plains and steppes is broken up by low hills which rarely rise above an altitude of 1,310ft.

DID YOU KNOW?

TRANSYLVANIA
This word means "beyond the forest" and refers to the region of central Romania. A high plateau surrounded by different mountains, it was the background for the well known character invented in 1897 by the British writer Bram Stoker, the terrible Count Dracula! This aristocratic vampire got his name from the Romanian word "dracul," meaning "dragon."

TIMISOARA
Located in western Romania, this city lies in the county of Timis, on the river of the same name. On December 16th 1989, it was, the scene of riots which led to the fall of the dictator Nicolae Ceausescu and his totalitarian regime. Timisoara was the first free city in Romania.

TIRASPOL
This is the capital of Transnistria (a region which considers itself as being independent from Moldavia, although at the international level it has not been recognised as such). Tiraspol is one of the few remaining cities to have preserved monuments of its Soviet past.

UKRAINE

This was a federated republic of the former Soviet Union until 1991, when it acquired its independence. Its area of over 370,000 sq miles makes it the second-largest European country after Russia. The Ukrainian landscape consists essentially of immense plains of black soil which are very fertile for agriculture.

What is the capital of Ukraine?

The capital, Kiev, lies on the river Dnieper. Its huge parks and historical buildings make it a magnificent city. It was one of the main religious centres in the Russian Empire, with a large number of churches, some dating from the 11th century. Of its many other monuments, the best-known is Kiev-Pechersk Laura with its catacombs – the oldest Orthodox monastery in Russia.

The Cathedral of St Sophia (11th century) in Kiev

What is the Crimea?

This autonomous region is a peninsula connected to the southern end of Ukraine. Its economy is essentially based on culture, mining, and tourism. Due to its climate and huge plains, it has a great many orchards (cherries, figs, apricots, peaches, etc.) and also grows wheat, almonds, barley, hemp, and tobacco.

Minsk has been the capital of the independent state of Belarus since 1991.

BELARUS

A state in eastern Europe, it shares borders with Latvia and Lithuania to the north-east, Russia to the east, Ukraine to the south, and Poland to the west. It has no sea access.

What is Polesia?

This is a swamp region shared by Ukraine and Belarus. With its terrain composed of peat and sand, it is a fairly inhospitable area. However, the Polesie National Park consists of forests containing nearly 140 species of bird and 40 species of mammal.

What is the capital of Belarus?

The capital is Minsk, which played an essential role in the dismantling of the former USSR. The Commonwealth of Independent States (CIS) treaty was signed here. Twelve of the fifteen former Soviet republics joined it to gain their independence in 1991.

The marshy region of Pripet in Polesia

DID YOU KNOW?

CHERNOBYL
This Ukrainian city became famous throughout the whole world on April 26th, 1986. One of the reactors of its nuclear plant exploded, irradiating the surroundings and leaving many victims. On the following days, a radioactive cloud floated over Europe, contaminating other countries like Scandinavia, Poland, Germany, Italy, and France.

UKRAINIAN ETHNIC GROUPS
After Russia, Ukraine is the most densely populated country in the former USSR. The majority of its population is Ukrainian, followed by the Russians. Its ethnic minorities are the Belarussians, Moldavians, Bulgarians, Poles, Hungarians, and the Crimean Tatars.

NAVAHRUDAK
This region, which formerly belonged to Poland, was annexed by the USSR after the Second World War and divided between Lithuania and Belarus. The illustration shows the ruins of Grand Duke Mindaugas' castle, which dates from the 13th century.

RUSSIA

With an area of over 10 million sq miles, this is the largest country in the world. Russia is in Eurasia, that is, its territory occupies a quarter of Europe and three-quarters of Asia. The Ural Mountains constitute the border between both continents. This country is so big that it has 11 time zones, which means, for example, that when it is noon at the eastern end of the country, it is 11pm and night at the western end!

The Peterhof gardens in St Petersburg

What is the capital of Russia?

Its capital is Moscow. It was the capital of the USSR between 1919 and 1991 and today has over 10 million inhabitants. The Kremlin, which means "fortress," is the seat of government institutions; the office of the president is in the Grand Palace. It stands on the Red Square and is also a huge historical and artistic complex.

The Cathedral of the Assumption in the Kremlin (Moscow)

What is St Petersburg?

This is the second-largest city in Russia and its biggest port. Founded in 1703 on the coast of the Baltic Sea by Tsar Peter the Great, it was the capital of Russia from 1712 to 1918. In 1914, its name was changed to Petrograd and then, 10 years later, it was re-named Leningrad. It was not until 1991 that it was again called by its original name. An architectural jewel, it is the cultural cradle of Russia.

Changing the guard at the tomb of the unknown soldier in Moscow

What is its longest river?

With a length of 2,300 miles, the Volga is also the longest river in Europe! It has its source in a small lake in the Valdai Hills north-west of Moscow. Then it flows south across the country and empties into the Caspian Sea through a large delta. The Volga is frozen over for 3 to 5 months of the year for a large part of its length.

Around June of each year, the Volga floods because of melting snow.

DID YOU KNOW?

LAKE BAIKAL
Located in the southern region of Siberia, this is the deepest lake in the world. It is also the largest freshwater lake in Asia. Its clear waters are the habitat for over 1,200 species of animal, some of which are only found in this spot.

SIBERIA
An icy region of Northern Asia, it was conquered by the Russians in the 16th century. The Trans-Siberian Railway, over 5,500 miles long, was built to cross the whole of Siberia, from Moscow to Omsk.

ASTRAKHAN
This city is situated in southern Russia in the Volga Delta. Founded by the Mongols in the 13th century, it was captured by Ivan the Terrible in 1556. Gradually, it came to play an economic role, because, although its port is blocked by ice for four months of the year, it exports the petroleum that is extracted in the region.

ASIA

The Himalayas are a mountain range with over 100 peaks higher than 20,000ft. One of these is Mount Everest, the highest mountain in the world!

With an area of about 27 million sq miles, this is the largest continent on the planet. It has almost 4 billion inhabitants, making it also the most densely populated one! Divided into six clearly distinct regions, it comprises 46 countries.

The Himalayan Mountains

What separates Asia from Africa?

It is the Red Sea. Its size (1,400 miles long and over 125 miles wide) makes it extremely important for trade. By sailing along this sea and then through the Suez Canal, ships from Asia can reach Europe very quickly.

The Red Sea is one of the warmest on our planet and is extremely salty.

Which is the most densely populated state in Asia?

China is the third-largest country in the world, after Russia and Canada. It is not only the most densely populated State in Asia but also on the whole planet! Of its 1.5 billion inhabitants (one-fifth of the world's population), about 13 million are concentrated in Shanghai and 11 million in Peking (called Beijing).

Why are the Himalayas called the "roof of the world"?

They are so called simply because this is the highest mountain range on the globe. The Himalayas include 9 of the 14 highest peaks in the world! Some of these are: Annapurna, Kanchenjunga, Dhaulagiri and, of course, Everest. The name "Himalaya" means "abode of snow" in Sanskrit.

These ruins in the desert of Syria, in the Middle East, bear witness to the glorious past of Palmyra, a Syrian city founded on an oasis in around 2,000 BC.

What is the Asian economy based on?

The economies of many Asian countries are based on agriculture. However, some countries, like Japan, China, India, and Israel have developed through technology and industry. Others, like the Arab Emirates, rely on their petroleum resources.

In 1405, Emperor Yongle decided to transfer the capital of the Chinese Empire from Nanjing to Beijing and build a city within a city: the Forbidden City. It was so called because only members of the imperial family, civil servants working at court, eunuchs, and servants were allowed to enter it!

DID YOU KNOW?

DUBAI
This city, in the north-west of the United Arab Emirates, is also the capital of the Emirate of Dubai, on the west side of the Persian Gulf. It is one of the major ports in the country and plays an indispensable part in trade with the other States. Dubai has been nicknamed "The Venice of the Gulf"!

BOMBAY
Renamed Mumbai in May 1995, this Indian city is a large commercial hub due to its huge harbor, its airport, and its many motorways and railways. Along with its financial center, industry is a very important element (shipbuilding, textiles, printing, chemicals, metallurgy, and even filmmaking)!

SHANGHAI
The most densely populated city in China, this is also one of the largest ports in the country. Its industries have made Shanghai a business center for trade and finance!

CHINA

The People's Republic of China lies in eastern Asia. It has close to 9,300 miles of land borders, which it shares with 14 countries: Russia, Mongolia, North Korea, Vietnam, Laos, Myanmar, India, Bhutan, Nepal, Pakistan, Afghanistan, Tajikistan, Kyrgyzstan, and Kazakhstan.

The Huang Ho is called "China's Sorrow" because of its frequent floods and their disastrous consequences.

What is the area of China?

If one includes its 2,900 islands, its total area is 5,950,000 sq miles. China is the third-largest country in the world, after Russia and Canada. Its landscape is largely mountainous: 84% of its mountains are over 1,600ft above sea level, and more than 43% are over 6,500ft high!

In the 18th century, over 60,000 servants and 9,000 women lived in the Forbidden City. It extends over 4 miles and contains 800 buildings with 9,000 rooms!

What are its two longest rivers?

The Yangtze, about 3,900 miles long, is not only the longest river in China, but also in all Asia! The second-longest Chinese river is the Huang Ho, 3,400 miles long. Its name means "Yellow River" because it carries alluvium in suspension in its flow, and this gives the water its very particular color.

What is its capital?

It is Beijing (formerly Peking), which literally means "northern capital." It is aptly named, as the city lies in the north-west region of the country. It has an area of 10,440 sq miles and 11 million inhabitants.

In China, the dragon symbolizes divine power.

How long is the Great Wall?

The first section of the Great Wall was completed around 210 BC, but was enlarged and consolidated in 1598 AD. Its length of 4,160 miles makes it the longest existing fortification in the world, and it can be seen from outer space!

View of the Great Wall of China

DID YOU KNOW?

HONG KONG
This territory has a special status in China. It was administered by Britain until 1997. With an area of 650 sq miles, Hong Kong consists of a part of the Asian continent as well as numerous surrounding islands and islets.

MACAU
This special administrative region of Asia was formerly under Portuguese rule. It was annexed by China in 1999. Its area is tiny, no more than 10 sq miles. It includes the Macau Peninsula and two islands, Taipa and Coloane.

TAIWAN
An island off the coast of the China Sea, Taiwan is claimed by China as its 23rd province. It has an area of 22,400 sq miles and its capital, Taipei, lies in its northern region. The island is highly industrialised and is one of the biggest exporting territories in Asia.

 # INDIA

Benares, officially Varanasi, on the left bank of the Ganges, is sacred for Hindus.

A country in southern Asia, India is bordered by the Oman Sea and Pakistan to the west, Tibet, Bhutan, and Nepal to the north, Myanmar (Burma), Bangladesh, and the Bay of Bengal on the east and, finally, the Gulf of Mannar and Palk Strait to the south.

What is the capital of India?

It is New Delhi, built between 1912 and 1929 near a site called Delhi in the north of the country, hence its name. Its architecture was designed by the British; this is why one finds buildings in the European style decorated with Indian architectural details. There is even a Triumphal Arch, erected in commemoration of the First World War.

India has a great variety of ethnic groups, languages, and religions.

Where is the source of the Ganges?

The 1,550-miles-long Ganges begins in the Himalayas and runs its course mainly in India, even though its delta is in Bangladesh. Hindus consider it a sacred river and bathe in it during purification rites.

New Delhi

Taj Mahal means "Palace of the Crown." It is one of the finest and best-preserved funerary monuments in the world.

What are castes?

These are closed social classes. Although this system was abolished by the republican constitution in 1950, there are still 1,600 communities in existence. Ethnic, religious, and linguistic differences still lead to the existence of many castes today (like the Untouchables).

What is India's demography?

With over 1 billion inhabitants (1/6 of the world's population), India is the second most populous country after China.

What is the Taj Mahal?

It was built in the city of Agra by Emperor Shah Jahan as a mausoleum for his favorite wife. Begun in 1632, this superb monument took over 20 years to build.

DID YOU KNOW?

THE BENGAL TIGER
This tiger lives only on the Asian continent. It can measure up to 9ft in length and weigh over 440lbs. Threatened with extinction, it is listed as a protected species.

GANDHI
Called the Mahatma, meaning "Great Soul," Mohandas Gandhi (1869–1948) was the leader of the nationalist movement which sought to free India from British rule. His action was based on the principle of non-violence and respect for individual freedom.

BOLLYWOOD
A mixture of the words "Hollywood" and "Bombay," this refers to the Indian film industry. Music and dance, which are an integral part of popular culture, are always present in these film productions.

OCEANIA

New Zealand consists of two islands. Most of the population live on North Island. South Island is very mountainous and has over 300 glaciers.

Oceania is a continent consisting of Australia, New Zealand, Polynesia, Melanesia, and Micronesia. It also includes thousands of islands scattered throughout the Indian and Pacific Oceans. Oceania was inhabited for thousands of years by indigenous tribes before being colonized by European settlers in the 16th century.

What is most famous monument in Australia?

This is, without a doubt, the Sydney Opera House. Designed by the Danish architect, Jorn Utzon, it has the world's largest pipe organ (with over 10,000 pipes). Its original architecture makes it one of the symbols of Australia and it was declared a World Heritage site by Unesco in 2007.

The great Barrier Reef contains many marine species, both animal and plant.

How long is the Great Barrier Reef?

With a length of 2,010km, this is the longest coral reef in the world. It lies off the coast of Australia and is an ecosystem rich in species of coral (nearly 400) and fish (over 1,500).

The Sydney Opera House has an astonishing roof: it resembles huge upright shells or enormous sails on a ship!

What is Uluru?

This is the aboriginal name for Ayer's Rock, a mountain in the center of Australia. Red in colour, Uluru stands in the middle of a desert plain. It is still sacred to the Aborigines.

Uluru or Ayer's Rock

Which is the highest mountain in New Zealand?

This is Mount Cook, 12,350ft high. Located on South Island, its summit is covered in eternal snow. The indigenous tribes call it "aorangi," meaning "snow piercer"!

The Fiji Islands are an archipelago of around 800 islands in Melanesia. Only about one hundred are inhabited.

Which islands make up Polynesia?

The word "Polynesia" comes from the Greek and means "many islands." It is aptly named, since Polynesia is a group of islets which emerge in the middle of the Pacific Ocean. Some, like Hawaii or Easter Island, are fairly large but others are simply little atolls where only coconut trees can be found!

DID YOU KNOW?

ABORIGINES

This word comes from the Latin "ab originis" meaning "from the origins" and is the name for the first people to inhabit Australia. Today, the Aborigines are still very attached to their traditions, which they hand down from one generation to the next.

THE BOOMERANG

The boomerang is a flying weapon thrown by Aborigines when hunting. Due to its curved shape, it rotates on its own axis when thrown and hits the target with force, even from a great distance. If it does not hit a target, it returns to the thrower's hand.

THE MAORI

The Maori are a New Zealand tribe of Polynesian origin. The traditional dance of Maori warriors, the Haka, is known to all rugby enthusiasts throughout the world, since the New Zealand team dances it before every match!

🇯🇵 JAPAN

This is an island state in eastern Asia. It lies in the Pacific Ocean and consists of a large number of islands, the four largest of which are Honshu, Hokkaido, Shikoku, and Kyushu. The country has a great many species of plants and animals, including the Japanese Macaque, which is found only on the island of Honshu and nowhere else!

Tokyo is a large city of over 12 million inhabitants.

Osaka, on the southern end of Honshu, is an important industrial center and harbor.

What is the vegetation of Japan?

Because of the heat, the humidity (caused by the large amount of precipitation) and its mountains, over 68% of the area of Japan is covered in forests. These consist of deciduous trees (which lose their leaves in autumn) and conifers (evergreens). There are plant species which are found only in Japan.

What is the capital of Japan?

Tokyo, meaning "capital of the East" is the capital; it is located on the island of Honshu. With an area of 373 sq miles, it consists of 23 special wards and is one of the most dynamic cities in Japan. It was formerly called Edo, but Emperor Mutsuhito renamed it Tokyo in 1868, when it was declared the capital of the country. In the heart of the city is a huge park surrounded by moats which the people are not allowed to enter, for the Imperial Palace lies in its center.

How is Japan governed?

It is a hereditary constitutional monarchy, that is, its emperors succeed each other from one generation to the next. However, their role is purely symbolic. The legislative power is in the hands of the two Houses of Parliament, the House of Representatives and the House of Councillors. The executive power is held by the Prime Minister and his cabinet, which is named by him.

On January 7th, 1989, Akihito became the 125th Emperor of Japan, following the death of his father, Hirohito.

What is its highest mountain?

Mount Fuji, 12,390ft, is the highest peak in Japan. Located on the island of Honshu, it is a volcano which has been inactive since 1707. It is considered sacred by the Japanese: several temples have been erected there and it is the destination of many pilgrimages.

Mount Fuji

Mount Fuji is the destination for pilgrimages by Shintoists and Buddhists.

DID YOU KNOW?

SUSHI
This is a typically Japanese dish, consisting of rice moulded into an oblong shape, on which raw fish is placed. Sometimes this is rolled up in a sheet of seaweed. Sashimi is raw fish cut into slices and eaten with white rice.

THE SAMURAI
They were initially Japanese warriors of noble origin. From the 11th century on, they formed a military class who served the Japanese feudal aristocracy, the daimyo. In 1869, the reforms brought in by Mutsuhito abolished the status of the samurai, who completely disappeared by 1871.

TEA CEREMONY
Tea, in particular, Ryokucha green tea, is an extremely popular drink in Japan. The tea ceremony, called chanoyu, is a veritable ritual which has come down through the centuries, with rules laid down by Sen no Rikyu in the 16th century.

AMERICA

The Great Lakes, in North America, spread over an area of 150,000 sq miles.

America consists of two continents which include North, Central, and South America. It was discovered in 1492 by Christopher Columbus. After that time, much exploration and colonisation occurred on its lands. Separated from Asia by the Bering Strait, America comprises 35 independent States. Its name comes from "Amerigo," the first name of Vespucci, an Italian explorer.

What is the national memorial of Mount Rushmore?

Giant sculptures on Mount Rushmore

This is a huge granite sculpture in South Dakota which depicts four United States presidents: Washington, Jefferson, Theodore Roosevelt, and Lincoln. It was carved between 1927 and 1941 by Gutzon Borglum, with the help of 400 workmen!

What are the Great Lakes?

These are five lakes: Ontario, Erie, Huron, Michigan, and Superior. Only Lake Michigan is located entirely on United States territory. The others are on the border between Canada and the United States. Together, these lakes form the largest stretch of fresh water in the world.

Why is the Amazon forest called the lungs of the world?

The Amazon plays an essential part in the ecological balance of the Earth. By means of its abundant vegetation, the forest transforms into oxygen a large quantity of the carbon dioxide that we release into the air through pollution.

The Moai, enormous stone statues, are aligned side by side on Easter Island.

The Amazon forest, with its 3,7 million sq miles, is the largest tropical forest in the world.

Where is Tierra del Fuego?

This archipelago lies at the southern tip of the American continent. Ferdinand Magellan was the first to discover it in 1520. He called it "Tierra del Fuego" (Land of Fire) because, as he observed it from a distance, he saw the many fires lit by the indigenous inhabitants.

DID YOU KNOW?

LAKE TITICACA
On the border between Bolivia and Peru, this lake is on a high plateau at 12,505ft. It is not only the highest navigable lake in the world but also the largest in South America. Fed by nearly 25 waterways, it has an area of 5,175 sq miles. For the Incas, this was a sacred place.

THE GRAND CANYON
In the Arizona desert, the Grand Canyon is an enormous gorge dug by the Colorado River over almost 6 million years. A most spectacular sight, it stretches for more than 275 miles and, in some spots, the chasm reaches a depth of 5,250ft.

ANGEL FALLS
Also called "Salto del Angel" (meaning "angel falls"), this is a waterfall in Venezuela. The water plunges 3,212ft from a high plateau, making it the highest waterfall in the world. It got its name simply because the person who discovered it was called Jimmy Angel!

THE UNITED STATES

The United States (or U.S.A.) is a federal republic in North America. It has land borders with Canada to the north and Mexico to the south. On the east lies the Atlantic Ocean and on the west, the Pacific. The area of the United States is 5,983,000 sq miles.

Manhattan skyscrapers

What do tourists visit in the United States?

They visit cities like New York (for its museums), Los Angeles (for its beaches), and Las Vegas (for its casinos). However, many tourists also go to the magnificent national parks: the Rocky Mountains, where Yellowstone, Monument Valley, and the Grand Canyon are found, and the Appalachians.

The Grand Canyon National Park in Arizona is one of the largest in the United States.

Where is San Francisco?

The city lies on a peninsula overlooking the Pacific Ocean to the west. However, to the east and north is a gulf, called San Francisco Bay. From 1933 to 1937, a huge bridge was built by J.B. Strauss to link the city of San Francisco with Marin County. It is called the Golden Gate. For many years, it was the largest bridge in the world.

What does the United States flag depict?

The 50 stars on the American flag symbolize the states which make up the United States; the thirteen red and white stripes represent the original 13 states.

Russian Hill is a residential area in San Francisco which provides a view of the entire bay!

What is its most densely populated city?

This is New York, with an area of 745 sq miles and a population of over 8 million. The city is divided into 5 administrative districts (boroughs): Manhattan, the Bronx, Queens, Brooklyn, and Staten Island.

But what is the capital of the United States?

The capital is Washington, where the headquarters of United States government institutions (the White House, Congress, the Supreme Court) are found, along with many ministries and federal bodies.

The White House is the official residence of the President of the United States of America.

DID YOU KNOW?

THE MISSISSIPPI
With its tributary, the Missouri, the Mississippi measures a total of 4,225 miles. It is one of the longest rivers in the United States. It takes its source in the State of Minnesota and empties into the Gulf of Mexico.

ALASKA
With an area of 943,240 sq miles and only 550,000 inhabitants, Alaska was admitted into the United States as its 49th State on January 3rd, 1959. Before the arrival of the Europeans, the country was inhabited by Aleuts, Inuits, and other indigenous peoples.

THE HAWAIIAN ISLANDS
The Hawaiian Islands are an archipelago in the Pacific Ocean. They became the 50th state on August 21st, 1959. The earliest inhabitants were the Polynesians, skilled navigators who arrived there in the 5th century.

MEXICO

Mexico is a country in North America with a common border with the United States, Belize, and Guatemala. It overlooks the Atlantic Ocean to the east and the Pacific to the west. Depending on one's altitude, the country has three kinds of climate: hot, temperate, or cold.

Mexico City is located on a huge plateau at an altitude of roughly 7,350ft.

What are its most famous archaeological sites?

These include the Pyramids of the Sun and the Moon in the sacred city of Teotihuacán and the ancient Mayan city of Chichén Itzá, in the northern region of the Yucatán Peninsula.

The Mayan Pyramid of Chichén Itzá is one of the most famous sites in the world.

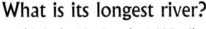

One of the peaks of the Sierra Madre

Where was Mexico City built?

It was built on the site of Tenochtitlán, the capital of the Aztec Empire. Although it was destroyed by the Spaniards in 1521, remains of the pre-Columbian civilization can still be seen in excavations and in various places in the city.

What is its longest river?

This is the Rio Grande, 1,925 miles long. It has its source in the state of Colorado (United States) and drains into the Gulf of Mexico. It is called Rio Bravo by the Mexicans.

What is its main mountain chain?

The Sierra Madre. One of its highest peaks is Colima (12,630ft), the most active volcano in Mexico.

Palenque is a Mayan archaeological site in the Mexican state of Chiapas.

Tenochtitlán was built on an islet on Lake Texcoco.

DID YOU KNOW?

ACAPULCO
In the southern region of the country, this city is on the shores of the Pacific Ocean. Its economy is based on tourism because, as it overlooks a gulf, it has beautiful beaches, many luxury hotels, casinos, and an undersea diving center.

VERACRUZ
It lies in the east of the country in a bay on the Gulf of Mexico. Founded by Hernán Cortès in 1519, it was used by the Spaniards as a base from which to conquer the country. Its harbor is one of the most important in Mexico to this day.

CANCÚN
Located on the Yucatán Peninsula, Cancún overlooks the Caribbean Sea. It consists of two sections: one contains the city's historical monuments while the other is a huge, modern tourist complex. In fact, due to its very pleasant climate, the economy of the city is based essentially on tourism.

AFRICA

Masks, which symbolize spiritual forces, play a fundamental part in initiation rites and burial ceremonies.

This is a continent of 53 countries, located in both the Northern and Southern Hemispheres. The equator runs through its centre. The natural surroundings, climate, and animal or vegetable species can vary greatly by location. Africa is called the "cradle of humanity" because the oldest human fossils were found there!

Tribal population from Kenya

Africa is populated by many ethnic groups: Maure, Tuaregs, Berbers, Pygmies, Bedouins, Nilotes, Bantu, Kongo, Lubas, Lundas, Tutsis, and many others.

How many countries lie on the equator?

There are six of them: Gabon, the Republic of Congo, the Democratic Republic of Congo, Uganda, Kenya, and Somalia.

What is its highest mountain?

Mount Kilimanjaro (19,340ft) in Tanzania. It is an extinct volcano whose summit is covered in eternal snows.

This illustration depicts the opening of the Suez Canal.

What is the Suez Canal?

This is a man-made canal, 100 miles long, which links the Mediterranean with the Red Sea. It was built to shorten the sea journey between Europe and America. Before its construction, ships had to sail around the whole continent of Africa, which took a long time. The canal was built from 1859 to 1869 by Ferdinand de Lesseps.

Which is its largest desert?

Extending over 5,6 million sq miles, it is the Sahara. It occupies the north of the African continent, stretching over 3,100 miles from the Atlantic Ocean (to its west) to the Red Sea (to its east). The Tuaregs, a semi-nomadic people who raise dromedaries, live in this arid region.

Dunes of the Sahara

DID YOU KNOW?

THE RIFT VALLEY

This 3,980-miles-long valley is, in fact, a series of depressions stretching from Syria to Mozambique. 50 million years ago, two tectonic plates on the earth's crust moved apart, gradually creating chasms and steep cliffs. The largest lake on the African continent is Lake Tanganyika, in the Rift Valley in East Africa.

SERENGETI NATIONAL PARK

Located in the north-eastern region of Tanzania, this park covers an area of roughly 9,134 sq miles. Created in 1941, its grasslands and wooded areas are the habitat for over 200 species of birds and 35 animals of the plains: gnus, antelopes, rhinoceroses, giraffes, elephants, lions, leopards, etc.

VICTORIA FALLS

The Victoria Falls are formed where the Zambezi River plunges into a gorge that is more than 325ft deep in some spots. At least 6ft wide, these spectacular waterfalls are among the finest in the world!

THE MIDDLE EAST

This term refers to a large geographical area with no precise borders. It is located approximately between the eastern Mediterranean (including the Middle East) and the Indian Ocean. The principal monotheistic religions originated here: Islam, Judaism, and Christianity.

Lake Urmia lies to the west of the Caspian Sea, not far from Tabriz.

Mount Demavend

A volcano which has been inactive for a very long time and is covered with eternal snow, it is the highest peak in Iran.

What is its highest mountain?

Demavend is a volcano in the Elburz mountain range in northern Iran. Its summit has an altitude of 18,602ft.

What is its largest lake?

Lake Urmia, in north-western Iran, is the largest lake and is named after the neighboring city. Surrounded by mountains, it lies at an altitude of 3,937ft. As its waters are very salty, no fish live in it, only some species of crustaceans. It is quite shallow, and its area of around 3,105 sq miles is growing smaller with the passing of time.

What is its largest island?

Cyprus, with an area of 5,750 sq miles, is the largest island in the Middle East. It is also the third-largest island in the Mediterranean. It contains many historical remains, some of which are very ancient. Archaeological excavations have shown that Cyprus was inhabited by pre-historic humans in the Neolithic age (about 9,000 years BC.)

Today, the Euphrates is at the heart of a great deal of political tension between Iraq, Syria, and Turkey, because its waters are essential to the irrigation of each country's crops.

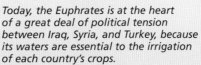

The fort of Paphos, dating from the 13th century

Beginning as early as the 8th century BC, Cyprus was colonized by many peoples: the Assyrians, Egyptians, Persians, Venetians and English. The island did not gain independence until 1959, and it still has many remains dating from these invasions.

What is its longest river?

The Euphrates. Over 1,680 miles long, it begins in Turkey and flows across Syria and Iraq. Along with another river, the Tigris, it forms a valley called Mesopotamia, called the "cradle of civilization." It is there that the earliest traces of the Sumerians (inventors of the oldest system of writing), Babylonians, and Assyrians were found. The Euphrates and Tigris join and empty into the Persian Gulf.

DID YOU KNOW?

SAN'A
This is the capital of Yemen, a state in the south-west of the Arabian Peninsula. Located on a plateau at an altitude of almost 3,546ft, San'a is a well-preserved historical center, with magnificent buildings, often geometrically shaped and decorated with ornate motifs.

JERUSALEM
This is the holy city for three major monotheistic religions: Judaism, Christianity, and Islam. It is the site of the Wall of Lamentations, where Jews come to pray; the Basilica of the Holy Sepulchre for Christians; and the Dome of the Rock Mosque for Muslims.

DUBAI
The economy of this city in the United Arab Emirates, like that of the rest of the country, is based on petroleum production. However, in the last few years, tourism has been rapidly growing, as this photo shows: the Burj Al Arab, a very luxurious hotel built on an artificial island in the harbor.

PEOPLE AND HISTORY

THE PHOENICIANS

The Greeks gave this people its name. The word "phoenix" means red – the Phoenicians were the first to discover how to manufacture a purple dye! It is believed that they made it from a sea snail called a murex. The Phoenicians were also mentioned in the Old Testament, where they were called Sidonians and became a very rich people around 1100 BC.

What made the Phoenicians famous?

Their fame was based on trade. The Phoenicians were excellent merchants who shipped large quantities of wood, particularly cedar, a precious wood. They also made embroidered fabrics dyed purple, objects carved in ivory or blown glass, and many other artifacts. Until the 5th century BC, they were unable to sell these articles, as money had not yet come into existence. So they would give them in exchange for others. This form of trade is called barter.

Where did they live?

Phoenician sculpture

In Phoenicia! This was a narrow strip of land on the east coast of the Mediterranean, most of which we now know as Lebanon. About 200 miles long, this land is not very wide, measuring a maximum of 15 miles! The Phoenicians were a prosperous people and were often attacked by neighbouring countries for this reason.

The Phoenicians bartered mainly artifacts with populations living around the Mediterranean basin.

What did they invent?

They invented an alphabet on which our own was based! Thanks to them, we can express words in written form. However, the Phoenician alphabet has only consonants – there are no vowels. During their travels, the Phoenicians brought their alphabet to other countries, including Greece, where vowels and various symbols were added.

The first Phoenician coins were minted around the 5th century BC.

They were known for another activity – what was it?

They were very good sailors and were therefore able to engage in trade with other countries. Thanks to the huge amount of wood they produced, they built ships which could sail all over the Mediterranean basin. According to the Greek historian Herodotus, a Phoenician expedition even reached Senegal in western Africa!

DID YOU KNOW?

CITY-STATES

Phoenicia was never a country as such, because its inhabitants lived in different conurbations (or large cities), each with its own leader. No one person ruled over the whole territory. These city-states sometimes entered into conflict with ach other. Among these were Byblos, Arados, Tyre, and Sidon.

TRADING POSTS

During their travels, the Phoenicians created trading posts, that is, they founded cities in distant countries to establish their trading activity. In order to exchange or sell their goods, they would travel to these trading posts where neighbouring merchants would come to barter or sell! The best-known were Utica, Carthage, and Cadix.

THE NORA STONE

Many Phoenician remains have been found at Nora, in Sardinia (Italy). They include the Nora Stone, a slab dating from the 9th century BC with inscriptions in the Phoenician alphabet. The Nora Stone is the oldest written document ever found west of the Mediterranean basin!

THE ETRUSCANS

The double flute was a favorite musical instrument with the Etruscans. Musicians would play it to entertain the guests during ceremonies and banquets.

The Etruscan civilization is believed to have begun around the end of the 9th century BC, because archaeologists discovered funerary objects and paintings from this time during their excavations. The palaces, temples, and other buildings from this epoch, built of brick or wood, have all been destroyed with the passage of time!

Where did they live?

They lived in a region called Etruria, hence their name. This region is near what we now know as Tuscany, in Italy. Although no official documents have been found, the Etruscans founded large cities: Cerveteri, Tarquinia, Chiusi, Arezzo, Volterra, and Pisa. Stone funerary buildings and many articles made of amber, silver, gold, and precious stones have been discovered there.

Fresco from the Tomb of the Leopards at Monterozzi, Tarquinia, in Italy (around 470 BC)

What role did women play?

In contrast to many other ancient civilisations, Etruscan women had a very important status: they held great authority within the family and took part in private and public activities. For example, they had the right to participate in banquets and ceremonies, just like men.

What is a necropolis?

In Greek, the word "necropolis" means "city of the dead." They are underground constructions near old cities. They contain tombs and are often covered with mounds of earth and stone (called tumuli). For example, the Necropolis of Tarquinia contains nearly 6,000 tombs with walls covered in bas-reliefs and superb frescoes!

Tomb near the Etruscan Necropolis at Volterra

Sarcophagus of the Spouses

DID YOU KNOW?

WHAT ELEGANCE!
The Etruscans were known for their refinement. In fact, they had a great influence on Roman civilization. Judging by paintings that have been found, they dressed most elaborately. We do know that their clothing was made of thick fabric embroidered with golden thread!

CERAMICS
The Etruscans developed their own method of manufacturing pottery by copying that of the Greeks. Their black, shiny ceramic pottery encrusted with metal is called "bucchero." The illustration shows a superbly decorated vessel for serving wine.

TOMBS
Furniture (tables, benches, etc.) was found inside them, placed exactly the way it was in the home of the deceased during their lifetime. In addition, there were vases, jewelry, objects for daily use, and even remains of food left next to the dead person so that he could continue his journey to the next world in peace!

THE SUMERIANS

Around 3,000 BC, this people settled in the basin
of Mesopotamia (in the south of modern Iraq),
in a region between two rivers: the Tigris and the Euphrates.
This was the first truly urban civilization and it marked the end
of the pre-historic period in the Middle East. The Sumerians
were excellent engineers and builders, as well as great astrologers.

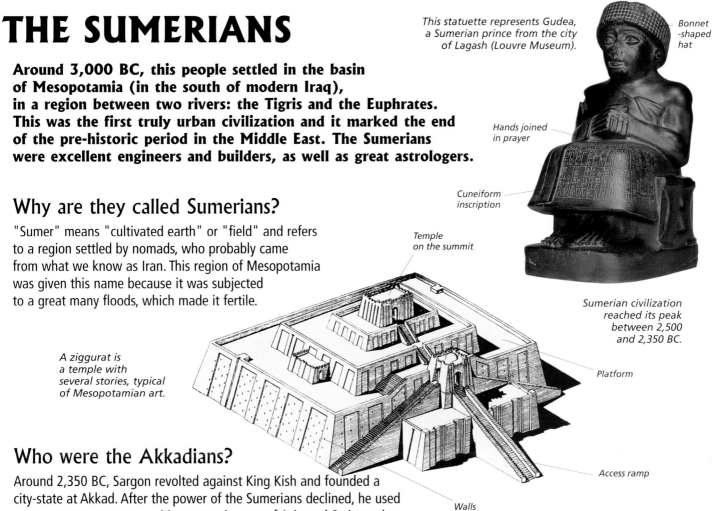

This statuette represents Gudea, a Sumerian prince from the city of Lagash (Louvre Museum).

Bonnet -shaped hat

Hands joined in prayer

Cuneiform inscription

Sumerian civilization reached its peak between 2,500 and 2,350 BC.

Temple on the summit

A ziggurat is a temple with several stories, typical of Mesopotamian art.

Platform

Access ramp

Walls

Why are they called Sumerians?

"Sumer" means "cultivated earth" or "field" and refers
to a region settled by nomads, who probably came
from what we know as Iran. This region of Mesopotamia
was given this name because it was subjected
to a great many floods, which made it fertile.

Who were the Akkadians?

Around 2,350 BC, Sargon revolted against King Kish and founded a
city-state at Akkad. After the power of the Sumerians declined, he used
a new strategy to conquer Mesopotamia, part of Asia and Syria, and
founded an empire:
the Akkadian Empire.

Cuneiform writing, invented by the Sumerians and later adopted by the Akkadians, Hittites, etc., included around 600 signs, usually inscribed on clay tablets.

How was Sumerian society organized?

It consisted of a nobility and a religious class, both privileged
classes. Originally, priests also held political power: the sovereign
(ensi) of each city-state was considered the representative
of the protective deity of the city. Later, political authority
was entrusted to military leaders. The middle class consisted
of merchants who played a fundamental role: since Sumerian
society had very few raw materials, they had to import them
from neighbouring countries. Finally, the peasants, shepherds,
and slaves were at the very bottom of the social hierarchy.

DID YOU KNOW?

SUMERIAN RELIGION
The Sumerians were polytheistic,
that is they believed in many
gods. The three major ones
were An (god of the sky),
Enki (god of the waters),
and Enlil (god of the wind).
Each city in the kingdom
had its own protective deity
which it worshipped as well,
in temples (called ziggurats).

THE WHEEL
Around 3,500 BC,
the Sumerians invented
the wheel. Carts on wheels
soon replaced the sled
as a means of transportation.
Paintings found on vases
dating back to 2,870 BC
show that the wheel was
used for war-chariots pulled
by onagers (large wild donkeys).

BABYLON
Founded by the Sumerians
around 2,300 BC, the city
of Babylon became the capital
of the kingdom of Hammurabi
in the 18th century BC.
Today, all that remains
of the city of Babylon are
its ruins in Iraq. In Sumerian
and Akkadian times,
Babylon was already
growing into a large city.

THE **ASSYRO-BABYLONIANS**

Babylonian civilization is thought to have developed around the 2nd millennium BC, when the Akkadians conquered the Sumerians. It reached its apex around 1,750 BC under the reign of Hammurabi, but fell under the control of the Assyrian empire several centuries later.

The Tower of Babel, a painting by Pieter Bruegel the Elder (1563)

Babylonian statue of a lion

How did the Assyrians treat their enemies?

They were cruel to them and boasted about it on the monuments on which they described their victories: villages were burnt, rebels impaled or walled up alive, and the heads of the corpses were used to crown the walls of the cities captured by the Assyrians!

Did the Tower of Babel really exist?

According to Genesis (the first book of the Bible), the Babylonians wanted to build a very tall tower to break open the gates to heaven and enter paradise directly! Displeased with this, God arranged for mankind to speak in different languages so that people would be unable to understand each other. Some historians think that the Tower of Babel was in fact the great ziggurat erected in honor of the god Marduk.

What was Babylonia?

Formerly called Sumer and then Akkad, this was a region of Mesopotamia which corresponds to southern Iraq. Babylonia consisted of a number of cities, including Ur, and is famous for the ruins it contains.

In Assyrian society, women had no rights or power; they had to obey their husbands, like slaves obeying their masters.

An Assyrian torturing a prisoner

Babylon also fascinated Cyrus the Great and Alexander the Great with its majestic Ishtar Gate, its temples, gilded palaces, and hanging gardens.

The hanging gardens of Babylon were considered one of the Seven Wonders of the ancient World.

DID YOU KNOW?

BABYLONIA
In old Babylonian, "bab-ilum" meant "Gates of God." It was in this ancient kingdom that the Sumerians invented a base 60 numbering system (called a sexagesimal system). Although we have now adopted the base 10 system, we still use base 60 in geometry (to measure angles) and to calculate time (1 hour equals 60 minutes)!

THE HAMMURABIC CODE OF LAW
Carved on a black basalt stone slab 7ft high, the Hammurabic code of law is one of the oldest legal codes ever found. Its upper section represents the Sun god, Shamash, handing the ring of legislative power to King Hammurabi.

CUNEIFORM WRITING
The Sumerians invented this system of writing, later used by ancient peoples of the Middle East. They used a stylus, or pointed stick, to mark characters onto tablets of clay or wax.

THE HEBREWS

In the Bible, God puts the faith of Abraham to the test by asking him to sacrifice his son Isaac.

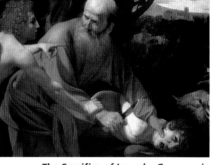

In ancient times, the Hebrews are thought to have settled in Mesopotamia and migrated to Palestine during the 2nd millennium BC. They were the first monotheistic people, believing in only one god: Yahweh, or Jehovah. This religion is the basis for Judaism, Islam, and Christianity. During the holocaust of the Second World War, the Nazis exterminated nearly 6 million Jews. The State of Israel was founded in May 1948: following a proposal by UNO, part of Palestine was given to the Jews.

The Sacrifice of Isaac by Caravaggio (Uffizi Gallery in Florence, Italy)

What is the diaspora?

This is a Greek word meaning "dispersal." In 586 BC, Jerusalem was captured by the Babylonians, the Hebrews were deported, and the Temple of Solomon destroyed. This is the diaspora mentioned in the Bible. In 539 BC, some of them were given permission to return to the land of Canaan in Judea. This kingdom became a Roman province in 63 BC and, more than a hundred years later, the Jews revolted but were again forced to flee and dispersed throughout the world.

Representation of ancient Jerusalem, with the Temple of Solomon in the center

Who was Solomon?

According to the Bible, Solomon was the third king of Israel. He ascended the throne around 970 BC, and had the Temple of Jerusalem built (later called the Temple of Solomon). He was a just and wise king. He made the city the religious and political center of the kingdom and ordered the construction of grand public buildings.

King Solomon bearing the insignia of royal power: the mantle, crown, and scepter

What was the Exodus?

Exodus is the name of the second book of the Torah (the Jewish Bible). It was given this name because it narrates the flight of the Hebrews from Egypt because they were being persecuted and enslaved by the pharaoh. Led by Moses, the Hebrews crossed the Sinai Desert to enter Canaan, which they then called Israel. During this journey, Moses received the Ten Commandments from Yahweh, which form the foundations of the Jewish religion.

Scroll of parchment from the Torah

DID YOU KNOW?

THE WALL OF LAMENTATIONS
Jews come from all over the world on a pilgrimage to pray at this holy place in Jerusalem: the Wall of Lamentations or Wailing Wall, the last remains of the Temple of Solomon (destroyed by the Romans in 70 AD).

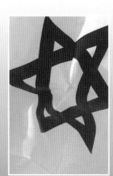

THE MENORAH
This is a seven-branched candelabrum. It is described in the biblical book of Exodus: it lit up the tabernacle or shrine, created by Moses, that the Hebrews transported through the desert to Jerusalem. It was then kept in the Temple of Solomon and represents the symbolic light of the Torah, which reflects the light of God.

THE STAR OF DAVID
In Hebrew, "Magen David" means "shield of David." Consisting of two superimposed triangles, one of which is inverted, this six-pointed star is one of the most important symbols of Judaism. During the Second World War, the Jews were forced to wear it sewn onto their clothes so that they could be recognised!

THE GREEKS

The Greeks were excellent artisans. They could make ceramic objects with extremely elaborate techniques of drawing and engraving. Below, a drinking-cup (called kylix) portrays a mythological scene.

Remains of human occupation have been found in Greece dating from around 8,000 BC. However, the Hellenes founded ancient Greek civilization as we know it far later. When they settled in the country and the surrounding islands of the Aegean Sea, they created a number of city-states which shared the same language and religion.

What is a polis?

A polis is an independent city, with its own politics, economy, and army. Protected by walls around its upper section, the city owned villages and farmlands round about. The people met regularly on a huge square (called the agora) to discuss politics or shop!

The Hellenic peninsula

Thebes
Delphi
Athens
Olympus
Sparta
Corinth
Crete

The polis consisted of two sections; the lower contained the agora and the upper the acropolis, where religious buildings were erected, protected by fortifications.

The Trojan Horse, a painting by Giandomenico Tiepolo (around 1760). According to mythology, the Greeks built an enormous wooden horse, inside which their warriors hid. The unsuspecting Trojans wheeled it inside their city walls. Once there, the Greeks came out and attacked them, capturing the city of Troy!

What is greek tragedy?

It is a style of theatrical drama, written in verse. These plays were put on before the public of Athens during the 5th century BC. The major authors were Aeschylus, Sophocles, and Euripides.

Statue of Poseidon

Deities and athletes were often represented in ancient Greek statues.

Who were the philosophers?

The best-known are Socrates and Plato. They were thinkers who devoted their whole lives to finding answers about love, justice, the origins of the world – in fact, about what makes a human being. Today, philosophy students still learn the works of these two great Greek thinkers!

What is polytheism?

It is the belief in several gods, and the Greeks worshipped many. According to mythology, these deities lived on Mount Olympus. Zeus was the god of the heavens and the supreme sovereign. Other examples were Hera, Zeus's wife; Athena, the goddess of wisdom; Poseidon, the god of the sea; and Hades, the god of the underworld.

DID YOU KNOW?

THE DISCOBOLUS
Carved by Myron around 460 BC, this bronze statue represents an athlete throwing a discus. Although the original has long been lost, we know this work because of the many copies made by the Romans.

GREEK ART
Over time, a good many of these works have unfortunately disappeared. However, through writings from the time or Roman copies, we know that the ancient Greeks were very gifted in all the arts: painting, sculpture, poetry, theater, etc.

HOMER
In Greek literature, Homer is the most famous of the epic poets. In the 8th century BC, he is thought to have composed the *Iliad* and the *Odyssey*, two works which narrate the heroic lives of men or demi-gods and their many extraordinary adventures.

HELLENISM

This term refers to the whole of ancient Greek civilization between the 4th and 1st centuries BC. Hellenism began with the conquest of the Persian Empire by Alexander the Great and ended with the arrival of Roman domination. During this period, Greek culture and science spread through all the countries of the Mediterranean basin and Asia Minor.

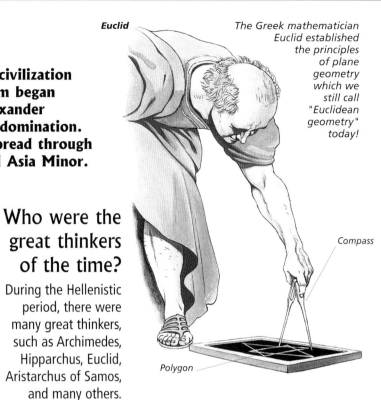

Euclid

The Greek mathematician Euclid established the principles of plane geometry which we still call "Euclidean geometry" today!

Compass

Polygon

Who were the diadochi?

The word "diadochus" means "successor" in Greek. On his death, Alexander the Great had no son, and therefore no direct heir. The empire he had built had already been divided into provinces, each of which was governed by one of his generals (the diadochi). However, some of them wanted control of the entire empire, and this led to many wars among the provinces for over 20 years!

Who were the great thinkers of the time?

During the Hellenistic period, there were many great thinkers, such as Archimedes, Hipparchus, Euclid, Aristarchus of Samos, and many others.

Which states were founded after the death of Alexander?

When the bloody wars of the diadochi were over, three great kingdoms were created: Macedonia, entrusted to Antigonos, became the dynasty of the Antigonides; Syria (Asia Minor, Mesopotamia, and Persia) came under the rule of the Seleucids; and, finally, Egypt was governed by Ptolemy. The sovereigns of these kingdoms were considered gods; they were patrons of arts and letters, but were also heroic warriors!

Library of Alexandria

When ships anchored in the port of Alexandria, their books were confiscated and copied, and the copies kept in the library.

The intellectuals of Alexandria had every available book they needed for their research, thanks to the library which contained the largest collection in the entire world!

DID YOU KNOW?

THE LIBRARY OF ALEXANDRIA
This was the largest library of antiquity, created by Ptolemy I, ruler of Egypt. Unfortunately, it was destroyed in 640 AD, but many works have been found in other libraries throughout the world, thanks to the copies made.

ARISTARCHUS OF SAMOS
In the 3rd century BC, this Greek astronomer was the first to make the hypothesis that the Earth revolved around the Sun! He also wrote a book on the distance of our planet from the Sun and Moon. His method was basically sound, but his calculations were not exact, due to a lack of accurate measuring instruments.

ERATOSTHENES
Appointed as head of the library of Alexandria around 240 BC, Eratosthenes was a well-rounded intellectual: a mathematician, geographer, astronomer, and even poet! He was the first to measure the circumference of the Earth fairly accurately. When he was about thirty, he became blind, stopped eating, and died in Alexandria.

THE PERSIANS

Darius I

Over 3,000 years ago, what we know as Iran was inhabited by several different peoples, including the Medes and Persians. After many battles, the Persians were able to found an immense empire whose borders went from India to Egypt in the 6th century BC.

Who founded the Persian Empire?

It was Cyrus the Great. A member of the Achaemenid dynasty, he reigned from 550 to 529 BC. During this time, many peoples were integrated into the empire: the Babylonians, the Syrians, and the Greeks of Asia Minor. Cyrus was a tolerant ruler: for example, he let the Jews of Babylon return to Palestine to rebuild the Temple of Solomon in Jerusalem. On his death, he was succeeded by his son, Cambyses.

Cyrus the Great

Also called the Immortals, the Melophores were a group of guards armed with spears and in charge of watching over the doors to the palace of the Persian ruler.

Who were the Achaeminids?

This was a dynasty which reigned over Persia from 550 to 331 BC. Its first ruler was Cyrus the Great (founder of the empire) and the last was Darius III, killed by his own men after their defeat by Alexander the Great.

This bas-relief in the royal palace in Persepolis depicts Darius the Great holding an audience with one of his subjects.

Who built Persepolis?

Located in the mountainous regions of south-west Iran, this city was founded by Cyrus the Great in 550 BC. His successors completed the task. Darius I made it the capital of Persia and had splendid buildings erected here, including the royal palace. The palace was set on fire and destroyed by Alexander the Great in 330 BC, and then abandoned. Archaeologists have found a large number of its remains.

Ruins of the royal palace of Darius I in Persepolis

DID YOU KNOW?

THE ARCHERS
The Persian army was very powerful due to the mobility of its cavalry and the accuracy of its archers. Legend has it that there were so many of them that, when they all released their arrows at once, the sky would darken!

ZOROASTRIANISM
This is the oldest of Persian religions, founded by the prophet Zoroaster. Its doctrines, collected in several holy books, explain the difference between good and evil: good comes from the god Ahura Mazda (creator of all things), while evil is represented by Angra Mainyu (the diabolical spirit).

THE PALACES OF THE KINGS
The royal palaces of Parsagades, Persepolis, and Susa are the finest examples of Persian architecture. Erected on immense artificial terraces, they had a huge central room called the apadana. This is where assemblies were held. The apadana was surrounded by a large number of smaller rooms.

THE EGYPTIANS

In ancient Egypt, workers, slaves, and even peasants (when they were not in the fields) worked on building the temples, pyramids, and canals.

The civilization of ancient Egypt was founded by a people who settled near the banks of the Nile River. It covered three main periods: the Old Kingdom, the Middle Kingdom, and the Early and Later Empires. During this time, 31 dynasties of pharaohs reigned, ending with the conquest by Alexander the Great in 332 BC.

Tutankhamun

How was Egyptian society organized?

The supreme head was the pharaoh, aided by viziers and other officials. The priests and scribes (men who wrote the official texts) were at the top of the social ladder. Next came the soldiers, workers, peasants and, finally, the slaves and prisoners.

Queen Nefertiti

Who was the pharaoh?

He was a ruler with supreme power: he took political decisions, led the armies, and was the religious head of the state. In addition, he was considered by his people to be the son of the Sun god, Râ, thus creating the link between humans and the world of the gods. On his death, the pharaoh was embalmed and surrounded with all his goods to help him in the next world!

Tutankhamun became king at the age of 9 and died around 20 years of age. It is not known whether this was a natural death or an assassination!

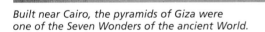
Khufu *Khafre* *Menkaure*

Built near Cairo, the pyramids of Giza were one of the Seven Wonders of the ancient World.

Why were the pyramids built?

To provide worthy tombs for the pharaohs. Inside, along with the funerary chamber, were a large number of corridors leading to rooms filled with great riches. This is why the pyramids were often robbed.

Satellite view of the Nile

Why is the Nile important?

Measuring 4,100 miles, the Nile is the longest river on the planet. When it floods, it deposits sediment (or silt) on the surrounding land, making it very fertile. As Egypt is almost a desert, ancient civilization was established on the river banks for survival.

DID YOU KNOW?

THE GOD HORUS
In mythology, this is the god of heaven. Born of the union between Isis (goddess of fertility) and Osiris (god of the kingdom of the dead), he was venerated in Egyptian civilization. Even the pharaohs identified with him. He is often portrayed as a falcon or a human body with a falcon's head.

CANOPIC JARS
When the ancient Egyptians embalmed their dead, they removed their entrails (liver, stomach, lungs, and intestines). Then each of these was put into a canopic jar which was placed near the coffin of the deceased.

HIEROGLYPHS
The word "hieroglyph" means "holy engraving" in Greek. This system of writing was very complex, as it had three categories of signs: they could represent an object, an idea, or a syllable (or even a consonant).

THE CELTS

Descendants of a number of different peoples, the Celts were warriors who spread throughout central Europe and then to the west and north during the 1st millennium BC. They never had a country or empire. In France, Switzerland, and Belgium, they were called Gauls; in Ireland, Gaels; in Scotland, Caledonians; in Spain, Celtiberians.

This painting by Lionel-Noël Royer, painted in 1899, portrays Vercingetorix laying down his arms at the feet of Caesar.

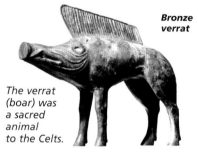

Bronze verrat

The verrat (boar) was a sacred animal to the Celts.

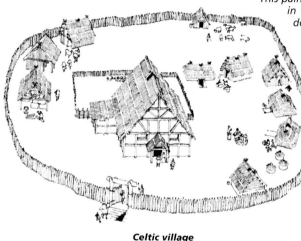

Celtic village

Were the Celts good artisans?

Yes, they were excellent metalsmiths, who could work metal to make arms and jewelry. They also adorned them with fine engravings, which made them famous for their artwork. The torc, for example, is a round necklace in gold or chiseled bronze. Only warriors and noble families wore them!

Very religious, Celtic warriors were certain that they were under divine protection.

What was a Celtic tribe?

This was a group of several Celtic families consisting of parents, children, grandparents, and in-laws. Each tribe was ruled by a king. The priest (called a Druid) played an important part in the group, and the bard was there to entertain members of the tribe.

What are dolmens and menhirs?

In Breton, "dol" means "table" and "men" means "stone." So, a dolmen is a monument made of rough stone put together to form a gigantic table. At the time, they were used as funerary chambers. Menhirs (from "men" and "hir", meaning "long stone"), on the other hand, are tall vertical blocks of stone.

Stonehenge, in south-west England, is a large megalithic complex (megaliths were huge, rough-hewn stones). They were built between 3,200 and 1,000 BC.

Who was Vercingetorix?

He was the head of the Arverni, a tribe from central Gaul. Vercingetorix succeeded in uniting all the Gallic tribes to defeat the Roman invaders, but he was beaten and taken prisoner by Caesar at Alesia. He was executed in Rome in 46 BC.

DID YOU KNOW?

The Celtic harp

MUSIC
The only traces we have of Celtic music are the instruments used, but we do not know the melodies played, as they were handed down from one generation to another without being written down.

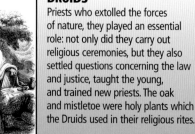

DRUIDS
Priests who extolled the forces of nature, they played an essential role: not only did they carry out religious ceremonies, but they also settled questions concerning the law and justice, taught the young, and trained new priests. The oak and mistletoe were holy plants which the Druids used in their religious rites.

THE CELTIC CROSS
This is a Latin cross surrounded by a ring which ends at its arms. It is a symbol of English and Irish Celtic Christianity, although it is possible that this cross had a different meaning for the Celts before they were converted to Christianity.

THE ROMANS

Ancient Rome was founded by a warlike people who settled on the plains of Latium (Italy) and conquered many lands around the Mediterranean. Originally ruled by kings, it was a republic for five centuries before finally becoming an empire which ended in 476 AD.

Janus is the god of doors and beginnings. As he was often thought of as the father of the gods, the Romans mentioned him first in all their prayers.

How was Rome born?

By conquering the region of the seven plains, the Etruscans made Rome a real city by leaving it much of their knowledge: the alphabet, and the art of building vaults or temples in which they were able to communicate with the gods! And 700 years later, Rome became an immense empire.

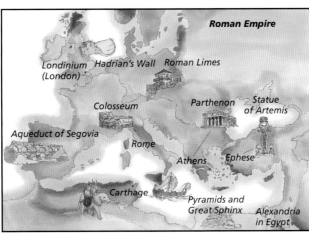

This map shows the Roman Empire as it was in the 2nd century, with its principal monuments and references to events in its history.

What was the Roman Empire?

It was a state ruled by an emperor who held supreme power: he dictated laws, handed out justice, named magistrates, led armies, and was also the religious leader. However, the senators and two magistrates (consuls) played a very important role: they were the mediators between the emperor, the nobles (called patricians), and the people (called plebeians). Rome was ruled by 87 emperors until its fall.

Which gods did they worship?

There were many, most from more ancient civilisations, like the Etruscans and Greeks. However, the Romans re-named them all: for example, Zeus, the king of the Greek gods, became Jupiter; Poseidon (the sea god) became Neptune, etc. The most worshipped deities were Janus, Jupiter (god of the heavens and master of the other gods), Juno (Jupiter's wife), and Mars (the god of war).

The thermes were huge structures where the Romans came to take baths, play sports, look after their bodies, and also discuss politics and other subjects.

DID YOU KNOW?

SPQR
This is the abbreviation of the Latin "Senatus Populusque Romanus" ("que," meaning "and," is run into the preceding word), which means "The Senate and the People of Rome." From the 3rd century BC, the motto "SPQR" was carved on temples and triumphal arches. It was the symbol of the Roman republic, and it was retained when Rome became an empire.

THE WOLF ON THE CAPITOL
This statue in the Capitoline Museum represents the wolf which is said to have saved and nursed two little boys, Romulus and Remus. According to the legend, the two brothers were the founders of Rome.

THE "GENS"
In high society, the Romans had three names, of which the "gens" was the second. It meant a clan or tribe, as it was used by a community of people who were not necessarily related.

THE ROMAN EMPIRE

The last consul of the republic was Julius Caesar. At his death in 44 BC, Octavius, his grand-nephew and heir, fought for power with Mark Antony for many years. In 31 BC, Octavius won and, four years later, set up a new political regime, the empire. On this occasion, he changed his name to Augustus, meaning "sacred."

Julius Caesar

Julius Caesar was never emperor but simply a consul, because the Roman Empire was founded just after his reign.

When was the Roman Empire divided?

Around 293 AD, it was divided into four regions, each governed by an emperor or his assistant. But this system (called a tetrarchy) did not last long: in 353, the empire was re-unified. Nevertheless, 42 years later, on the death of Theodosius I, the empire was again split up, this time into two large parts. These were ruled by the sons of the deceased: one, called the Western Roman Empire, was under the rule of Honorius and the other, the Eastern Roman Empire, was governed by Arcadius.

Only wealthy citizens could afford to build a Roman villa, with its very comfortable interior and rich decoration.

Who gave the rights of the city to the inhabitants of the empire?

It was Caracalla. In 212, he issued an edict allowing all free men to be citizens of the empire: this included the right to own property, to vote, to fight in the army, to appeal against a court decision, etc.

The Romans built great works like these ruins of the camp of Diocletian (2nd century).

Palmyra, in Syria

When was the Roman Empire at its largest?

This was under the reign of Trajan, emperor from 98 to 117 AD. Its territory extended from the west of Great Britain to North Africa and included Spain, Germany, Egypt, and all the countries of the Middle East. In addition, three more provinces were created at this time: Assyria, Mesopotamia, and Armenia.

Bust of Caracalla

DID YOU KNOW?

LIMES
"Limes" means "border" in Latin. As early as the 1st century, the Romans built long walls, watchtowers, and forts on part of their borders. In this way, they delimited the borders of the empire and defended it against invaders. The term "limes" also refers to natural borders, such as a river or mountain.

THE BATTLE OF ACTIUM
This was a naval battle which took place on September 2nd, 31 AD in the north-west of Greece. It opposed the fleet of Octavius (later called Augustus) and that of his great enemy, Mark Antony (the ally of Cleopatra, queen of Egypt). Octavius won the battle, and made Rome an empire four years later.

THE BARBARIANS
In the 4th and 5th centuries, the Western Roman Empire was attacked by barbarians (foreigners) on a large number of occasions, and in 476, the last emperor was deposed, bringing the empire to an end.

THE BYZANTINE EMPIRE

In 395, after the death of Theodosius, the Roman Empire was split into two parts. His two sons divided power between them and Arcadius took over government of the Eastern Roman Empire, called the Byzantine Empire. Its capital was not Rome but Constantinople.

Mosaic in the basilica of Hagia Sophia in Istanbul depicting Constantine, the founder of the city

How was Constantinople founded?

In 326, the Roman emperor Constantine the Great decided to found a city on the site of an ancient one called Byzantium. It was not called Constantinople until 330 in homage to its founder, and today it is called Istanbul!

Why did the Byzantine Empire cease to exist?

By capturing Constantinople on May 29th, 1453, Mehmet II, the Ottoman Turkish sultan, brought the Byzantine Empire to an end.

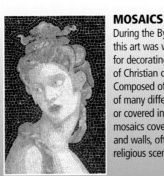

Club — Turban — Cloak — Saber — Babouche

Mehmet II made Constantinople the capital of the Ottoman Empire and re-named it Istanbul.

Who were the main enemies of the empire?

All through its history, the Byzantine Empire was subjected to many threats: over a period of less than three centuries the Goths (Visigoths and Ostrogoths), Huns, Lombards, Avars, Slavs, and Arabs invaded it or attempted to conquer its territories. For example, the Arabs laid siege to Constantinople for 4 years (from 674 to 678) but did not succeed in conquering it!

Janissaries were the elite troops in the Ottoman army, created to defend the Islamic cause.

Emperor Justinian

Who was Justinian I?

Also called Justinian the Great, he was an Eastern Roman emperor who re-conquered part of the Western Roman Empire. In order to govern this large territory effectively, he created a code of law (called the Justinian Code) so that everyone would have the same legal system. It took over 10 years to compile this enormous work!

After a siege of 7 weeks, Mehmet II took Constantinople.

DID YOU KNOW?

HAGIA SOPHIA
Completed in 537, it was built on the site of a church of the same name by order of Emperor Justinian. During its history, the basilica was destroyed and rebuilt. In 1453, following the conquest of Constantinople, the Turks added minarets and turned it into a mosque. Today, it is a museum.

MOSAICS
During the Byzantine Empire, this art was widely practised for decorating the interiors of Christian churches. Composed of tiny glass cubes of many different colours or covered in gold leaf, mosaics cover ceilings and walls, often depicting religious scenes.

VARANGIANS
These were Vikings who arrived in northern Russia by boat in the 9th century and began trading with the inhabitants. Then they settled there, created the first Russian state. They attempted to take over Constantinople on a number of occasions until 972.

THE BARBARIANS

The ancient Greeks and Romans called all foreigners "barbarians."

The prosperity of the Western Roman Empire attracted neighbouring peoples, called barbarians by the Romans: the Huns, Visigoths, Ostrogoths, and Franks had no qualms about crossing the borders of the Empire to capture its territory and settle there. In 476, the empire, weakened by political dissension and successive attacks, was unable to resist any longer and surrendered to the barbarians.

Banquet at the court of Attila

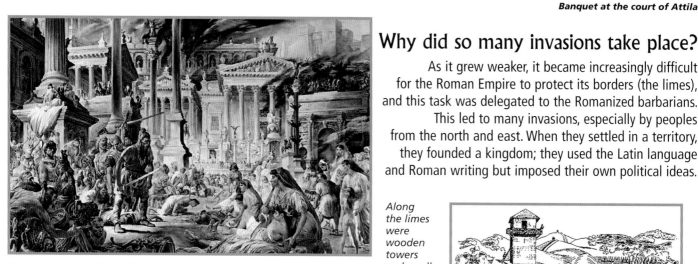

When Rome was pillaged in 410, Galla Placidia, the daughter of Emperor Theodosius I, was kidnapped. She later married Athaulf and so become queen of the Visigoths.

Why did so many invasions take place?

As it grew weaker, it became increasingly difficult for the Roman Empire to protect its borders (the limes), and this task was delegated to the Romanized barbarians. This led to many invasions, especially by peoples from the north and east. When they settled in a territory, they founded a kingdom; they used the Latin language and Roman writing but imposed their own political ideas.

Along the limes were wooden towers and small forts.

Who were the barbarians?

The barbarians were not a single homogeneous group but included many Germanic tribes (from Germany, the Baltic lands, Poland, etc.). These peoples were confronted by the incursions of other populations, like the Visigoths, who were attacked and pushed back toward the Roman Empire by the Huns. Once they had invaded other countries, the barbarians founded great civilisations, like those of the Franks and Visigoths.

Crown

When did the sack of Rome occur?

In 408 and 409, Alaric I, king of the Visigoths, attempted to capture Rome, but was unsuccessful. However, in 410, he blocked the city by closing off the roads as well as access to the Tiber. On August 24th, Alaric took Rome and pillaged it for three days. The city was again sacked by the Vandals in 455 and the Suebi in 472.

DID YOU KNOW?

ATTILA
Attila was the king of the Huns, one of the most powerful barbarian peoples of his time. He brought together the nomadic Asian tribes to form a huge army and then attacked the Western Roman Empire.

ODOACER
In 476, the barbarian King Odoacer deposed the last Western Roman Emperor Romulus Augustulus. He was proclaimed regent of Italy by Zenon, the Eastern Roman Emperor. However, he was assassinated by one of his numerous enemies in 493.

ALARIC I
He was the leader of the auxiliary troops of mercenaries who fought for Theodosius I. On the death of Theodosius, he became king of the Visigoths and ordered the sack of Rome, which lasted for three days.

THE VIKINGS AND NORMANS

Originally from Scandinavia (Norway, Sweden, and Denmark), the Vikings were great explorers and merchants who sailed the seas. Toward the end of the 8th century, they had run out of land and needed new trading outlets. So they decided to leave their own country to pillage neighbouring lands and settle there.

The Vikings had several types of ships: drakkars were long and fast, ideal for war expeditions. Knarrs were smaller and used for transporting goods. Still others were used only for funeral rituals.

The Vikings were not only good traders, but also excellent carpenters and fine fishermen.

How far did the Vikings travel?

From the end of the 8th to the 11th century, the Vikings explored a large number of lands. Those from Denmark went to western Europe and down as far as the Mediterranean coast; the Swedes went east, reaching Russia and Constantinople; and the Norwegians explored Greenland and North America at least five centuries before Christopher Columbus!

Who were the Normans?

The Normans, or "men of the north," were Vikings who settled on the north coast of France. To prevent them from attacking the whole territory, Charles III (the "Simple") decided to give this land to the leader of the Normans, Rollon, and proclaimed him duke of Normandy in 911. William the Conqueror, another duke of Normandy, invaded England and ruled it from 1066 to 1087. Around the same period, mercenary Normans conquered southern Italy and Sicily to found a kingdom in 1130. It was taken over by the German Hohenstaufen family 64 years later.

How did Viking warriors fight?

Stern (back) of a drakkar, the Viking warship

Their warships (called drakkars) allowed the Vikings to land on foreign coasts and launch surprise attacks. The warriors were protected by an iron helmet on their heads and a metal coat of mail on their chests. They fought with swords, a round shield, a pike, or a large ax (called a Dane ax) held with both hands.

The Bayeux tapestry depicts the Battle of Hastings in 1066: William the Conqueror invaded England and became king.

DID YOU KNOW?

TRADE

The Vikings were excellent merchants who traded not only with northern Europe but also with countries as far afield as the Arab world. These Scandinavians sold animal furs, walrus ivory, and whale oil.

RUNES

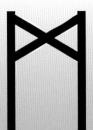

Mannaz, a rune symbolizing man

These are the characters used in the ancient alphabet of the Germanic peoples. Runic inscriptions have been found throughout the whole of western Europe, on stone monuments and different metal objects like spearheads or amulets. The majority were found in England and Scandinavia.

CHESS

In 1831, on the Island of Lewis (Scotland), 78 pieces of a Viking chess-set were washed up from the sea onto the shore. The pieces were carved from walrus ivory or whales' teeth. This is one of the largest chess-sets of the Middle Ages ever found.

THE CRUSADES

A Knight Templar dressed in a long tunic and mantle, both bearing a red cross

These were military expeditions organized by the Christian church to "free holy places from the infidel." They took place between the 11th and 13th centuries; Christians and Muslims fought to capture the Holy Land and especially Jerusalem, the Holy City, so important to both these religions.

How did the Crusades originate?

The Seljuks (a Turkish dynasty) conquered Syria and Palestine, capturing Jerusalem in 1078. Several years later, the Byzantine Emperor Alexios I Komnenos asked Pope Urban II to help him recapture the territories which had fallen into the hands of the Turks. Alexios offered to reunite the Church (then divided into the Eastern and Western Churches), but with his military help. This is how the First Crusade began in 1096. Of course, Urban II wanted to recover Jerusalem, but he also wanted to stop the invasion of the Turks, who were persecuting large numbers of Christians in the Byzantine Empire.

Book illustrating various stages in the battle of the crusaders against the Muslims

During the First Crusade, the city of Jerusalem was taken by the crusaders after a 48-day siege. On July 15th, 1099, nearly all the Muslim inhabitants were massacred.

Who were the Templars?

The order of the Temple was founded in 1119 to defend pilgrims. At once monks and soldiers, the Templars made vows of chastity, obedience, and poverty, handing over all their goods to the order. The order was abolished in 1312 for political rather than religious reasons.

Crusader helmet

How many Crusades took place?

There were eight crusades against the Muslims. However, others were organized by the Catholic Church: in France against the Albigensians, and in Bohemia against the Hussites. The last one, in Spain against the Moors, was called the "Reconquista" (meaning "reconquest" in Spanish).

DID YOU KNOW?

THE KRAK DES CHEVALIERS
This fortress, built by the Knights Hospitaller in Syria, is surrounded by two walls which protect a chapel and dwellings. In 1142, the crusaders settled there and remained for 129 years before it was taken by the Muslims. "Krak" comes from the Arabic "karak," meaning "fortress."

RICHARD THE LION-HEARTED
King of England between 1189 and 1199, Richard I led the Third Crusade and conquered the city of Acre, in Palestine. A valorous horseman, he could be cruel but left several poems in his hand-writing and was the hero of many legends.

SALADIN
Of Kurdish origin, this Muslim sultan reconquered most of the territories that the Christians had succeeded in taking during the Second Crusade. However, during the Third Crusade, he fought against Richard the Lion-hearted. In 1192, they signed a peace treaty stating that the Muslims could keep Palestine and Syria.

THE ARABS

In the 8th century BC, this civilization settled in a mountainous region in the south of the Arabian Peninsula. Excellent farmers, they quickly learned to irrigate their crops, mainly spices and herbs, in order to sell them to neighbouring countries. Islam, the religion of the Arabs, was founded in Hejaz and the merchant city of Mecca.

Caliph Ali with his retinue

What is the Arab world today?

During their history, the Arabs conquered many countries: the majority of the Arab-speaking population is found in Saudi Arabia and Algeria, the United Arab Emirates, Yemen, Syria, Jordan, Lebanon, Egypt, Palestine, Libya, Sudan, Tunisia, Morocco, and in parts of other countries (Iraq, Eritrea, and Israel).

Archangel Gabriel brings the revelation of God to Mohammed.

Who was Mohammed?

Born in Mecca around 570, he was a merchant who had a vision of the Archangel Gabriel and other divine revelations when he was 40. After his death in 632, those close to him decided to write about his life. This is how the Koran was created with Allah as the only God.

Who were the Caliphs?

After the death of the prophet Mohammed, the caliphs directed the Arab people to go into the desert and preach the religion of Islam. The first four were Abu Bakr (the prophet's father-in-law), Omar I, then Othman, and finally Ali, both Mohammed's sons-in-law. Later, the caliphate became an institution, and dynasties were founded over time. However, it was totally abolished by the Turks in March 1924.

Charles Martel at the battle of Poitiers in 732

Who defeated the Arabs at Poitiers?

As early as the 7th century, the Arabs conquered many lands and attacked Europe on a number of occasions. However, when they reached Poitiers in 732, the Frankish army, led by Charles Martel, stopped them, putting an end to the Islamic invasion of France.

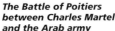

The Battle of Poitiers between Charles Martel and the Arab army

DID YOU KNOW?

MOSQUES
These are Islamic places of worship; the inside is covered in carpets and outside is a fountain where the faithful can purify themselves. On top of a minaret, a man called the muezzin calls them to prayer five times daily.

NUMBERS
The base 10 numeral system was invented in India and, thanks to Arab mathematicians, spread throughout Europe from the 13th century. It completely replaced Roman figures. This system, called a decimal system, allows us to write numbers using only 10 symbols.

CALLIGRAPHY
In Muslim culture, calligraphy plays a fundamental part. It is considered an art taught to men by Allah and is therefore a way to honor him. From the 12th century on, the books of the Koran were written with beautiful decorative letters.

THE MONGOLS

Originally, the Mongols were a tribe whose members fought among themselves. However, in the early 13th century, they made up an immense nation, thanks to Genghis Khan. Once united, these tribes were a formidable army. The Mongol Empire stretched from eastern China to the Caspian Sea. Over the course of time, it became divided. Today, the Mongols have a population of around 3 million, the majority of whom are Buddhists.

Mongolia shares borders with China, except to the north, where it borders Russia. Its landscape consists of steppes, lakes, and mountains.

Who was Genghis Khan?

A member of a powerful tribe from southern Mongolia, Temüdjin was a great conqueror. When he founded the Mongol empire in 1206, he proclaimed himself Genghis Khan, which means "universal war lord." He chose Karakorum as the capital of his empire. He undertook the conquest of part of China, Korea, and the territories which are now Iran and Iraq. Genghis Khan was also a great legislator: he established a code of law, called yasak, which every one of his subjects had to respect.

A remarkable military leader, Genghis Khan died in 1227. His best-known descendant was his grandson, Kubilai Khan, who founded the Yuan dynasty in China.

Were the Mongols originally a single people?

No. Around the year 1000, nomadic tribes, who raised horses and cattle, roamed the steppes of central Asia. They lived in tents, traveled on horseback, and dressed in animal skins. They lived on meat, milk products, and fermented drinks. They traveled about ceaselessly, looking for new pastures or villages to pillage. Today, many Mongols still live a nomadic life, just like their ancestors.

The Mongol bow was small and easily handled but powerful. The skilled warriors used it both on horseback and on foot!

Were the Mongols good warriors?

Yes; by uniting them, Genghis Khan made the Mongols an army of formidable warriors. While relatively small for the time, this army was powerful due to the skill of its archers on horseback. A horseman usually owned several horses so that they could rest after a long journey or a battle. Very often, the soldiers would take the enemy by surprise, leaving him no chance of survival.

DID YOU KNOW?

HORSES
For Mongol tribes, the horse was an extremely important animal, because it enabled them to get around quickly. Today, it is still a widespread form of transport in Mongolia. In fact, Mongol children learn to ride from a very young age!

THE YURT
The traditional dwelling for Mongol tribes is a circular tent with a round opening on the top. It has a wooden framework, covered in skin or felt to protect against cold and wind. Its door always faces south.

TRADITIONAL CLOTHING
Their coat (called a deel) is made of sheepskin, or silk for grand occasions. In winter, it is lined with wool and held by a leather belt. During periods of extreme cold, the Mongols (men and women) wear felt or woollen boots and silk hats lined with fox- or sable-fur.

THE CHINESE

We know that humans inhabited China over 460,000 years ago, because archaeologists have found remains and bones from this time. Before becoming the Republic of China, the territory was ruled by several great dynasties. Today, with its billion and a half inhabitants, it is the most densely populated country in the world. Its major religions, often called philosophies, are Confucianism, Taoism, and Buddhism.

Dragon mask

In Imperial China, mandarins were high dignitaries of the court.

Mandarin's hat

This life-size statue is one of 8,000 soldiers who stood guard before the tomb of Emperor Shi Huangdi.

How did China gets its name?

Its name comes from the Qin dynasty, which reigned from 221 to 207 BC. Emperor Qin Shi Huangdi unified the country, which had previously consisted of separate states. Not only did he make China an empire, but he also decided that everyone should adopt the same system of writing, weights, and measure, a very practical step for trade within the country. Even the length of cart axles was standardized so that vehicles could travel along all the roads of the Empire!

Confucius

Who was Confucius?

Born around 551 BC, Confucius was a thinker who founded Confucianism, one of the most widely followed philosophies in China. A wise man, he and his disciples went into exile in the other states of what was to become China, There, he preached his teachings: virtue, respect, and justice. Misunderstood, he returned to his native country and there taught his philosophy as well as writing. On his death, he left 3,000 pupils, 72 of whom preached the "religion" of Confucius.

The Analects are a collection of thoughts by Confucius, written by his disciples.

How is the Chinese calendar divided up?

According to legend, the first Chinese calendar was introduced around 210 BC by Huangdi (the "Yellow Emperor"), who is considered the father of Chinese civilization. This lunar and solar calendar consists of years of different lengths, associated with animals (12 years of 12 lunar months and 7 years of 13 months).

The Great Wall of China is said to be the only building that can be seen from the Moon!

Why was the Great Wall built?

With a length of 4,163 miles, it was erected to protect the country from foreign invasion, essentially from the north. Every 650 ft, this wall has 40-foot-high watchtowers where the Chinese soldiers took turns in looking out for the enemy.

DID YOU KNOW?

THE HAN DYNASTY
The Han dynasty governed China for four centuries, from 206 BC to 220 AD. It turned the empire into a unified, powerful state, but this was divided into several kingdoms following enemy attacks. At the end of the 2nd century BC, a university was created to teach the words of Confucius.

THE TANG DYNASTY
The first Chinese code of government was written under this dynasty (around 625 AD). It is a text about legal institutions founded on principles compiled under the preceding dynasty, the Sui. Created by Li Yuan, the Tang dynasty ruled China from 618 to 907.

THE MING DYNASTY
It was founded by a former Buddhist monk, Zhu Yuanshang, after the period of Mongol domination. It existed from 1368 to 1644 and encouraged literature and art. For example, a 15th century emperor decided to collect over 22,780 works on Chinese knowledge. In addition, its artisans were famous for their richly decorated porcelain objects.

PRE-COLUMBIAN CIVILISATIONS

These are civilisations which existed before the arrival of Christopher Columbus in America. They are thought to have been founded by people from Asia who came there about 70,000 years ago, when the Bering Strait was frozen and could be crossed on foot! The earliest remains from the great Pre-Columbian cultures, however, date from the 3rd century.

Hernán Cortès in the presence of the Aztec ruler, Montezuma II

Who were the Aztecs?

The Aztecs were a people who dominated south and central Mexico from the 14th century on. They created a great empire which was destroyed by Spanish conquerors two centuries later.

Who were the Incas?

Founded in the 12th century by the Quechua (a people from Peru), this civilization consisted of great farmers and excellent builders. Although they did not know about the wheel or writing, the Incas built huge stone edifices, like the immense city-fortress of Machu Picchu. The Inca Empire came to an end in 1572.

Depending on the periods, Pre-Columbian civilisations practised the arts of sculpture, weaving, frescoes, and making metal objects. They have left us a huge heritage from their history.

Who were the first conquistadors?

They were Spanish adventurers who set off to invade and conquer America in the 16th century. The word "conquistador" means "conqueror" in Spanish. Although they were not warriors, they could be very violent. Along with conquering land, their main aim was to convert the Amerindians to Catholicism. The best-known conquistadors were Hernán Cortès and Francisco Pizarro, who captured the empires of Mexico and Peru respectively.

Machu Picchu

Built at an altitude of over 600ft, the city of Machu Picchu was discovered on July 24th, 1911 by the American explorer Hiram Bingham.

Who were the Mayas?

Historically, they were a people from the Yucatán peninsula. They invented hieroglyphics to inscribe their religion, rites, and history on stone and in manuscripts made of leaves covered in a film of lime. They were also known for their architecture, particularly their temples.

In Mexico, the step pyramid of Chichén Itzá has a temple on top of it, like most Pre-Columbian pyramids.

DID YOU KNOW?

PRE-COLUMBIAN RELIGION
These civilisations were polytheistic, that is, they believed in a number of gods. To the Aztecs, sacrifices were necessary to feed and appease their gods. The Incas sacrificed living animals daily to the Sun. However, when natural disasters or great turmoil occurred in the empire, they also offered human sacrifices.

THE PIEDRA DEL SOL
From the Spanish for "Sun stone," this circular carved stone rock depicts deities and symbols linked with the Aztec cycle of seasons. It is over 11ft in diameter and weighs 24 tons! It was carved in the early 16th century during the reign of Montezuma II, but was not discovered until 1791.

THE MESOAMERICAN BALLGAME
This is thought to have been a ceremony rather than an actual sport, played on a rectangular field. The players had to pass a ball through a hoop set high above them, using only their elbows, thighs and hips. When the match was over, the captain of the losing team was decapitated and his head impaled on the wall of the playing field.

THE DISCOVERY OF AMERICA

During the summer of 1492, three small sailing ships, called caravels, set off from the coast of Spain on a perilous voyage in search of the shortest route to the Orient and its fabulous riches. We owe the discovery of the Americas and their colonization by Europeans to Christopher Columbus, who led this mission.

Christopher Columbus

How long did Christopher Columbus's voyage last?

The expedition led by Columbus left Spain on August 3rd, 1492 and disembarked on Guanahani, an island in the Bahamas, at dawn on October 12th of the same year. Columbus immediately took possession of the island and called it San Salvador. In all, Columbus carried out four expeditions to the New World. He discovered Cuba (which he re-named Juana), the Dominican Republic and Haiti (under the name Hispaniola), Jamaica, the islands of Trinidad and Margarita, Venezuela, Panama, and Honduras.

The caravel was a fast, light sailing ship used in Spain between the 15th and 16th centuries.

Large square sail

Quarterdeck

Foredeck

Hold

Why did Christopher Columbus think he had reached India?

Christopher Columbus thought that the Earth was 25% smaller than what was generally believed at the time and that it consisted mainly of land above sea level. He therefore concluded that he would be able to find a shorter route to reach Asia by navigating westward. In fact, he thought for a long time that he had landed in a new region of Asia, not realizing that he had discovered the New World.

Christopher Columbus planned to reach India by a fast route to speed up and increase trade with Europe. Instead, he found a new continent!

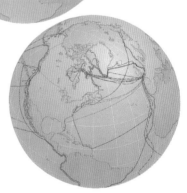

Amerigo Vespucci

Why was the new continent called America?

Amerigo Vespucci (1454-1512) was an Italian navigator who took part in two expeditions to the territories discovered by Christopher Columbus. Unlike Columbus, Vespucci was convinced that they were not in Asia, but in a new world. The German geographer and cartographer Martin Waldeseemüller, who translated the accounts of Vespucci's travels, suggested that the new lands be called America, in memory of the explorer. First attributed only to South America, the name gradually came to be used for the whole continent.

DID YOU KNOW?

ISABELLA OF SPAIN
Called "the Catholic," she became queen of Castile in 1474 and contributed to the birth of the Spanish nation. She financed Christopher Columbus's expeditions after he had been refused help by his own country, Italy. Isabella also introduced the Inquisition, a cruel church tribunal that hunted down heretics.

NEW PRODUCTS
Among the new food products imported from the Americas were potatoes, corn, tomatoes, turkeys, cocoa, and tobacco.

FRANCISCO PIZARRO
The conquistadors were explorers who conquered territories in the New World in the name of Spain and Portugal. Francisco Pizarro was one of them. He landed in America in 1510, conquered the Inca Empire and founded the city of Lima, the modern capital of Peru, in 1535. Most conquistadors were thirsty for wealth, and pillaged and massacred the indigenous populations.

THE REFORMATION

The Reformation was a 16th century revolutionary religious movement. Through it, the Christian world was divided in two and the Protestant Church was born. It all began in Germany, when the theologian Martin Luther nailed his 95 Theses, condemning the sale of indulgences, to the door of the church in the castle of Wittenberg.

Born in 1483 in Eisleben, Germany, Martin Luther became a priest and devoted all his time to studying the Bible. He soon disagreed with Catholic teaching and initiated the Protestant movement.

What was the sale of indulgences?

Indulgences were sold to enable the faithful to buy redemption from their sins by donating money to the clergy. God would then pardon them and they would go to heaven. In other words, serious sins, like murder, could be forgiven for a sum of money, which was unthinkable for some Christians.

In this lithograph, Martin Luther burns the bull (papal letter), called Exsurge Domine, which condemns his 95 theses. This occurred at Wittenberg, the city where Luther is buried.

What was Martin Luther's reform?

In the Catholic religion, as in many others, man must live a blameless life in order to go to heaven. Some Popes of Luther's time asked their faithful to pray but also to give money to the Church so that God would forgive them. Luther disagreed with this, saying that not money, but only God could save man by forgiving his sins.

What were the consequences of the Reformation?

There were many, but the most important was the division of Western Christianity into Catholics and Protestants. Several European regions established their political and religious independence from the Catholic Church. In addition, Protestantism led to a number of disasters, the best-known being the Saint Bartholomew's Day massacre in Paris, when thousands of Protestants were killed during the night of August 23rd-24th, 1572, and the Thirty Years' War (1618-1648), which began in Germany and spread through the whole of western Europe.

In 1525, Luther married Katharina von Bora, with whom he had six children.

DID YOU KNOW?

POPE LEO X
Leo X, whose real name was Giovanni de' Medici, became Pope in 1513. He opposed the 95 Theses of Luther by writing a papal bull condemning and excommunicating him in 1520. This portrait of him, painted by Raphaël around 1518, is in the Uffizi Gallery in Florence, Italy.

HANS HOLBEIN
This German painter is one of the greatest masters of Renaissance portrait-painting. Between 1523 and 1526, he illustrated the first German translation of the Bible by Martin Luther.

CALVINISM
John Calvin was a French religious reformer. A supporter of the Reformation, he took up the defense of the Protestants when they were persecuted by King Francis I. He wrote an important work, "Institutes of the Christian Religion," on his own interpretation of the Bible. This doctrine is called Calvinism.

THE AMERICAN CIVIL WAR

In the United States, Abraham Lincoln, an opponent of slavery, was elected president in 1860. In February 1861, seven southern states agreed that they wanted independence in order to defend their interests. So they formed the Confederate States of America and elected Jefferson Davis president of this coalition. Four other states joined them some months later. The Confederacy fought against the northern states, which were referred to as the Union.

A great American president, Lincoln freed the slaves long before the war was over. He was assassinated by a Confederate sympathizer on April 14th, 1865, five days after the war ended!

What were the major battles?

Many battles took place during the Civil War: the battle of Bull Run, the first great combat, which was won by the Southern side; Chattanooga, which eliminated the Confederate citadels and enabled the Union Army to go farther into the south of the country. Gettysburg was the war's real turning-point, causing the largest number of deaths of this war.

The United States at the time of the Battle of Gettysburg (July 1863)

■ Union States
■ Slave states that remained in the Union
■ Western Territories
■ States of the Confederacy

What was the main cause of this war?

The main reason for the conflict between the North and the South was slavery: the Confederate states made their living largely from farming, and they needed slaves to work on their plantations. The northern states had no interest in having slaves, as they were industrial areas, where mechanized labor was being fully developed.

How did the war end?

By taking over strategic Southern ports, the Union won the war. The Confederates eventually ran out of supplies and laid down their arms in April 1865. The 4-year war produced numerous casualties: nearly 620,000 men perished. In the South, many towns and plantations were destroyed, but the slaves were free at last!

Battle of Gettysburg

This battle lasted 3 days and was a decisive one in the Civil War.

DID YOU KNOW?

ULYSSES GRANT

He played an active part in the Civil War as the commander of the Union Army. After Grant captured Richmond, the Confederate capital, Robert E. Lee, the Southern commander, surrendered to him in April 1865. Grant later became president of the United States from 1869 to 1877.

THE RAILROAD

The Civil War was one of the first conflicts to use industrial means of transport: in this case, railroads. The railraod was used to transport troops and arms on both sides.

ROBERT EDWARD LEE

He was commander of the Confederate Army. His strategy and attack tactics were studied for many years, because they consisted of analyzing enemy weaknesses and anticipating their actions. However, he was beaten at Gettysburg (1863), and finally capitulated at Appomattox (1865) to General Grant.

THE FRENCH REVOLUTION

From 1789 to 1799, France went through a period of turmoil which led to the end of the old régime, abolishing the privileges of the nobles and the king. The French revolted against the absolute monarchy which was oppressing them. "Liberté, Egalité, Fraternité" (liberty, equality, fraternity) was their motto and it is still that of France today. At the end of this revolution, the Republic was born.

Portrait of Louis XVI painted by Joseph-Siffred Duplessis in 1777

What caused the Revolution?

In 1789, the people were suffering not only because of a financial crisis, but also from famine due to poor harvests. In addition, unlike the nobility and clergy, they had to pay taxes to the king. Discontented with the way their country was being run, the oppressed people revolted.

The storming of the Bastille. This fortress on the eastern outskirts of Paris had 8 well-guarded crenellated towers. It was destroyed by the Parisian rebels.

When did the Revolution break out?

On July 14th, 1789, the Parisians stormed the Bastille prison, where opponents of the régime had been imprisoned since the time of Louis XIII. When the attack took place, there were only seven prisoners to be freed. Since 1880, this has been celebrated as a national holiday in France.

Marianne, the symbol of the French Republic

What was "the Reign of Terror"?

This was a period from September 5th, 1793 to July 27th, 1794. The Jacobins, led by Robespierre, guillotined all who were thought to be enemies of the Revolution. Danton and many Girondins died because of it. On July 28th, Robespierre himself was guillotined and the "Terror" was over!

Why did Louis XVI call the Estates General?

Because the kingdom was bankrupt, Louis XVI called the Estates General on May 5th, 1789. They represented the church, the nobility, and the Third Estate (the people). He thought that this assembly would support him against Parliament, which had rejected his tax reforms. However, this turned out not to be the case, because, in the end, the Estates General turned against him!

Robespierre, Saint-Just and Couthon

DID YOU KNOW?

THE JACOBIN CLUB
They were part of the "society of friends of the Constitution" and were so called because they met at a Dominican convent in Paris. Republicans and democrats, they soon opened their doors to the "sans-culottes" and women. After the fall of Robespierre, the club was closed.

THE GUILLOTINE
This machine for cutting off people's heads was invented in 1789 by a doctor, Joseph Guillotin, after whom it was named. This form of capital punishment was applied under the Revolution, as it was considered the most humane: the condemned suffered less than through hanging. The guillotine was used until 1981, when the death penalty was abolished in France.

THE TENNIS COURT OATH
On June 20th, 1799, the deputies of the Third Estate gathered in a tennis court at Versailles and solemnly pledged "never to disband without giving France a constitution"!

THE INDUSTRIAL REVOLUTION

In earlier times, the economies of western countries relied essentially on agriculture. However, from the end of the 18th century, society became industrial, populations moved to the cities, and work was done by machines.

The Industrial Revolution made England the most powerful nation in the world in the early 19th century, and London became a great metropolis.

How did the Industrial Revolution begin?

The Industrial Revolution began in Great Britain around 1780: its coal and iron mines made it possible to develop industry and urbanization. Industrialisation then spread to the rest of the United Kingdom, western Europe, and the United States in the 19th century.

In what way did cities change?

People living in the countryside migrated to the cities to work in the factories. Thus, over time, the cities evolved very rapidly: not only from the building of railway stations, but from the construction of suburban housing designed to accommodate a segment of the population that was becoming steadily more important.

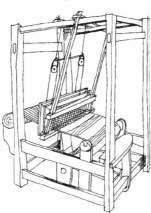

Mechanical weaving loom

Industrialisation led to massive exploitation of people in mines and factories.

How did work develop?

Small business grew and became huge factories. Initially, however, especially in the textile industry – spinning and weaving – people worked at home or in very small factories. However, once mechanized labor was introduced, many of these small factories closed to make way for large ones.

DID YOU KNOW?

MANCHESTER
Located in north-western England, Manchester was the world's main cotton manufacturing center, thanks to the steam-driven machines used for spinning and weaving. This is a great example of industrialization!

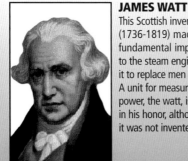

JAMES WATT
This Scottish inventor (1736-1819) made fundamental improvements to the steam engine, enabling it to replace men and animals. A unit for measuring electrical power, the watt, is named in his honor, although it was not invented by him.

THE RAILWAY
The first railways were English, used for transporting ore. Richard Trevithick designed the first steam engine in 1804 to transport 10 tons of steel over 9 miles. This began a revolution in transportation.

ITALIAN UNIFICATION

In the very early 19th century, the territory of Italy was divided among the Austrians, the Savoy-Carignano dynasty and the Bourbons, along with some independent principalities. From 1815, revolutionary movements attempted to unify Italy, to no avail. However, the Risorgimento ("Resurgence") had begun. It led to Italy's becoming a nation in its own right in 1861.

Count Camilo Benzo of Cavour was an important political figure in the unification of Italy.

How many wars were fought to gain Italy's independence?

There were three. All played a fundamental part in unifying Italy under one flag and one political authority. The kingdoms of Sardinia and Piedmont fought against Austria in 1848-49, 1859-60 and later, in 1866, to retrieve the last territories (Lazio and Veneto).

The Battle of Magenta (June 4th, 1859) was a significant episode in the second war of independence.

When was Italy unified?

Naples was conquered on November 7th, 1860 through the military operation (called the Expedition of the Thousand) led by Garibaldi, and after several other battles. On March 17th, 1861, the first Italian parliament proclaimed Piedmont-Sardinia part of the Italian kingdom with Victor Emmanuel II as its ruler.

Historic meeting between Garibaldi and Victor Emmanuel II at Teano

Why was Garibaldi called the "hero of two worlds"?

A key figure in Italian unification, Garibaldi owes his nickname to his action in Europe for the unification of Italy, as well as in South America. In fact, in 1835, he took part in the insurrection of the Rio Grande do Sul in Brazil against the Brazilian government. He also fought for the independence of Uruguay.

Mazzini claimed that Italy had to be united under a republic and not a monarchy.

Who were the main fighters for Italian unification?

Giuseppe Mazzini (1805-1872), Genoese patriot and writer, founder of two revolutionary movements: Young Italy (Giovine Italia) in 1831 and Young Europe (Giovine Europa) in 1834. Giuseppe Garibaldi (1802-1882), an Italian general and patriot, organized the Expedition of the Thousand, which was supported by the Count of Cavour. In 1847, the poet Goffredo Mameli (1827-1849) wrote the words to the Italian national anthem "Fratelli d'Italia", set to music by Michele Novaro.

Giuseppe Mazzini

DID YOU KNOW?

VICTOR EMMANUEL II
The last sovereign of the kingdom of Sardinia, he succeeded his father Charles Albert of Sardinia in March 1849. Later, he joined with political militants for the unification of Italy, like Prime Minister Camilo Benzo, Count of Cavour. On March 17th, 1861, he was proclaimed King of Italy by the new parliament.

THE EXPEDITION OF THE THOUSAND
On May 6th, 1860, about one thousand volunteers embarked on two ships in Genoa on the orders of Giuseppe Garibaldi. In October, their military expedition put an end to Bourbon domination of the kingdom of the Two Sicilies, which was annexed to Piedmont.

SECRET SOCIETIES
These were associations, the largest one being the Carbonari, who worked secretly against the established order and were instrumental in bringing about Italian unification.

THE RUSSIAN REVOLUTION

In Russia, an early revolution took place in 1905, but the most important one occurred in 1917, in two episodes. The first, in February, overthrew the Tsarist regime and established a provisional moderate government; the second (called the October Revolution) was organized by Lenin's Bolshevik party. When he took power, he created the Russian Soviet Federative Socialist Republic, which became the USSR (Union of Soviet Socialist Republics) in 1922.

A member of the Romanov dynasty, Nicholas II was the last Tsar of Russia.

What led to the February Revolution?

At the very beginning of the 20th century, although the Russian economy was flourishing, the peasants (85% of the population) and the workers were living in poverty. Despite their demands, Tsar Nicholas II did nothing to help his people. Events came to a head during the First World War. The successive defeats of the army with high numbers of dead and wounded, the lack of food, and the emergence of many trade unions and co-operatives (to make up for the failures of those in power) led to the revolt by the people, with the support of the army, in February 1917.

Lenin

Who led the October Revolution?

It was Vladimir Ilyich Ulyanov, known as Lenin. The leader of the Bolsheviks (the radical Russian Social Democratic Labour party), he wanted the war to end, the soviets to take power, the peasants to take over the land and, finally, the workers to control industry.

What happened after the February Revolution?

Now alone, Tsar Nicholas abdicated. On March 2nd, 1917, the first provisional moderate government was formed under the leadership of Prince Georgi Lvov. Among the many changes he brought in were freedom of association and expression. This led to the creation of large numbers of soviets (people's assemblies) throughout the entire country, with power similar to that of the temporary government. Later, this would be led by Alexander Kerensky, who was opposed to the Bolsheviks.

Lénine

Lenin

Occupation of the Winter Palace at Petrograd (now St. Petersburg)

DID YOU KNOW?

THE RED ARMY
This was the name given to the Russian (later the Soviet) armed forces between 1918 and 1946. The color red was chosen by the revolutionary movement. Its chief missions were to protect the Russian revolution from its enemies and defend the country's borders.

THE SOVIETS
These were assemblies of Russian workers and soldiers of the revolution. Following Lenin's slogan "All power to the soviets," they became the institutions on which the new Soviet State was based after the Bolshevik revolution.

THE WINTER PALACE
This three-storied baroque palace was built in 1762. It was the residence of the Tsar at Petrograd (St. Petersburg). It became the seat of the provisional government after the fall of the Tsar and was stormed by the Bolsheviks during the night of October 24th-25th, 1917. Today it is the Hermitage Museum.

THE FIRST WORLD WAR

This was the first armed conflict to involve countries from all over the world: thirty-two nations took part. Two enormous blocs were opposed: the Allies (coalition of the Triple Entente) and the nations of the Triple Alliance. Called the Great War, it ended on November 11th, 1918 with the victory of the Allies.

The assassination of Archduke Franz Ferdinand of Habsburg at Sarajevo

Trenches were dug to protect the soldiers and allow them to rest when they were not needed to fight on the front. However, as these were not built to last, the men lived in appalling conditions and suffered terribly.

How did the First World War begin?

On June 28th, 1914, Archduke Franz Ferdinand, the heir to the Austrian throne, and his wife were assassinated by a Serb at Sarajevo (in Bosnia-Herzegovina). The Austro-Hungarian Empire therefore declared war on Serbia. The war extended to the whole of Europe and the rest of the world because of the various alliances among the major countries: Germany on one side, and France, Russia, and the United Kingdom on the other entered the war at the beginning of August.

What were these alliances?

At the end of the 19th century, the countries of Europe entered into alliances to protect each other. On the one hand, there was the Triple Entente (the United Kingdom, Russia, and France), and on the other, the Triple Alliance (Germany, Austria-Hungary, and Italy).

A mortar, a weapon used extensively during the First World War

Projectile

Short cannon

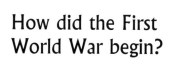

Here, in the Somme region, French and British troops fought against the Germans.

When was the Armistice signed?

The Allies, who won the war, signed the armistice with Germany on November 11th, 1918 in a railroad carriage in a forest in Compiègne, France. This ended the First World War.

DID YOU KNOW?

THE RED BARON
This nickname was given to Baron Manfred von Richthofen, a German pilot who shot down 80 allied planes single-handed during the Great War. However, his own plane was shot down over enemy territory in 1918.

THE SINKING OF THE *LUSITANIA*
On May 7th, 1915, the British transatlantic liner *Lusitania* was torpedoed by a German submarine. It sank in twenty minutes off the south coast of Ireland, causing the death of nearly 1,200 people, including 128 American civilians. This event was one of the reasons why the United States eventually entered the war.

WEAPONS
The First World War was the first conflict in which planes, tanks, and chemical weapons were used. The latter included mustard gas – called yperite – which caused suffocation and deadly burns.

THE SECOND WORLD WAR

This was the second conflict in history involving countries from every continent in the world. On one side, Great Britain, France, the United States, and the Soviet Union fought against Germany, Italy, and Japan. This was the most destructive war ever: it caused over 60 million deaths and many cities were completely destroyed.

Hitler and Mussolini (giving the fascist salute) watching a parade

What caused this conflict?

During the First World War, the Treaty of Versailles, signed on June 29th, 1919, was a severe punishment for Germany: it was occupied and had to pay the Allies a huge indemnity as well as returning Alsace and Lorraine to France. These sanctions enabled Hitler to come to power. He wanted to make Germany a huge country inhabited only by people of a pure race (which he called the Aryan race). After annexing Austria and overpowering Czechoslovakia (whose Sudetenland region he incorporated into Germany), Hitler invaded Poland in 1939. In the face of these invasions, France and Great Britain declared war on Germany on September 3rd, 1939.

German 88-mm anti-tank cannon

On April 25th, 1945, the Soviet Red Army entered Berlin, completing the defeat of the Nazis. Here, a Russian soldier raises the Soviet flag on the roof of the Reichstag (Parliament).

When did the Second World War end?

It ended in Europe on May 8th, 1945 with the surrender of the German Third Reich. In the Pacific, it ended on August 15th of the same year with the Japanese capitulation, signed on September 2nd with the Americans. Less than one month earlier, Japan had undergone the only two atomic bombings in history: on August 6th at Hiroshima and August 9th at Nagasaki.

Adolf Hitler

Why did Italy join forces with Germany?

Since 1925, Italy had been a dictatorship under the Fascist Party led by Benito Mussolini. The Duce's ("Leader") dreams of grandeur and conquest, which were opposed by the League of Nations (the forerunner of the United Nations) and the Allies (France and Britain), made Mussolini turn to Hitler for support. In addition, Mussolini believed that the Germans and Italians would win the Second World War. But this was not to be!

DID YOU KNOW?

THE HOLOCAUST
This was the extermination of the Jews by the Nazis during the Second World War. Hitler wanted to get rid of them all by deporting them to concentration camps and killing them in gas chambers. Nearly 6 million Jewish men, women, and children died.

THE INVASION OF NORMANDY
In the largest amphibious operation of all time, American, British, and Canadian troops landed in Normandy in June 1944. With the help of the French resistance, the Allies gradually freed France from the grasp of the Germans.

THE ATOMIC BOMB
The Italian physicist Enrico Fermi was one of the first scientists to develop a system for achieving nuclear fission. However, he did not take part directly in building the atomic bomb used against the Japanese during the Second World War.

HISTORICAL CHARACTERS

RAMSES II

Bust of a statue of Ramses seated. The pharaoh holds a scepter in his right hand.

The son of Seti I, Ramses II was the third ruler of the 19th Egyptian dynasty. He was one of the best-known of the pharaohs; considered a god, he was a brave soldier and great builder. He brought riches and well-being to his country. Ramses II lived longer than any other Egyptian ruler (to at least 90 years of age) and had the longest reign: 66 years! He left behind many magnificent remains.

The famous Battle of Kadesh which took place around 1274 BC

Against whom did he fight at Kadesh?

Against the Hittites. They controlled northern Syria, which Ramses II wanted to annex into his kingdom. A large number of battles took place over many years, the most important being the Battle of Kadesh, as it put an end to this long conflict. According to bas-reliefs and Egyptian writings, Ramses II defeated the Hittite King Muwatalli.

Which city was founded on the Nile delta?

Pi-Ramses, also known as Per-Ramses, meaning "city of Ramses." It was the political and economic capital of the pharaoh, as it was located on a strategic site: the Nile delta, from which the country could easily be defended and trade carried on. However, Thebes remained the most important city in Egypt because of its religious rituals.

Mummy of Ramses II, discovered in 1880

What did Ramses II look like?

By examining his mummy and one of his statues, 110 French researchers made a study of the physical appearance of this ruler in 1976. Using new technology, it was learned that he had red hair and white skin. He was nearly 6'2" tall, which was very rare at the time. Later, his face was reconstituted from a mummified skull and a three-dimensional representation made.

Many paintings of Nefertari show the queen deified, just as the king was.

How many wives did he have?

Legend has it that he had about one hundred wives and concubines, and as many children. His greatest wives were Nefertari and Isis-Nofret. The successor of Ramses II was Mineptah, his thirteenth son, who only acceded to the throne at sixty years of age, due to his father's long reign.

DID YOU KNOW?

THE RAMESSEUM
Located near Thebes, this is the mortuary temple of the great Ramses. It consists of several buildings, including a main temple with a huge hypostyle hall, that is, a room with a ceiling supported by enormous columns.

ABU SIMBEL
In the south of the country is one of the most gigantic archaeological sites of the pharaonic era. Ramses II had a huge temple (dedicated to him) cut into the rock of a mountain, as well as a smaller one for his wife Nefertari.

PEACE WITH THE HITTITES
When the war against the Hittite kingdom was over, a peace treaty was signed with Ramses II: it defined the Syrian land borders of each side. In addition, to seal the peace, the pharaoh married the daughter of the Hittite King Hattusili III.

ALEXANDER THE GREAT

Alexander is considered the greatest victor of antiquity.

Born in 356 BC, he was the son of Philip II, King of Macedonia. Aristotle, the great Greek philosopher, was his teacher; with him he studied science, medicine, and literature. During his reign, Alexander succeeded in creating a huge empire from the eastern Mediterranean to India.

Head of Alexander the Great

The Battle of Issos (333 BC) against the Persians and their ruler Darius III

What was his first victory over the Persians?

The Battle of the Granicus River in north-western Asia, in May 334 BC, was the first decisive victory over the Persians.

When did Alexander accede to the throne?

After the assassination of his father Philip II, Alexander was proclaimed king by his army in 336 BC. Aged barely twenty, he wanted to make Macedonia an empire. He was called Alexander the Great due to his ambitions and numerous victories.

How far did Alexander's army go?

In 326 BC, Alexander reached India by defeating King Poros. He wanted to go even further, but his army of over 35,000 men refused to follow him. He had to turn back, and the borders of his empire ended there.

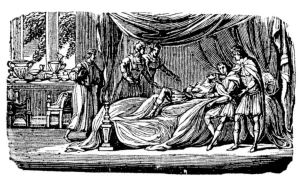

Alexander the Great on his deathbed

Where did he die?

At only 33 years of age, he died at Babylon, after a raging fever. He died in June 323 BC and was later buried in the city of Alexandria, in Egypt.

Detail from the sarcophagus of Alexander the Great (Istanbul Archaeological Museum)

DID YOU KNOW?

THE BURNING OF PERSEPOLIS

After defeating the Persians, Alexander and his army destroyed Persepolis (which means "city of the Persians"). Although he rarely used such methods, Alexander ordered his soldiers to set fire to the entire city. Today, only its ruins remain.

ALEXANDRIA IN EGYPT

This is the city that Alexander founded in 332 BC. He decided to make it the most beautiful city in the world. He named it Alexandria after himself, but other ancient cities in other parts of the globe also bear this name after Alexander's victories.

ADORATION OF THE KING

Like the Persian kings, Alexander demanded that his subjects worship him: they had to lie before him on the ground or kiss his fingers to show their submission to his authority. Many statues were erected in honor of his bravery.

ARCHIMEDES

Archimedes, painting by Domenico Feti

Born in 287 BC at Syracuse in Sicily (Italy), Archimedes was one of the most gifted scientists of all time. A mathematician, physicist, and talented inventor, he studied in Alexandria, Greece, for many years. His discoveries were of ground-breaking importance for the development of science at the time and remain so today.

Archimedes invented his theories or machines by observing everything around him, even when in his bath.

What is his most famous phrase?

Archimedes was the inventor of the precursor of the pulley and lever. He invented machines which enabled a single person to lift very heavy weights. When he made this discovery, Archimedes is said to have exclaimed: "Give me a lever long enough and a fulcrum on which to place it, and I shall move the world."

Cylinder

Very excited at his discovery, Archimedes jumped out of his bath and ran naked into the street, crying "Eureka"!

Spiral

Archimedes's screw turned by hand.

What is Archimedes's screw?

Also called the screw pump, this is a device used for extracting liquids or solid particles. It consists of a huge continuous spiral inside a pipe placed in the substance to be extracted. As it turns, this large "screw" scoops up a certain amount of the substance and brings it to the top end of the tube. Archimedes' s screw is still used in many machines today.

What is Archimedes's principle?

A law of physics stating that any object wholly or partially immersed in a fluid is buoyed up by a force equal to the weight of the fluid it displaces. If the liquid displaced is heavier than the object placed in it, the object will float (like ships). But if the object (a pebble, for example), is heavier than the liquid displaced, it will sink! According to legend, Archimedes discovered this principle when taking a bath and cried "Eureka!", which means "I've found it" in Greek.

DID YOU KNOW?

HIERO'S CROWN
At Syracuse (Italy), the tyrannical King Hiero commissioned a goldsmith to make him a crown. However, he suspected the goldsmith of not using all the gold he had given him. So the ruler told Archimedes to prove that he was right or wrong!

THE MIRRORS
As legend has it, mirrors were used during the attack on Syracuse to set fire to the sails of Roman ships. They were able to concentrate the sun's rays and reflect them onto a precise point so as to set the enemy ships on fire.

π
3.1415
926535
897932384

GREEK PI
This is a Greek letter which corresponds to "p" in our alphabet. However, in geometry, it also corresponds to the number 3.1415926, etc. Pi enables the circumference of a circle (distance around it) to be calculated in terms of its diameter (the straight line through its center).

127

HANNIBAL

Born in 247 BC, he was a general in the army of Carthage, a prosperous Phoenician city which controlled the coasts of northern Africa as well as a part of Italy and Spain. During the Second Punic War, he defeated his enemy, Rome, several times. However, when his brother Hasdrubal was killed trying to bring him reinforcements in Italy, Hannibal and his army had to flee to Africa. In the face of this defeat, Hannibal was forced to go into exile and committed suicide in 183 BC to escape the Romans.

The crossing of the Alps by Hannibal, with his army of 40,000 men as well as their elephants, was a very dangerous undertaking. Nearly half of them had died by the time Hannibal arrived at Rome!

What military tactic did he use?

Rather than confront the enemy, Hannibal would surround it in order to attack it by surprise on several fronts. By using this effective tactic, he was able to defeat the Romans on a number of occasions.

Hannibal riding his elephant Sorus across the Alps. 19th century fresco (Capitoline Museum in Rome)

Cornelius Scipio was a Roman politician and general. He defeated Hannibal at Zama (Africa) in 202 BC, in a battle that ended the Second Punic War. Scipio was given the title "Africanus" following this victory.

How did he reach Italy?

The Second Punic War began in 218 BC. Rather than reaching Italy directly by ship, which would have let the enemy see them approaching, Hannibal went through Spain, crossing the Alps on elephants. The animals and men accompanying him were certainly not prepared for such a journey!

When was he defeated?

From 207 BC, Hannibal could no longer count on the help of his brothers, who had been defeated by the Romans: Hasdrubal near the Metauro River and Magon in Liguria (a region in southern Italy). So he returned to Africa to help the Carthaginians, who were under attack by Scipio. But Hannibal finally met defeat at Zama in 202 BC.

Was he a good strategist?

Yes, undoubtedly. During his different campaigns, he succeeded in defeating a Roman army far more powerful than his own, by using his military strategy. Although he was never able to conquer Rome, his ambushes and surprise attacks were most certainly the greatest war operations of ancient times.

DID YOU KNOW?

HANNIBAL'S TWO BROTHERS
Hannibal entrusted Hasdrubal with leading his troops in Spain, and Magon, the youngest of the three sons of Hamilcar Barca, took part in the Battle of the Trebia (218 BC in Italy).

THE MERCENARY WARS
During the First Punic War, Carthage enlisted many foreign soldiers in its army. However, these mercenaries were never paid, and this led to a conflict between 241 and 238 BC. Hamilcar Barca, the father of Hannibal, Hasdrubal and Magon, put an end to this war by killing nearly 40,000 insurgents.

WAR ELEPHANTS
Elephants were occasionally used as war machines in the ancient world. Only males were used, as they were heavier and more aggressive than females, and so far more effective in stamping on the enemy! Toward the end of the 15th century, firearms replaced elephants in combat and with good reason: every time a cannon was fired, they would flee, crushing everything in their path!

JULIUS CAESAR

A member of a noble family, Julius Caesar (whose full name was Gaius Julius Caesar) was born in Rome around 100 BC. First a quaestor, he then became consul and dictator of the Roman Republic for life. He undertook great reforms which gave him increasing power. He was assassinated by a group of senators in March 44 BC.

Defeated, Vercingetorix surrendered to Caesar and was strangled in prison in 46 BC.

What is a triumvirate?

In ancient Rome, the triumvirate was a group of three people who held political power. Julius Caesar was a member of the first triumvirate, along with Pompey and Crassus, creating an alliance of political strength, military prestige, and financial power.

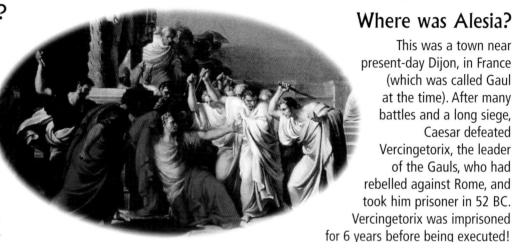

Initially, Pompey was Caesar's ally, but later became his chief adversary.

On the Ides of March in 44 BC, Caesar was assassinated by conspirators led by Marcus Junius Brutus and Gaius Cassius Longinus.

Where was Alesia?

This was a town near present-day Dijon, in France (which was called Gaul at the time). After many battles and a long siege, Caesar defeated Vercingetorix, the leader of the Gauls, who had rebelled against Rome, and took him prisoner in 52 BC. Vercingetorix was imprisoned for 6 years before being executed!

Bust of Pompey

What region was called "Britannia" by the Romans?

It was Great Britain! In 55 BC, Julius Caesar crossed the Channel to explore this unknown land. He made the journey again the following year to try and conquer it, without success. However, he did manage to set up diplomatic and trade relations with the local populations.

Caesar defeated Pompey at Pharsalus (in Greece) in 48 BC.

Bust of Caesar

What caused the civil war?

Following the death of the triumvir Crassus, Caesar had to confront Pompey, as both wanted to rule Rome. This civil war began in January 49 BC. After several battles, Caesar defeated Pompey at Pharsalus (in Thessaly, Greece) in 50 BC. Pompey sought refuge in Egypt, where he was assassinated; and Caesar came to power.

DID YOU KNOW?

CLEOPATRA
Queen of Egypt at 17 years of age, Cleopatra was forced to give up the throne, but retrieved it with the help of Caesar. She became his mistress and bore him a son, Caesarion. After the death of the dictator, she went back to Egypt and married Mark Antony, but committed suicide with him after his defeat at the battle of Actium in 30 BC.

POMPEY
A politician born in Rome in 106 BC, he led several expeditions to the East, from which he returned as victor. In 60 BC, he formed the first triumvirate with Crassus and Caesar. However, from 49 BC, he engaged in battle against Caesar in a bid for power, but was defeated. He fled to Egypt, where he was assassinated.

THE RUBICON
This is the former name of a river in the center of Italy which flows into the Adriatic. Roman troops were forbidden by law to cross it. However, Julius Caesar crossed it with his army in 49 BC, when the Roman senate gave its powers to Pompey. This started a civil war and caused Caesar to utter his famous phrase "alea jacta est," meaning "the die is cast."

MOHAMMED

Born in Mecca around 570, he was a merchant until the age of 40. After receiving divine revelations, he became a prophet and preached the religion of Islam, an Arabic word meaning "submission." On his death in 632, a mosque was built over his tomb which became the destination for pilgrims.

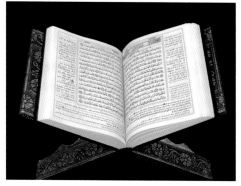

The Koran is the transcription of the message of Allah revealed by the Archangel Gabriel to the prophet Mohammed.

What is in the Koran?

After the death of the prophet, his disciples decided to write down the revelations he had received from Allah. The Koran is divided into 114 chapters, called surahs, which are themselves divided into verses, called ayah. The surahs are not set out in the chronological order in which they were revealed but according to their length, from the longest to the shortest, with one exception: the first surah is relatively short. They speak of the life of the prophet and rules for life, whether religious or moral.

A stone cube-shaped building, the Kaaba stands in the center of the Grand Mosque in Mecca (Saudi Arabia). It represents the "house of God" and holds the Black Stone found in the desert and believed to have been brought by the Archangel Gabriel; it is a sacred place for all Muslims.

Who revealed the word of Allah to Mohammed?

It was revealed by the Archangel Gabriel. During his travels through the country, Mohammed took refuge in a grotto not far from Mecca. He had a vision of the archangel and heard his first revelation: "There is only one Lord, one God: Allah." A long period of time passed between this and the other revelations; they then continued until the prophet's death. This is how the religion of Islam was born.

The sacred esplanade of the Grand Mosque in Mecca, with the Kaaba, worshipped by the Muslim faithful, in its center. Today, wherever they may be in the entire world, Muslims face the Kaaba when praying to Allah.

Why did Mohammed leave Mecca?

At the time, the inhabitants of Mecca (a trading city) opposed Mohammed and his disciples. This is why they left and settled in a small oasis 215 miles from Mecca in 622. Known as the Hijra, the prophet's exile enabled him to create the first Muslim community and found the Islamic calendar.

DID YOU KNOW?

THE UMMA
This term refers to the Muslim faithful, that is, the world Islamic community. It began with the Hijra, when Mohammed settled in Medina in 622.

ABU BAKR
He was the first caliph. He followed Mohammed to Medina and later gave him his young daughter, Aïsha, to marry. The Sunnis consider him the first man to convert to Islam.

THE CALIPHS
In Arabic, "caliph" means "successor." The caliphs were the successors of Mohammed who preached the Islamic religion after the prophet's death. Initially, caliphs were elected, but later the title was handed down from one generation to another. The caliphate was completely abolished in March 1924.

Papal coat of arms

THE POPES

The Palace of the Popes was the papal residence between 1309 and 1377.

The Palace of the Popes at Avignon

"You are Peter, and upon this rock I will build my Church." According to the Gospel, Jesus spoke these words to his disciple Peter. This is how the most important institution of the Catholic Church, the papacy, was founded.

When Rome was captured by Piedmontese troops, Pope Pius IX withdrew to the Vatican, where he was a virtual prisoner until his death in 1878.

When were the Church States founded?

Toward the end of the 8th century, the Carolingians offered the Popes their protection, granting them large territories in the center of Italy, which later became the Church States. Today, the Vatican is an independent state – the smallest in the world – within Rome. The Church States were under the absolute authority of the Pope.

Who was the Antipope?

He was a Pope whose election was disputed by Rome. In 1378, following conflicts inside the Church and the Hundred Years' War, a new Pope was elected even though the Pope in office was still alive. He was therefore considered an antipope, since he had not been approved by the whole Church. From 1378 to 1418, Christianity sometimes had as many as three Popes at a time.

St. Peter's Basilica in the Vatican

Why was Clement V famous?

He was the first Pope to establish his seat at Avignon, in Provence, where he had sought refuge from the turmoil in Rome. The six Popes who succeeded him stayed in Avignon, residing in a huge palace called the Palace of the Popes. When Gregory IX transferred his papal seat back to Rome, Avignon became the residence for several antipopes.

DID YOU KNOW?

THE CONCLAVE
After the death of a Pope, the cardinals gather to elect a new pontiff. Derived from the Latin "cum," meaning "with" and "clavis" which means "key," the word conclave is very apt, as the meeting takes place behind locked doors and no cardinal has the right to leave until the new Pope has been elected.

THE LATERAN
The Basilica of St. John Lateran in Rome is a cathedral, which stands next to a palace that was the official papal residence until it was destroyed by fire in 1308, causing the pontiff to flee to Avignon. Although the palace was restored and altered, no Pope ever lived there again.

THE COUNCILS
Also called synods, the councils were assemblies of bishops and ecclesiastics who gathered together to discuss and make decisions on religious questions (morality, discipline, faith, etc.).

CHARLEMAGNE

Born in 742, Charles, called "magne" (from the Latin "magnus," meaning "big"), was the son of Pepin the Short and Bertrada of Laon (also called Bertha Broadfoot). He was king of the Franks and then of the Lombards, as well as ruler of the Western Empire, which later became the Holy Roman Empire. Charlemagne died in 814, and was canonized in 1165 by the antipope Pascal III at the request of King Frederick Barbarossa of Germany.

In 774, Charlemagne came to the help of Pope Hadrian I, who was under attack by the Lombards. (Illustration by Antoine Vérard in the Grandes Chroniques de France, around 1492.)

What was the Carolingian dynasty?

This was the second royal dynasty of the Franks, succeeding the Merovingians in 751. The last of this line was deposed in 987 by the Capetians. Pepin the Short was the first of this dynasty. However, his eldest son Charles united a large section of Western Christianity and called this dynasty after himself: "Charles" is "Carolus" in Latin; hence, the name Carolingians.

Charlemagne was a great conqueror and so became the ruler of the Western Empire.

Ruler of the Western Empire, Charlemagne established residence in a palace at Aachen.

How did Charlemagne become emperor?

As soon as he invaded a territory, he would force the people to adopt the Christian religion. The new Pope, Leo III, was looking for strong support, which he received from Charlemagne. In gratitude for all the services he had rendered the Church (by spreading the faith and protecting Rome), the Pope crowned him Emperor of the West.

Although he was able to speak several languages, Charlemagne did not know how to write. To sign documents, he simply drew the central square and his officials completed the signature.

Bust of Charlemagne

When was he made emperor?

On Christmas night of the year 800, Charlemagne entered St. Peter's Basilica in Rome dressed in Roman attire. He was declared Emperor of the West by Pope Leo III, in exchange for his allowing papal authority over the State of Rome. Much is known about this emperor, because Eginhard wrote his biography in a work called "The Life of Charlemagne."

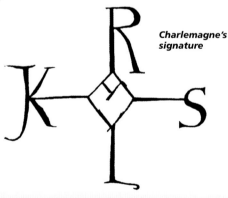

Charlemagne's signature

DID YOU KNOW?

RONCESVALLES
Described in an 11th century "chanson de geste" (epic poem) called *The Song of Roland*, the Battle of Roncesvalles was lost by Charlemagne. On August 15th, 778, his rear guard, led by Roland, was surprised by the Gascons (Basques), who refused to submit to the king of the Franks.

THE MISSI DOMINICI
In groups of four (two ecclesiastics and two laymen), these men were named by the ruler and were in charge of administrating the territory, which was divided into counties. Their role was to mete out justice and pass on the emperor's orders. At the first sign of a problem, the missi dominici had to refer back to the ruler and apply the punishment he decided.

AACHEN (AIX-LA-CHAPELLE)
This is Charlemagne's throne in the Palatine chapel of the Cathedral at Aachen. This western German city became the residence of the ruler. He had many buildings erected here, including the cathedral and a fine palace.

GENGHIS KHAN

Genghis Khan means "universal warlord" in Mongolian: this is the honorary title which Temüdjin bestowed on himself when he founded his empire. The son of a Mongol tribal leader, he was born around 1167 and succeeded his father at the age of 13. Over twenty years later, in 1206, he created an empire by imposing his authority on the whole of Mongolia.

The Mongols were excellent archers, remarkably accurate in their shots, even while galloping!

Genghis Khan was a bloodthirsty conqueror but also a great legislator: he created a code of law which all the inhabitants of his empire had to respect.

Why was the Mongol Empire great?

Once he had established the capital of his kingdom at Karakorum, Genghis Khan led his army to conquer China and Korea, invading the kingdom of Khwarezm, which lay in present-day Iran and Uzbekistan. By the time of Genghis's death in 1227, the Mongol Empire extended from the Caspian Sea to Eastern China!

What is Samarkand?

This is a city in modern Uzbekistan. Formerly known as Maracanda, it was almost totally destroyed by Genghis Khan in 1220. Formerly, Samarkand had been an important trading city, because it was on the Silk Road which linked China and the Roman Empire.

Bibi Khanum is a jewel of Islamic art. Built at Samarkand, this mosque is the mausoleum of the Mongol conqueror Tamerlane (Timur) (15th century).

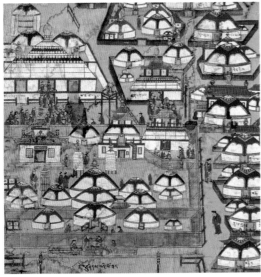

Karakorum, the capital of the Mongol Empire

What was his first conquest?

Genghis Khan began by attacking the kingdoms closest to his empire, in northern China. His excuse was that he needed the fertile Chinese lands as pastures for his horses. After several defeats, he managed to penetrate the territory of the Jin dynasty and take its capital, Yanjing (today's Beijing).

DID YOU KNOW?

THE MONGOL ARMY
As they traveled, the Mongol warriors took with them three or four horses each. In this way, they were able to have a fresh horse ready each day during long journeys or when engaged in battle.

THE SONS OF GENGHIS KHAN
The Mongol Empire that Genghis Khan built during his lifetime was divided among his three sons on his death. Brave warriors, they were as bloodthirsty as their father. But Genghis's most famous descendant was his grandson, Kubilai Khan.

MONGOL CLANS
Mongol tribes were nomadic and divided into clans with a very strict hierarchy. The most powerful of these controlled tribal activities and decided where they would go and whom to fight.

133

MARCO POLO

Born in Venice around 1254, Marco Polo was a merchant, explorer, and great expert on the East. He was the first European to describe the Mongol Empire and China. Thanks to the confidence which he inspired in Emperor Kubilai Khan, he was able to visit many places completely unknown to Westerners.

The Venetian merchants Niccolo and Matteo Polo, Marco's father and uncle respectively, handed down to him their passion for traveling when he was very young. Freed from prison in 1299, Marco Polo returned to Venice, where he died in 1324.

MATTHEVS RICCIVS MACERATENSIS QVI PRIMVS E SOCIETAE
ESV EVANGELIVM IN SINAS INVEXIT OBIIT ANNO SALVTIS
1610 ÆTATIS 60.

What did Kubilai Khan ask of Marco Polo?

When Marco Polo's father and uncle returned from their first voyage, Kubilai Khan gave them a letter for the Pope, asking him to send 100 Christian wise men to convert the population to Christianity. When the Polos returned to China, they took with them not 100 men but a vial containing holy oil from Jerusalem representing Christ!

Before the period of great explorations, The Travels of Marco Polo was the first account containing information about the East.

Where did he write his work?

During his imprisonment at Genoa, Marco dictated to his fellow prisoner Rustichello da Pisa the texts which were to become the explorer's literary work. Called *The Travels of Marco Polo*, it is an account of his travels in the Far East, from beginning to end. At that time, many Europeans did not believe the stories of his adventures.

In 1267, Matteo and Niccolo Polo returned from Cambaluc (as the Mongols called Beijing) with a letter for the Pope.

How long did he stay in China?

Twenty-four years. He left Venice in 1271 and returned in 1295. During this long period, Marco Polo became ambassador to Kubilai Khan and explored the entire Mongol Empire.

After spending 24 years in the East, the Polos weighed anchor to return to Venice.

DID YOU KNOW?

GENOA PRISON
In 1298, Marco Polo was captain of a Venetian galley, and took part in a battle between Genoa and Venice. After the Genoese victory, he was held prisoner for one year before returning to his country.

KUBILAI KHAN
The grandson of Genghis Khan, he was the first emperor of the Yuan dynasty. During his reign, he continued the work of his grandfather, that is, the conquest of China. Marco Polo was a member of his court, where he carried out administrative and diplomatic tasks.

THE SILK ROAD
This is an ancient trading route linking China and the Mediterranean. It was first mentioned by the geographer Ferdinand von Richthofen in one of his books. Its name comes from the trade in silk, which was a very expensive, precious material in Roman times. In addition, its manufacture remained a mystery to Westerners.

LEONARDO DA VINCI

Self-portrait of Leonardo da Vinci at 60, in the Royal Library of Turin

Born in Italy, Leonardo da Vinci (1452-1519) was an engineer, scientist, architect, painter, and sculptor. He was one of the most creative people of the Renaissance. Leonardo was interested in a great many things, from mechanics to anatomy, optics to mathematics, and was entirely self-taught. He designed prototypes for flying machines and nautical and military devices.

What is his most famous painting?

Although Leonardo painted many works, his most famous is undoubtedly *the Mona Lisa*. Painted between 1503 and 1506, it is known throughout the world and represents a woman with a mysterious smile. The work is displayed in the Louvre Museum in Paris, in a room especially set aside for it.

The Gioconda is also called the Mona Lisa, the name of the wife of the Marquis Francesco del Giocondo, but it is not certain that she is the one in the painting. The Gioconda is a small oil-painting on wood (30 x 20 inches).

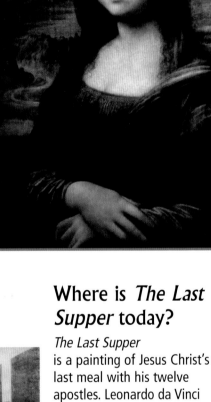

Who were his patrons?

Ludovico Sforza "The Moor," Giuliano de' Medici and Francis I (King of France) successively helped Leonardo da Vinci create his works.

Which flying machines did he create?

By observing birds, Leonardo learned that there was nothing mysterious about flying, contrary to the opinion of scientists of the time. He understood that the shape of a wing and its "mechanical" movement enabled birds to move through the air! So he sketched a large number of flying machines, like the ornithopter and many others. Even though none of them was ever built because it was impossible to do so, Leonardo's studies allow us to understand certain principles of aerodynamics. In fact, some of his ideas were used to invent machines like the helicopter rotor.

Where is *The Last Supper* today?

The Last Supper is a painting of Jesus Christ's last meal with his twelve apostles. Leonardo da Vinci painted it for the refectory of the convent of Santa Maria delle Grazie, in Milan. It is still there today.

Sketch of a mechanical wing

DID YOU KNOW?

LADY WITH AN ERMINE
This is an oil-painting on wood executed by Leonardo in 1490. The woman is thought to be Cecilia Gallerani, the mistress of Ludovico "The Moor" (one of the artist's patrons). It measures 21 x 15 inches and is in the Czartorycki Museum in Krakow, Poland.

WAR MACHINES
Throughout his life, Leonardo lived under the protection and funding of rich patrons who commissioned not only paintings but also war machines. He made several sketches of machines like cannons, catapults, and even a sort of armored tank like those we have today.

THE CODICES
They are part of Leonardo's works. Only about 7,000 of the 13,000 pages he is believed to have written have been found. These writings and sketches are divided into ten Codices, the most famous being the *Codex Atlanticus*. They were written in Leonardo's quite peculiar form of writing, that is, from right to left. It can only be read using a mirror. As he was left-handed, this allowed him to avoid spreading wet ink from his pen onto the page.

MICHELANGELO

A gifted but tormented artist, he is a genius of Western art.

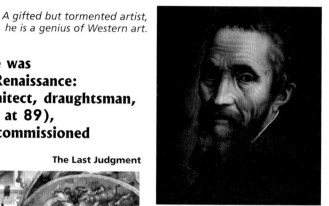

Born in 1475 in Caprese (a little village in Italy), he was one of the most gifted and significant artists of the Renaissance: a wonderful sculptor and painter, he was also an architect, draughtsman, and even poet! During his long life (he died in 1564 at 89), Michelangelo worked mainly in Rome and Florence, commissioned by the papacy and the Medici family.

Self-portrait of Michelangelo Buonarroti, called Michelangelo

What is the Sistine Chapel?

Built in 1475, it is a Palatine chapel in the Vatican, consisting of a large room, 130ft by 44ft. In 1508, Pope Julius II asked Michelangelo to paint a gigantic fresco on the ceiling. He finished this in 1512. Then much later, in 1535, he executed *The Last Judgment* on one of the walls of the chapel choir; this took him 6 years to finish!

The Last Judgment

This imposing fresco (45ft x 40ft) portrays Christ in the center, with the saved souls (on the left) rising to heaven while the damned (on the right) descend into hell.

This 13.5-ft-high, white marble statue symbolizes the strength and invincibility of the Florentine republic.

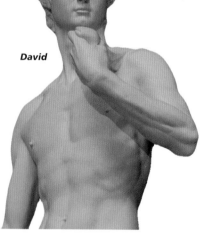

David

What architectural works did he design?

On the death of the architect Sangallo the Younger in 1546, Michelangelo was commissioned to take over his work on the dome of St. Peter's Basilica in Rome, as well as the Palazzo Farnese. He also designed the Capitol buildings, today Rome's administrative center.

The dome of St. Peter's Basilica is around 134ft in diameter. Michelangelo designed this large cupola to lighten the structure.

What is his most famous sculpture?

It is *David*, completed in 1504. This statue represents the hero of the Old Testament before his battle against his enemy Goliath. It was placed in the center of the Piazza della Signoria, opposite the Florence Town Hall (the Palazzo Vecchio). Today it can be seen in the Galleria dell'Accademia, in Florence.

DID YOU KNOW?

JULIUS II
Pope from 1503 to 1513, he was a great patron of the arts. He not only took care of Church business, but also commissioned works from great artists like Bramante, Raphaël, and Michelangelo. For example, Michelangelo decorated the ceiling of the Sistine Chapel and carved statues for the Pope's tomb.

MOSES
This statue was originally intended to adorn the tomb of Julius II. Initially, it was to have included over forty statues, but, for various reasons, only a few were finished by Michelangelo. More than 7.5ft high, *Moses* was carved between 1513 and 1516. Today, this work stands in the church of St. Peter in Chains in Rome.

Façade of the Palazzo Vecchio

MICHELANGELO AND LEONARDO DA VINCI
During the early 16th century, they were both in Florence, each working on a fresco for the Council Room in the Palazzo Vecchio. These works no longer exist, as the room was repainted by Giorgio Vasari in 1556.

CHARLES V

Portrait of Charles V by Rubens

Charles V, the son of Philip I of Habsburg and Joanna of Castile-León, was born in 1500. He became King of the Netherlands at 15, King of Spain at 16 and finally, Emperor of the Holy Roman Empire at 19, making him one of the most powerful European rulers of the time!

How large was his territory?

It extended over three continents: Charles V owned some areas of America and Africa, as well as a large part of Europe: Castile and Aragon (in Spain), the Netherlands, Flanders, Alsace, Franche-Comté, the states of Naples, Sicily and Sardinia, and finally, all the lands which the Habsburgs already owned before he came to power!

From 1520 on, Charles V had to deal with several rebellions within his kingdom, including the Castilian War of the Communities, in Spain. This battle ended in a bloodbath on April 23rd, 1521 at Villalar, when the rebel leaders were decapitated.

What occurred at Worms?

On April 17th, 1521, Martin Luther was called before the Diet (political assembly) at Worms, in Germany. He defended the theses of the Reformation before Pope Leo X and Charles V. Charles let him go free, but on May 25th, the Diet voted an edict rejecting Luther and ordering the destruction of all the books they considered heretical.

Portrait of Charles V

What were the Landsknechts?

This German word, meaning "servant of the country," referred to German mercenaries; their main weapons were the harquebus and the pike. To defeat the allies of Francis I, King of France, Charles V lured them to him by offering them fabulous booty. On arrival in Rome, they devastated the city and captured Pope Clement VII. However, when they realized how little they were actually being paid, they mutinied.

Pope Leo X at the Diet of Worms

DID YOU KNOW?

CLEMENT VII
Pope from 1523, he sided with Francis I against Charles V. However, in 1527, Rome was besieged by the imperial army, which included the Landsknechts. The Pope was imprisoned in the Castel Sant'Angelo for 7 months, and was then forced to submit to Charles V and the Holy Roman Empire.

THE BATTLE OF PAVIA
One of the first battles between Charles V and Francis I took place at Pavia, south of Milan. Francis, who led the French army, was taken prisoner by the emperor. Forced to sign the Treaty of Madrid, the French King gave up all his demands concerning Italy and Burgundy.

ABDICATION
Tired of the endless wars inside the empire and on its borders, Charles V handed over the Netherlands and Spain to his son, the future King Philip II, in 1555. The following year, he abdicated in favor of Ferdinand I, his brother, and withdrew to a monastery until his death in 1558.

ELIZABETH I

Born in London in 1533, she was the daughter of King Henry VIII and his second wife, Anne Boleyn. She was the last member of the Tudor dynasty to sit on the throne of England and Ireland. During her long reign (from 1558 to 1603), the country flourished, establishing itself as a great naval and economic power.

Portrait of Elizabeth I

What was her religion?

Initially, she was a Protestant, later converting to Catholicism during the reign of her half-sister Mary Tudor. However, Elizabeth returned to the Protestant faith once she was on the throne. Between 1559 and 1563, she approved a good many religious reforms which imposed Anglicanism as the state religion. Catholics and Puritans were then closely watched and often severely persecuted.

Elizabeth I was called the "Virgin Queen" because she never married or had children.

Gold coin with the effigy of Elizabeth I

Which queen did Elizabeth I have executed?

After having her husband assassinated, Mary Stuart, Queen of Scots was imprisoned in 1567. She managed to escape and sought refuge with her cousin Elizabeth I of England. When she realized that Mary was involved in plots to have her dethroned, Elizabeth threw her into prison and condemned her to death. Mary Stuart was decapitated in February 1587.

Elizabeth died on March 24th, 1603 at the age of 70. She was succeeded by her cousin James I, son of Mary Stuart.

Why did war break out between Spain and England?

One of the causes was the execution of the Catholic Mary Stuart by the English. In addition, the explorer Francis Drake, in the service of Elizabeth I, intercepted a Spanish convoy and took its gold. Philip II, the Catholic ruler of Spain, sent his "invincible armada": over 130 ships with nearly 30,000 men set sail in May 1588. But the Spanish fleet was defeated by the powerful English navy.

The Queen's signature

DID YOU KNOW?

HENRY VIII
King of England from 1509 until his death in 1547, Henry VIII was the second monarch of the Tudor dynasty. In 1534, he also became the religious ruler, rejecting the Pope's authority. This later led to the birth of the Church of England. He was nicknamed "Bluebeard" because he had six wives, two of whom he executed.

PRIVATEERS
These were sea-adventurers in the pay of the government: the ruler gave them written authorization to pillage enemy ships. This authorization was called a letter of marque or "lettre de course" in French, giving rise to the term "corsair."

THE TOWER OF LONDON
Declared a World Heritage site by Unesco in 1988, this medieval complex consists of a number of fortified buildings. Formerly, the Tower of London was used as a prison for members of the nobility. Many were executed here, like Anne Boleyn, mother of Elizabeth I.

WILLIAM SHAKESPEARE

A great English poet and dramatist, he was born at Stratford-upon-Avon in 1564. Considered one of the greatest writers of the English language, he began as an actor and became an author: he wrote a collection of roughly 150 sonnets in addition to tragedies and entertaining comedies. He died in his native town in 1616 at the age of 52.

The originality of William Shakespeare's works made them a great success with his contemporaries.

Engraving of Shakespeare by Martin Droeshout (1623)

When did he settle in London?

He went to the capital to make his fortune around 1588. He was an actor in several theatrical companies. In 1594, he joined the company called the "Lord Chamberlain's Men" and in 1599 became a shareholder with the new troupe at the Globe Theatre. He became famous and created many works, some of which were performed at the court of Queen Elizabeth I.

Portrait of the young William Shakespeare

Which character said the famous words: "To be or not to be"?

It was Hamlet, hero of the tragedy of the same name. Tormented by this deep philosophical question, Hamlet lived in a state of indecision which made him incapable of taking action. "To be or nor to be, that is the question" is often said today when referring to a difficult moral decision.

What are his best-known works?

They have been translated into many languages and performed all over the world. The best-known are the tragedies *Romeo and Juliet, Hamlet, Macbeth, Othello,* and *King Lear,* and the comedies *A Midsummer Night's Dream, The Comedy of Errors,* and *As You Like It.*

In 1595, Shakespeare wrote Romeo and Juliet, *inspired by an English poem by Arthur Brook.*

In the tragedy Othello (around 1604), the hero Othello, blinded by jealousy, kills his wife Desdemona in their nuptial bed and ends up killing himself.

DID YOU KNOW?

CHRISTOPHER MARLOWE
An English playwright and poet, Marlowe was a great dramatist of the Elizabethan era and a contemporary of Shakespeare. His most famous work is *The Tragical History of Doctor Faustus,* in which the hero offers his soul to the devil in return for being served by a demon for 24 years.

PRIVATE LIFE
Very little is known of Shakespeare's private life. We do know that, in 1582 (aged 18), he married a 26-year-old farmer's daughter, Anne Hathaway. Three children were born of this marriage. When he became rich, he bought a large property at Stratford-upon-Avon, where he retired in 1612 and died four years later.

GLOBE THEATRE
This is the London theater where William Shakespeare's company performed on numerous occasions. It burnt down accidentally during one of their last performances. It has since been rebuilt and can be visited today.

GALILEO

Born in Pisa, Italy in 1564, Galileo Galilei was a great physicist and astronomer. In his youth, he followed his father's advice and studied medicine. Nevertheless, he gradually turned his attention to mathematics and philosophy. In fact, he became a mathematics teacher in his home town at the age of 36. He was one of the founders of modern physics and died in 1642.

Portrait of Galileo painted by Domenico Robusti in 1605

What instrument did he use for observing the sky?

He used a refracting telescope equipped with high-precision lenses. In 1610, he published his discoveries in a book called *Sidereal Messenger* (*Sidereus Nuncius*), in which he demonstrated the existence of new stars and the structure of the Milky Way.

Galileo did not invent the refracting telescope, but improved it to magnify images 20 times.

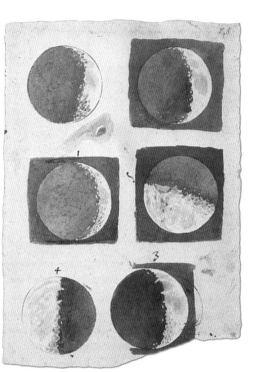

In 1616, Galileo drew the phases of the Moon.

When did he say "and yet it moves"?

At the age of 70, Galileo was condemned to life imprisonment on June 22nd, 1633. On that day, he supposedly said to the court of the Inquisition "And yet it moves," meaning that the Earth revolves around the Sun and not the contrary! His sentence was fairly quickly commuted and he was sentenced to house arrest.

Galileo studying the sky with his refracting telescope

Why was he put on trial?

He was tried on "serious suspicion of heresy." He agreed with the theories of Copernicus, and declared that the Earth revolved around the Sun (heliocentrism), whereas the Church opposed this, certain that the Earth was the center of the universe and that the Sun revolved around it. This was called geocentrism.

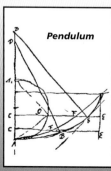

In 1633, the Church forced Galileo to recant his heliocentric view.

DID YOU KNOW?

HIS WRITINGS
He was the author of many works, the major ones being *Sidereal Messenger* (*Sidereus Nuncius*), about the Milky Way, *The Assayer* (*Il Saggiatore*), on the comets, and *Dialogue Concerning the Two Chief World Systems*, which deals with tides.

THE REFRACTING TELESCOPE
The first one was invented in Holland by Hans Lippershey in 1608 and appeared in Italy the following year. Galileo improved it and managed to enlarge 20 times the image of the star he was studying. This allowed him to observe mountains and craters on the Moon and to discover Jupiter's four largest satellites.

THE PENDULUM
By observing the back-and-forth movement (complete oscillation) of two pendulums – one made with a stone, the other with a cork, and each attached to a string – Galileo realized that they both moved at exactly the same speed, even though the arc described by the cork pendulum was far smaller than the one produced by the stone.

LOUIS XIV

During his long reign, Louis-Dieudonné (also called Louis the Great), made France a leader of political and cultural life in Europe.

Louis XIV was born in 1638, the son of Louis XIII and Anne of Austria. His second name was Dieudonné (God-given), because his parents had thought that they would never be able to have children. In fact, Louis-Dieudonné was born 23 years after their marriage! On his father's death, he became king at 5 years of age, but his mother acted as regent with Cardinal Mazarin until Mazarin died in 1661. Louis XIV then began governing France.

Why was he called the Sun King?

Louis XIV himself chose the Sun as his emblem because, to him, this star was the source of all life and also represented Apollo, the God of Peace and the Arts in Greek mythology. In fact, already at the age of 15, the monarch dressed up as the Sun for the *Ballet Royal de la Nuit* (Royal Ballet of the Night).

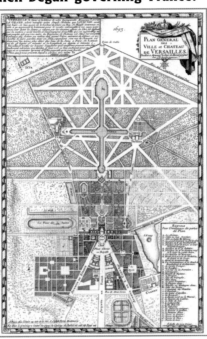

Louis XIV turned his father's hunting pavilion into the Château of Versailles, which became his royal residence and a showplace for the king's grandeur.

Louis XIV, King of France, painted by Hyacinthe Rigaud in 1701, in the Louvre Museum, Paris

Why did he move to Versailles?

Ever since the Fronde, the civil war that took place when he was very young, Louis XIV had wanted to leave Paris. He had a simple hunting lodge turned into the Château of Versailles (this took 20 years)! Once he had moved there, the court joined him in 1682 and remained there.

Who was Mazarin?

An Italian cardinal, he was a statesman who served France. A skilled diplomat and politician, he was a minister during the reign of the young Louis XIV and governed the country from 1643 until his death in 1661.

Painting of the young king on horseback

How long did he reign?

His reign was the longest in French history, lasting over seventy-two years. On his death in 1715, he was succeeded by his great-grandson, Louis XV.

Initially a councillor to the Pope, Mazarin was later called on by Richelieu (Louis XIII's minister) to succeed him.

DID YOU KNOW?

THE FRONDE
This was a revolt between 1648 and 1653 led by the privileged classes (members of parliament and the nobility), which degenerated into civil war. It broke out in response to the levying of new taxes both to finance the Thirty Years' War and Mazarin's increasing power, in other words, that of royalty to the disadvantage of the nobility and parliament.

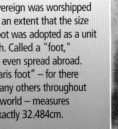

HIS FOOT
The sovereign was worshipped to such an extent that the size of his foot was adopted as a unit of length. Called a "foot," this unit even spread abroad. The "Paris foot" – for there are many others throughout the world – measures exactly 32.484cm.

ABSOLUTISM
This term refers to the absolute monarchy. When Louis XIV officially took over the reins of French government in 1661, he said to his ministers: "L'État, c'est moi" ("I am the State"). During his reign, France became a political and administrative model for all 18th century European monarchies.

PETER THE GREAT

Portrait of Peter the Great painted by Paul Delaroche in 1838, over 100 years after the Tsar's death

Pyotr Alexeyevich of the Romanov family was born in Moscow in 1672. Also called Peter I or Peter the Great, he ruled over Russia from 1682 with his half-brother, Ivan V, who was too sickly to govern. He had himself proclaimed Tsar (emperor) of the country in 1721. On his death four years later, he was succeeded by his wife Catherine I.

How did he change Russia?

By introducing many reforms, political, social, and economic. One such reform was the creation of a Senate to manage the financial, administrative, and legal affairs of the nation. One of his social reforms was to send young people abroad to learn crafts and trades in the West and bring their expertise back to Russia.

Peter I traveled extensively to learn naval techniques for his fleet.

What city did he build?

St. Petersburg. In 1703, he decided to build this city, which would become the capital of Russia in 1712. Construction work killed several thousand people who died in the marshes of the Neva River. Renamed Leningrad on Lenin's death in 1924, it regained its original name of St. Petersburg in 1991.

What was the Great Northern War?

In the 17th century, Sweden colonized a large number of territories in Poland, Norway, Saxony, and Denmark. To halt this expansion, Russia declared war on Sweden in 1700. The conflict ended in 1721; victorious Russia took control of a large part of the Baltic coast. Following his success, Peter I was proclaimed Tsar!

Peter the Great was a good sailor and ship's captain. He even came to Europe to learn the carpenter's trade in order to be able later to monitor the construction of his ships!

Cathedral of the Saviour on Blood in St. Petersburg

DID YOU KNOW?

THE CONDEMNATION OF HIS SON
Alexis Petrovich had always had a difficult relationship with his father, Peter the Great. He fled Russia to escape his father's authority but was betrayed, found, subjected to a trial, and condemned to death on July 7th, 1718. His friends and counsellors were also condemned either to the death penalty, forced labor, flogging, or deportation.

THE BOYARS
These were Russian nobles who were military leaders. From the 18th century on, they became great landowners, and as such, belonged to the ruling class. They were easily recognizable by their long beards. However, to make his country more obviously western European, Peter the Great forced all his boyars to shave their beards or pay a fine!

CHARLES XII
King of Sweden from 1697, he was a great conqueror. He fought against Russia during the Great Northern War but was defeated. Despite his zeal for battle, he was responsible for his country's losing its position as a great Baltic power.

GEORGE WASHINGTON

A general in the American army during the Revolutionary War, George Washington was born in Virginia in 1732 and died there in 1799. He was the first president of the United States of America. His face is carved on Mount Rushmore along with those of Abraham Lincoln, Thomas Jefferson, and Theodore Roosevelt.

George Washington at Princeton, New Jersey (painted by Charles Willson Peale)

When were the United States declared independent?

On July 4th, 1776, by their adoption of the Declaration of Independence, the 13 American colonies under British domination broke away from their fatherland, England. After several years of war, Great Britain recognised America's independence in 1783.

In 1783, he retired with the intention of taking care of his plantations in Virginia. Nevertheless, he returned to politics 4 years later by becoming the president of the Philadelphia Convention.

How often was he elected president of the United States?

Washington had two terms in office. He was first elected on February 4th, 1789 and then again three years later. After his second mandate ended in 1797, he retired to his estate at Mount Vernon and died there on December 14th, 1799.

When did war break out between England and its American colonies?

On May 10th, 1775, the Second Continental Congress (assembly of delegates from the British colonies in America) voted that the colonies would no longer be under English domination and that each would form its own government. Although the English King made an attempt at reconciliation with his colonies, he finally declared war on them.

During a huge storm, General Washington crosses the Delaware River with his men on Christmas Eve of 1776. The following day, he was victorious at the Battle of Trenton, taking over 900 prisoners. (Painting by Emmanuel Leutze.)

DID YOU KNOW?

YORKTOWN
This is a city in Virginia where troops led by George Washington crushed the English army on October 19th, 1781, forcing them to capitulate. Nearly 2 years later (on September 3rd, 1783), England signed the treaties of Paris and Versailles, thus ending the American Revolutionary War.

LAFAYETTE
He was a French general (1757-1834) who supported the English colonies during the Revolutionary War. In 1777, he was appointed a general in the American army and became George Washington's friend. On his return to France, he took part in the French Revolution.

THE DECLARATION OF INDEPENDENCE
Adopted by the Continental Congress on July 4th, 1776, this document proclaimed the independence of the 13 American colonies from their English fatherland. Most of it was written by Thomas Jefferson. By the time of this declaration, the American colonists had been at war with Britain for over a year.

NAPOLEON

On June 2nd, 1800, Napoleon took Milan. Twelve days later, he arrived at Marengo (in Piedmont), where he had to retreat before the Austrian army.

Named Louis Napoleon Bonaparte, he was born on August 15th, 1769 at Ajaccio in Corsica. He began as a corporal but became a general after taking power in 1799 following the French Revolution. Later crowned emperor, he took the name Napoleon I and ruled over Europe until 1815. The regime he established was called the First Empire.

Bonaparte crossing the Alps at the St. Bernard Pass (painted by J.L. David)

When did he become emperor of France?

He established a political regime (called the Consulate) in November 1799, along with Sieyès and Ducos. Three months later, he was appointed first consul, which gave him a great deal of power. He then proclaimed himself emperor with the blessing of Pope Pius VII on December 2nd, 1804.

Napoleon is named head of the Egyptian Campaign in May 1798.

Napoleon on the imperial throne, painted by Jean Auguste Dominique Ingres in 1806

How far did his empire extend?

By 1810, when Napoleon married Marie-Louise (the daughter of the Emperor of Austria), his empire had reached its greatest extent. From Hamburg (in Germany) to Italy, Napoleon had succeeded in forming alliances with other countries. Only Great Britain refused to become a part of Napoleon's sphere of influence. For this reason, the emperor decreed a continental blockade; that is, he forbade any country under French control to have economic connections with Britain!

What was the Battle of Waterloo?

On June 18th, 1815, the British and Prussian (German) armies fought against Napoleon's troops at Waterloo (in present-day Belgium). This was Napoleon's greatest defeat after the one in Russia. In fact, the Battle of Waterloo brought about the emperor's fall!

Where was he exiled to?

Abandoned by the French bourgeoisie and his army, he retired to the island of Elba in 1814, the allies having left it to him as his only kingdom. However, after his return and his defeat at the Battle of Waterloo, he was exiled to the island of St. Helena (in the Atlantic Ocean), where he died in 1821.

DID YOU KNOW?

THE NAPOLEONIC CODE
Also called the "French Civil Code," it was adopted on March 21st, 1804. It consists of a number of legal articles put down in writing so that every citizen might know his rights. Though it has gone through many alterations, the Napoleonic Code is still in use in France today.

THE COUP D'ETAT
The 18th Brumaire of the year 8 in the French Republican calendar corresponds to November 9th, 1799. This was when Napoleon set up a temporary government (the Consulate) led by three men, including himself. This brought an end to the French Revolution, which had lasted for ten years.

THE RUSSIAN CAMPAIGN
In April 1812, Tsar Alexander I of Russia broke the treaty he had signed with Napoleon at Tilsit. Not only was the Tsar worried by the dividing up of Poland, but he also shattered the bloc the Continental powers had formed against Great Britain. War was declared! After several victories, Napoleon and his Great Army were defeated by the cold Russian winter and headed back toward France. Thousands of soldiers died during this retreat.

CHARLES DARWIN

Born in 1809, he was a British naturalist who turned the scientific and religious world of his time on its head. After studying medicine, he almost became a clergyman. Instead, he decided to explore the world. For many years, he observed fossils, rocks, plants, and animals in the various countries he visited. This gave him a great amount of information for his research.

At Plymouth, the Beagle set sail on December 27th, 1831 with Darwin aboard. He embarked as its naturalist, but without pay.

What was his theory?

The theory of the evolution of species. A species changes (evolves) over generations into a new species or several new species. If a new species can adapt successfully to its surroundings, it can reproduce in enough numbers to form a population; otherwise, it dies (theory of natural selection). This theory implies the hypothesis that all primates, including man, have a common ancestor.

Where did he observe little-known species?

Darwin visited Cape Verde, the Falkland Islands, and Australia. Nevertheless, it was in the Galápagos Islands in the Pacific Ocean that he was able to study wide varieties of turtles and birds.

This caricature of Darwin as a monkey was published in the London Sketchbook *in 1874.*

The Galápagos Islands

In mid-September 1835, the Beagle dropped anchor at Chatham on Turtle Island, near the Galápagos Islands.

Where is Darwin buried?

On his death on April 19th, 1882 at Down House, he was given a national funeral in London. His body lies in Westminster Abbey, near the physicist Isaac Newton.

Westminster Abbey

Who opposed this theory?

With his theory, Darwin was searching for the origins of man, who, according to him, was a distant cousin of the ape. Christians opposed this idea because it contradicted the Bible's position that man was created by God.

DID YOU KNOW?

THE ORIGIN OF SPECIES

Darwin's book *On the Origin of Species by Means of Natural Selection* was published in 1859. Although it brought him great fame, he scandalized public opinion with his theories. Yet his theory is still valid and most scientists agree with it.

HIS JOURNEY

During his five years of travels, Darwin explored the Canary Islands, San Salvador, the coasts of South America, New Zealand, Mauritius, and the Cape of Good Hope. He took notes during his long voyage and returned to England in 1836 to study them.

THE ROYAL SOCIETY

Founded in 1660, the Royal Society is the English Academy of Science. It includes scientists like Isaac Newton, Edmond Halley, Albert Einstein, Charles Darwin, and many others. Today, many scientists still belong to it, like Steven Hawking, the famous physicist.

ARCHITECTURE

PYRAMIDS

History's most famous pyramids were built by the ancient Egyptians. These monuments were tombs for their kings, called pharaohs. However, other civilisations also built pyramidal edifices, mainly temples.

The Sphinx is an enormous statue with a lion's body and a human head which guards the entrance to the Giza pyramids. It is believed to have been built on the orders of the pharaoh Khafre.

How were the Egyptian pyramids built?

We do not know for sure; we have only theories about this. The Egyptians probably used ramps to raise the enormous blocks of stone. Initially, the pyramid was built in the form of a staircase, but the steps were then filled in to obtain a smooth surface. One thing is certain: thousands of workers took part in constructing these tombs.

Inside corridors

King's chamber

Queen's chamber

Steps

Fake funeral chamber

Illustration of construction work on the pyramid and its interior

The blocks of stone were transported to the site on sleds.

What did the Egyptian pyramids contain?

Naturally, there was a burial chamber, where the mummified body of the pharaoh was laid to rest. He was surrounded by many treasures, which attracted robbers. This is why the architects included a number of traps and dead-end corridors in the tomb.

The body of Tutankhamun was not placed inside a pyramid but in a tomb in the Valley of Kings (Thebes).

Which are the most famous pyramids?

The most famous pyramids are at Giza, near Cairo. The whole complex included the three impressive tombs of the pharaohs Khufu (the Great Pyramid), Khafre, and Menkaure. The Pyramid of Khufu is, in fact, the only one of the Seven Wonders of the World that can still be seen today.

DID YOU KNOW?

THE MESOPOTAMIAN PYRAMIDS
The Ziggurat is a terraced pyramid with a temple on top. This is a typical construction of the Mesopotamian civilization; its shape symbolizes the desire of man to get close to heaven.

Pyramid of Chichén Itzá, Mexico.

THE MAYAN PYRAMIDS
Mayan pyramids are also terraced with a small temple at the top. Some tombs have been found inside them, but they were used more as places of worship than for burial. The most famous are at Uaxactun, Copan, Naranjo, and Palenque.

THE LOUVRE PYRAMID
This glass pyramid, designed by the architect Leoh Pei Ming for the Louvre Museum in Paris, was inaugurated in 1989. Its purpose is to create a new space as a dialog between antiquity and modernity.

TEMPLES

The term "temple" generally refers to a religious building where a deity is worshipped. The Mesopotamians were among the first to build them. However, the best-known are probably those erected by the Greeks from the 5th century BC on.

What were Greek temples used for?

The Greek temple usually had two main functions: to hold the statue of the god and to contain the city's treasures. Generally rectangular in shape, it had a central room, the naos, or sanctuary, which contained the statue. This room was surrounded by imposing columns.

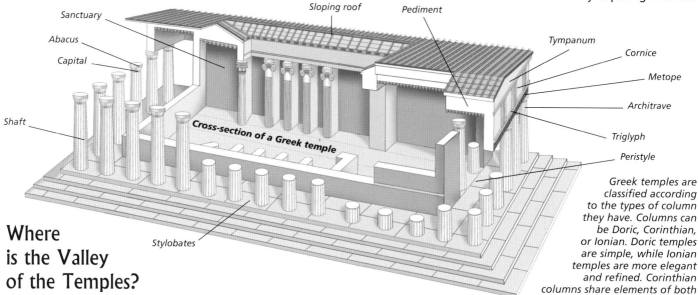

Sanctuary · Abacus · Capital · Shaft · Sloping roof · Pediment · Tympanum · Cornice · Metope · Architrave · Triglyph · Peristyle · Stylobates

Cross-section of a Greek temple

Greek temples are classified according to the types of column they have. Columns can be Doric, Corinthian, or Ionian. Doric temples are simple, while Ionian temples are more elegant and refined. Corinthian columns share elements of both the other styles.

Where is the Valley of the Temples?

The Valley of the Temples is in Agrigento, in Sicily. The valley includes about ten Greek Doric temples, erected between the 5th and 4th centuries BC, when Sicily was under Greek domination. The site offers a wonderful view of the sea and has become one of the island's major tourist destinations. The Valley of the Temples has been included in the World Heritage site list by Unesco.

Greek temples were decorated with mythological figures and scenes.

What was the Parthenon?

The Parthenon is a temple dedicated to the goddess Pallas Athena ("guardian of the city"), built by order of Pericles in the 5th century BC. A major monument of classical Greek art, it became the symbol of the supremacy of this civilization. Exceptionally large, it contained a colossal gold and ivory statue of the goddess. It became a church, a mosque, and an ammunition dump, as a result of which it was partly destroyed by an explosion in 1687. Many of its statues are today in the British Museum in London.

DID YOU KNOW?

BOROBUDUR
This is the name of a gigantic Buddhist temple in Indonesia, built in the 8th century. It is adorned with 1,640 bas-reliefs portraying the past lives of the Buddha and 504 statues of him.

THE PANTHEON
The Pantheon in Rome was erected in 27 BC and dedicated to all the Roman gods. It later became a Christian church and today contains the tombs of such illustrious people as Raphaël. Other cities, for example Paris, also have their Pantheons.

THE SHWEDAGON PAGODA
This is a Buddhist monument erected in Burma in the 11th century. It is bell-shaped and rests on a brick terrace. It is thought to have been built to house a jaw-bone and tooth belonging to the Buddha.

THE COLOSSEUM

Located in the center of Rome, the Colosseum is the best-known Roman amphitheater. Construction began in 72 AD, using the spoils of the conquest of Jerusalem. It was inaugurated by Emperor Titus in the year 80 in a three-month celebration with ceremonies and public games.

How was the Colosseum designed?

This edifice, inspired by the Greek model, served as both a stadium and a theater. It formed an ellipse of colossal dimensions: 164ft high, with a perimeter of 1,720ft. Its three rows of seats could house 50,000 spectators, who were seated depending on their social status. The Colosseum and its famous arched façade served as a model for many other Roman amphitheaters in Italy and France.

Fighting gladiators

In the Middle Ages, the Colosseum became a huge quarry for materials which were used by the Popes to erect the Barberini Palace, Piazza Venezia, and St. Peter's Basilica.

Ancient Roman coin with the head of Vespasian

What shows took place there?

The Colosseum was a center for shows and games such as the munera, ferocious battles between gladiators, and the venatio or animal fighting. The Romans found these combats most entertaining. The munera ended in the 5th century AD, and the venatio continued for another 200 years.

The center of Rome has been on the Unesco World Heritage list since 1980.

Who had the Colosseum built?

Emperor Vespasian began its construction in 72 AD and it was inaugurated by his son Titus 8 years later. Both were members of the Flavian dynasty, which gave the arena its Roman name "Amphitheatrum Flavium". Domitian, Titus's successor, had a fourth story added. This was damaged by many earthquakes. It was later abandoned and some of its materials were used for other constructions! It was not until the 18th century that the building was placed under Church protection and renovated.

DID YOU KNOW?

NAUMACHIA
Naumachia were naval battles involving several boats. To create these, the arena was flooded to form an artificial lake. The combatants were often prisoners of war or people condemned to death.

THE DECAY OF THE COLOSSEUM
The end of the Roman Empire was marked by earthquakes in 442 and 508, which severely damaged the Colosseum. The amphitheater was later used as a cemetery, a fort, and a quarry.

THE COLOSSEUM TODAY
The ruins of the Colosseum still stand today. They can be visited on two levels and provide tourists with attractive views of the city through their interior arcades. Temporary exhibitions and shows are also held there.

FORTIFICATIONS

Fortifications are constructions intended to protect a place or a position from possible attack. They can be permanent fortifications, which require huge resources, or campaign fortifications, which are usually improvised, although campaign fortifications can be improved to become permanent ones.

The Great Wall of China is dotted with watchtowers and bastions.

What was the purpose of fortifications?

Fortifications could have two roles: to act as obstacles to delay an approaching enemy, or to provide protection for those under attack. The best-known fortified edifice is the castle.

What is a siege?

This is a military operation consisting of encircling a fortified position to isolate and thus weaken it.

Example of a typical medieval fortress surrounded by a moat

Corner Tower
Walkway
Crenellations
Turret
Arrowslit
Upper Bailey
Drawbridge
Moat
Keep
Lower Bailey

What is the largest fortification in the world?

It is the Great Wall of China, 4,163 miles long. Made of stone, brick, and earth, it can measure up to 26ft high in some places. It protected the kingdoms of several dynasties of Chinese emperors. Its ruins have been listed as a Unesco World Heritage site since 1987. This is said to be the only human work visible from the Moon.

What were the results of the invention of the cannon?

To reduce the impact of cannon shots, castle walls were made thicker and rounder. However, as cannons gradually became more powerful, fortifications became obsolete as a means of defense and castles were no longer built.

The cannon spread throughout Europe towards the end of the 14th century. Large balls of stone or iron were used as projectiles.

DID YOU KNOW?

THE KEEP
The castle's highest tower is called the keep. It was the residence of the lord. During a siege, it became an observation and shooting post. It was also used as the last refuge if the rest of the castle fell into enemy hands.

THE WALLS
The Palestinian city of Jericho had very ancient walls with towers, which were initially built of stone and brick. With the development of artillery, it became necessary to reinforce them with iron and concrete.

ARROWSLITS
These are openings along fortification walls. They allowed the besieged a view of their enemy and to throw projectiles at them. There are different types of arrowslits for various projectiles: vertical for archers, horizontal for crossbows, and rounded for harquebuses.

CATHEDRALS

A cathedral is a Christian place of worship. It differs from a church in that it is the seat (headquarters) of a bishop. Cathedrals are often majestic monuments, adorned with stained glass and sculptures. They exist all over the world, in various architectural styles.

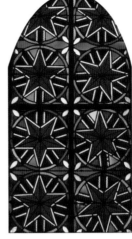

Gothic stained glass window

What were stained glass windows used for?

Stained glass windows are decorative panels made of pieces of coloured glass. In religious buildings like cathedrals, they had symbolic value, because light was considered a manifestation of the divine. Some portrayed biblical scenes and thus passed on a message to the faithful, most of whom were illiterate.

Notre-Dame de Paris

Which cathedral is also the title of a famous novel?

Notre-Dame de Paris is one of the most famous cathedrals in the world and a symbol of the city of Paris. It is also the title of a novel by Victor Hugo, published in 1831, which tells the story of Quasimodo and Esmeralda.

Plan of a cathedral

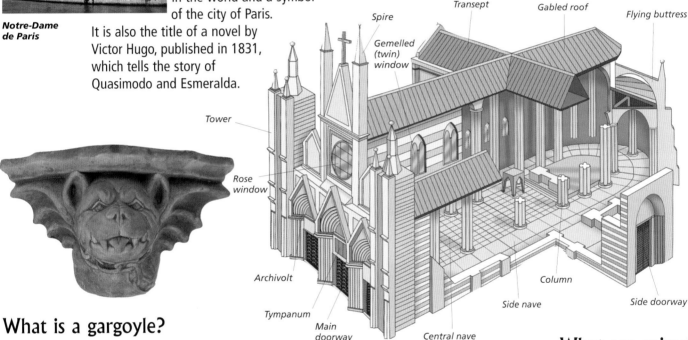

Spire
Gemelled (twin) window
Transept
Gabled roof
Flying buttress
Tower
Rose window
Archivolt
Tympanum
Main doorway
Central nave
Column
Side nave
Side doorway

What is a gargoyle?

A sculpture which often represents a grotesque face, a gargoyle in fact served as a drain that allowed rainwater to run off at a safe distance from the walls of the building.

What are spires?

Spires are architectural elements, conical or pyramidal in shape on a square base, which decorate the tops of bell-towers. The Duomo (Cathedral) in Milan, Italy, is adorned with so many spires that it has been nicknamed the "marble hedgehog."

DID YOU KNOW?

THE NAVE
The nave is the central section of a church, where the faithful gather for ceremonies and services. The original meaning of the word "nave" is "ship." This word was chosen in memory of Jesus, who is said to have taught his apostles the principles of his religion from a boat on the Sea of Galilee.

CROSS-SHAPED GROUND-PLAN
Churches often have cross-shaped ground-plans. This could be a Latin cross (with cross-pieces of different lengths), as shown here, or a Greek one (cross-pieces of equal length). Catholic churches are often built facing east, so that the worshippers look toward the place where the Sun rises.

APSE
The apse is the end of the church, behind the choir. It is often semicircular, although square or rectangular apses also exist.

AQUEDUCTS

An aqueduct is an artificial channel for transporting water. The water can be brought from its source to supply a city or irrigate crops, for example. Some aqueducts are supported by bridges, with a very characteristic architecture, often in the shape of arches. These are called bridge-aqueducts. Aqueducts can also run underground.

The Pont du Gard is the tallest Roman bridge aqueduct still in existence.

When were the first irrigation networks created?

The ancient civilisations of India and Mesopotamia already built aqueducts for their water supply. However, the best-known aqueducts of antiquity are those made by the Romans. In fact, some sections of these are still used today in certain Italian cities, for example, to supply water to their fountains.

A complex system of canals supplied water to the ancient city of Babylon.

What is the world's largest aqueduct network?

The largest aqueduct network in the world is in southern California. The water is drawn from the Colorado River, which has huge reserves, supplying 134 million cubic feet daily.

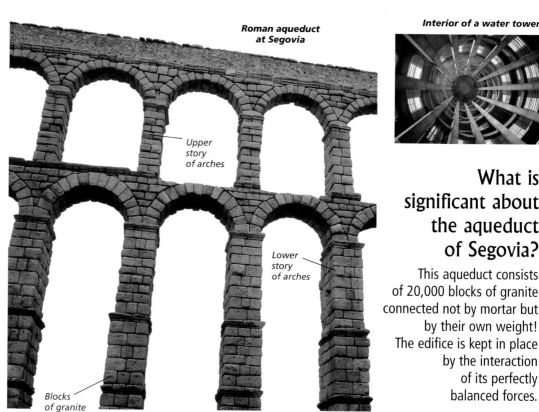

Roman aqueduct at Segovia

Upper story of arches

Lower story of arches

Blocks of granite

The bridge is 2,900ft long and has 128 arches.

Interior of a water tower

What is significant about the aqueduct of Segovia?

This aqueduct consists of 20,000 blocks of granite connected not by mortar but by their own weight! The edifice is kept in place by the interaction of its perfectly balanced forces.

DID YOU KNOW?

WATER SUPPLY STRUCTURES
These are structures used for holding water, generally dams. They can impound rainwater, surface water, underground rivers, or seawater.

WATER TRANSPORTATION STRUCTURES
These include all the structures required to transport water, from supply structures to distribution networks.

DISTRIBUTION NETWORK
The impounded water is treated and stocked in reservoirs or water towers. It is then distributed by means of a dense network of canals.

BRIDGES

Bridges are a means of crossing an obstacle (watercourse, railway, etc) by passing over it. As you study the history of bridges, you can admire the development of their construction techniques. From the first rudimentary wooden bridges to the iron ones of today, there have been a number of stages, some of which are major technical achievements.

What was the Romans' favorite type of bridge?

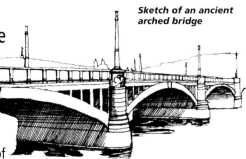

Sketch of an ancient arched bridge

The masonry bridge refers to a large category of bridges which were made fashionable by the Romans. They are sometimes called arched bridges, as they consist of one or more stone arches. Some are still standing today.
One is the Pont du Gard, in France.

A natural rock bridge, formed by erosion

The Golden Gate Bridge in San Francisco, in the United States

Brooklyn Bridge in New York spans the East River to link Brooklyn with Manhattan Island.

What is a drawbridge?

A drawbridge is a mobile bridge which can be raised or lowered. All castles had a drawbridge for crossing the moat. When the bridge was drawn up, it prevented enemies from entering.

How is a suspension bridge designed?

As its name suggests, the deck of a suspension bridge is not placed on pillars, as in the traditional bridge, but suspended in the air. It is held up by gigantic cables attached to pylons. This kind of bridge allows for longer main spans (length of the deck between two pylons). However, there are some disadvantages, such as up-and-down movement in high winds, which caused the spectacular collapse of the Tacoma Narrows Bridge in Washington State, USA, in 1940.

A movable bascule bridge, inspired by castle drawbridges

DID YOU KNOW?

THE RIALTO BRIDGE
A famous symbol of Venice, this bridge was the only crossing-point over the Grand Canal until the 19th century. It is one of the most visited tourist monuments in the city.

THE AKASHI KAIKYO BRIDGE
The Akashi Kaikyo bridge, the world's longest suspension bridge, was opened to traffic on April 5th, 1998 in Japan. It links the city of Kobe, on Honshu Island, with Awaji Island. It was designed to resist earthquakes and violent winds.

THE PONTE VECCHIO
The Ponte Vecchio ("Old Bridge") is the most famous bridge in Florence, Italy. Built in 1345, it is the only one of the city's bridges to have withstood the bombings in 1944.

THE EIFFEL TOWER

The Eiffel Tower is known the world over and is for many the symbol of Paris, if not of France. Originally erected as the entrance arch for the 1889 Universal Exhibition in Paris, it was only intended to stand for 20 years. However, its scientific potential and usefulness as the tallest monument in the Paris region saved it from destruction. Today, visitors come to see it from all over the world.

Gustave Eiffel took part in building the Statue of Liberty in New York.

Gustave Eiffel

The Eiffel Tower opened on March 31st, 1889.

Woman at the 1889 Paris Exhibition

Who designed the Eiffel Tower?

The Tower is named after its designer, Gustave Eiffel. An engineer who specialized in metal structures, he had designed a number of bridges and viaducts before taking on the Tower. He also set up the first aerodynamic laboratory and contributed to the rise of aviation.

What are the statistics of the Eiffel Tower?

Comprising 18,000 pieces of iron and 2,500,000 rivets, the Eiffel Tower stands 984ft tall – not counting the broadcast antennae on top of it, which make a total of 1,050ft. It weighs 7,000 tons, which, in fact, make it a relatively light structure. The walk to the very top has 1,665 steps!

What did Parisians think of the tower?

The Eiffel Tower met with the opposition of the literary and artistic elite of Paris, who called it a "useless, monstrous" eyesore. However, criticism died down once the Tower was completed, because of its huge popular success.

Guy de Maupassant opposed construction of the Eiffel Tower.

DID YOU KNOW?

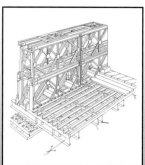

ASSEMBLY
50 engineers and designers made 5,300 sketches. Around a hundred workers made over 18,000 different pieces in their workshops. 132 people were involved in their assembly.

HITLER IN PARIS
During the Second World War, the Eiffel Tower was involved in the resistance movement! Legend has it that the French put its lifts out of action during Hitler's visit to Paris to prevent him from visiting the top!

THE EIFFEL TOWER AND THE CHRYSLER BUILDING
The Eiffel Tower was considered huge at the time of its construction, which left many people amazed. In 1929, it lost its title of the world's tallest building (which it had held for 40 years) when the Chrysler Building in New York, a 1,046ft-high skyscraper, was completed. Nowadays, skyscrapers twice as tall are being built!

SKYSCRAPERS

"Skyscraper" is the name given to any building consisting of many stories with a height of over 490ft, as they seem tall enough to touch the sky.

Chicago's 17-story Monadnock Building, completed in 1893, stands 220 feet metres high.

Where were skyscrapers first built?

In 1871, a terrible fire broke out in Chicago, in the United States. A new kind of structure had to be invented to re-house the residents, one that was solid, quick to build, and occupied as little space as possible on the ground. Baron Jenney took advantage of the invention of mechanical lifts to design high-rise buildings in steel rather than wood, and skyscrapers were born. Other American cities soon followed the fashion, in particular, New York.

The Empire State Building, the tallest in New York, measures 1,453ft, including the antenna.

Why are skyscrapers in fashion?

Skyscrapers have many disadvantages: they are costly to build and can have a negative environmental footprint. Yet, skyscrapers continue to fascinate people and are often a sign of economic health and pride in the countries which decide to build them. In fact, many countries compete in the race to build the tallest skyscraper.

What invention led to the birth of skyscrapers?

The lift is an essential element in the design of buildings as tall as skyscrapers. It would take too much time and energy to climb dozens of stairs.

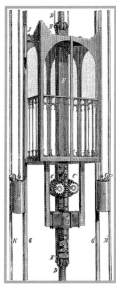

The lift was patented by Elisha Otis in 1861.

Which city is famous for its skyscrapers?

The city of New York, and particularly the area of Manhattan, cannot be dissociated from its famous skyscrapers, the headquarters of many large businesses. It is home to the Empire State Building and Ground Zero, the site of the former World Trade Center, which was destroyed in the attacks of September 11th, 2001.

Manhattan

DID YOU KNOW?

STEEL
At the end of the 19th century, a new process made it possible to manufacture large quantities of steel. This metal, both lighter and sturdier than iron, was used to build increasingly taller skyscrapers.

RECORDS
Located in the heart of the capital of Taiwan, *Taipei 101* is a 101-story skyscraper which stands 1,667ft high. It is one of the world's tallest buildings, after the Tower in Dubai, which is 2,683ft tall.

SEATTLE
Seattle is a city in the north-west of the United States. A large number of skyscrapers have been built there. The best-known landmark is a tower with a platform on top, called the Space Needle. However, despite its height of 597ft, it is not a skyscraper.

INVENTIONS AND DISCOVERIES

MEASURING TIME

From early in the history of mankind, people wanted to measure time, especially in order to organize city life. They began by observing nature and its phenomena: the seasons, the lunar cycle, the shifting of shadows throughout the day. They gradually invented more and more elaborate devices for measuring time: the sundial, the clepsydra, the mechanical clock, and the atomic clock.

Hourglass

Time is also a philosophical concept that continues to raise many considerations and questions.

What people divided the day into 24 hours?

The Sumerians and Babylonians were the first to divide the day into 24 hours, the hour into 60 minutes, and the minute into 60 seconds. They probably picked these numbers because they are divisible by 2, 3, 4, 6, and 12. The day is the period of time during which the Earth makes one complete rotation on its axis.

Medieval illustration showing an armillary sphere

What is a clepsydra?

The clepsydra is a water clock using the same principle as the hourglass. The flow of a thin stream of water establishes a period of time. This device probably originated in Egypt, but it was adopted and improved by the Greeks, who used it to limit the length of time an orator could speak.

Stylus

The sundial shows the time of day by means of a rod called a stylus, which casts a shadow on a marked surface when it is placed in the sun.

Sun dial

What civilian calendar do we use today?

Most of the Western world uses the Gregorian calendar, introduced by Pope Gregory XIII in the 16th century. It is a solar calendar, based on the time it takes the Earth to revolve around the sun – 365.24221935 days of 24 hours each. Since the year cannot be divided into 365.24221935 days, each year lasts 365 days. Every 4 years (except for centenary years that are not divisible by 400), one day (February 29th) is added. This is called a leap year.

Dial   *Mechanism*

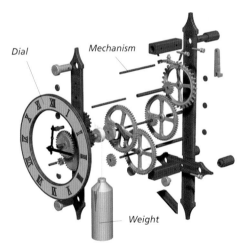

Weight

In 1657, the Dutch physician Huygens applied the law of pendulum oscillations described by Galileo to build the first pendulum clock.

DID YOU KNOW?

TIME ZONES
Since 1884, the world has been divided into 24 time zones. Each zone is determined by its meridian (an imaginary line connecting the North and South Poles). The basic meridian, or meridian zero, is the one that passes through the royal observatory at Greenwich (photo at left), in the suburbs of London.

LATITUDE AND LONGITUDE
The astrolabe is an instrument for measuring the positions of the stars. In the 16th and 17th centuries, it allowed navigators to determine their latitude. Measuring longitude had to wait for the work of the English clockmaker John Harrison, in the 18th century.

Astrolabe

THE WATER CLOCK
Ctesibios was a Greek physician of the 3rd century BC. He became famous for improving the clepsydra, which up to then had not been very accurate, into a true water clock with a constant flow. This clock was connected to a cylinder marked with the hours.

NUMBERS

Numbers are words or symbols that are used to indicate quantities. Since antiquity, calculating has been a fundamental necessity. Numerals were conceived in order to facilitate trade, permit land and time to be measured, and to study astronomic phenomena. The decimal system we use today is derived from Indian and Arab number systems.

The abacus is a device used since ancient times for arithmetic calculations. It is able to perform the 4 basic operations using whole numbers.

Abacus

Different systems for writing numbers: from top to bottom, Egyptian, Babylonian, Roman, Chinese, Indian, Mayan, Arabic, and Thai.

Who invented zero?

Zero, which represents a null amount, was invented well after the other numbers. The Indians introduced it into their number system around the 5th century BC. They called it "sunya," meaning "empty." The Arabs learned of it in the 8th century, and it was introduced into Europe three centuries later, along with the other numerals.

0 symbol

What does calculation mean?

"Calculation" comes from the Latin "calculus," meaning "pebble." In the oldest counting systems we know of, such as that of the Sumerians, pebbles were used to make simple calculations. The word "count" also comes from Latin.

When did numbers appear in human history?

The Sumerians, a people who settled in Mesopotamia in the 4th millennium BC, were the first to use written symbols to represent numbers. They represented one with a line, ten with a circle, one hundred with a ball, etc. These symbols were probably scratched on clay tablets.

On a tape measure, numerals are used for measuring length.

Who invented the first calculator?

In 1642, the French philosopher and scholar Blaise Pascal created the first automatic calculating machine in order to help his father. Called the Pascaline, it could do addition and subtraction. Some years later, the German mathematician G.W. Leibniz improved on Pascal's device by building a machine that could also solve multiplication and division problems.

DID YOU KNOW?

THE PYTHAGOREAN TABLE
This is a table with both rows and columns that shows the products of multiplications. The disciples of Pythagoras used it to avoid arithmetic errors, and named it the "Pythagorean Table" in honor of their teacher.

PERFECT NUMBERS
A number is said to be perfect when it equals the sum of all its divisors except itself. An example? Six is a perfect number because it is divisible by 1, 2, and 3, and is equal to the sum of those numbers (1 + 2 + 3 = 6).

Clock with Roman numerals

ROMAN NUMERALS
The Romans used seven letters of the alphabet which they combined, according to precise rules, to write numbers. So, I equaled 1, V equaled 5, L equaled 50, C equaled 100, D equaled 500, and M equaled 1,000.

THE ALPHABET

The alphabet is a group of graphic signs for writing down sounds. Combined in many different ways, they can form all the words of a language. The word "alphabet" comes from the first two letters of the Greek alphabet, alpha and beta. The English alphabet is derived from Latin and contains 26 letters.

Originally, the Latin alphabet consisted entirely of capital letters; lower-case letters appeared in the Middle Ages.

The Arabic alphabet consists of 28 letters, only three of which are vowels.

Which is the most widely used writing system in the world?

The Latin alphabet is the most widely used. Inspired by the Greek alphabet, it was invented by the ancient Romans to write their language, Latin. It is used by the large majority of languages in central and western Europe, and also in regions colonized by Europeans. Some languages, particularly in Africa, that had no writing systems have adopted it too.

Is Chinese writing alphabetical?

Chinese writing is not alphabetical because the characters it uses represent not sounds, but words or ideas. It is one of the most complicated writing systems in the world, but also one of the most beautiful. In China, writing can be an art: calligraphy.

The most ancient Chinese writings we know of date from the 14th century BC. They are divinations carved onto turtle shells and the shoulder blades of cattle.

Are all languages written from left to right?

English, like all European languages, is written from left to right. But there are also languages that are written from right to left, like Arabic and Hebrew, or from top to bottom, like Korean. Some languages have even tried boustrophedon, which alternates left-to-right and right-to-left lines.

DID YOU KNOW?

BRAILLE
This is a system of writing for the blind, which is read by touching. It consists of 63 symbols made up of a series of raised dots, with a maximum of six. It was invented by Louis Braille in 1829.

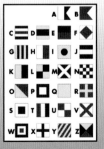

THE DIGITAL ALPHABET
Sign language is a means of communication through gestures, used by the hard of hearing. It is a language in its own right, with its own dictionary, grammar, and alphabet, called the digital alphabet. Here a hand is forming the letter "i."

THE NAUTICAL ALPHABET
This is an international code of maritime signals in which each little flag represents a letter of the alphabet, a number, or an entire message.

PRINTING

Printing encompasses the methods of reproducing text and pictures, usually on paper. This procedure, basic to publishing, is today industrialized on a huge scale. But this was not always so.

Before the invention of printing, if you wanted to reproduce a book, you had to copy it! In the Middle Ages, for example, some monks spent all their time doing this: they were called scribes, and their copies were called manuscripts.

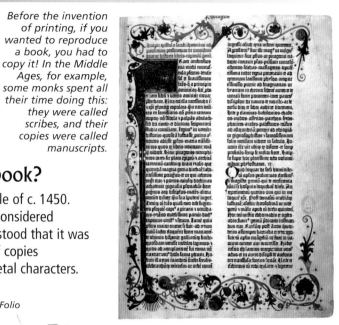

What was the first printed book?

The first printed book was Gutenberg's Bible of c. 1450. Gutenberg, a German printer, is generally considered the inventor of Western printing. He understood that it was possible to publish an unlimited number of copies of the same work by means of movable metal characters.

Gutenberg did not sign a single one of the printed books attributed to him!

Gutenberg's Bible, called the 42-line Bible, printed in Mainz in 1455.

How are books printed today?

Printing is now done by huge and often complex machines called presses. There are many printing methods, of which offset is the most widely used. But the basic principle remains the same: the inked pad.

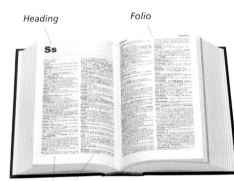

Heading   Folio

Ss

Columns of text

Offset machine operators

Are the pages of a book printed in order?

No! Presses print large sheets containing many pages all at once. The sheet is then folded in such a way that the pages are in correct order, in the form of a booklet. The final book is made up of these booklets bound together.

Who invented movable type?

Gutenberg modernized the technique by using metal, but he did not invent it! That was done in the 11th century by the Chinese. Bi Sheng had had the idea of making porcelain blocks in the shape of written characters; after being fired to harden them, they were put together on a supporting surface, inked, and finally pressed against a sheet of paper.

Old printing workshop

DID YOU KNOW?

ABCD EFGHIJK LMNOP QRSTUV WXYZ

Helvetica

HELVETICA
This is a style of typographic characters. It was designed in 1957 by the Swiss typographer Max Miedinger, and was very successful during the 1960s and 1970s. Many signs, such as subway/underground signs in the world's largest cities, are printed in Helvetica.

ALDE MANUCE
He was the greatest Italian typographer and the first modern editor. As a printer in Venice, he made known many books in Greek, Latin, and contemporary languages. He also published the greatest work of the humanist Erasmus of Rotterdam, In Praise of Folly (1511). He also invented italic letters and pocket-sized books.

LETTERPRESS
This is a printing procedure widely used for important printing projects that demand high quality of reproduction (stamps, catalogs, etc.). The ink is transferred directly from an engraved metal cylinder to the paper.

GUNPOWDER

Also called black powder, gunpowder was history's first explosive, and was the only one known for centuries. Invented around the 9th century by the Chinese, who used it for fireworks, it was probably imported to Europe by the Arabs around the 13th century. During the 20th century, it was gradually replaced by other substances such as pyroxyl powder.

Fireworks display

The Chinese were the first to use black powder in fireworks.

What is gunpowder made of?

Gunpowder is made up of saltpeter, charcoal, and sulfur, mixed in different proportions according to how it will be used. The saltpeter gives the mixture a salty taste. One anecdote tells that soldiers, when they had no salt at the front, used black powder to salt and preserve their food!

Ancient barrels used to hold gunpowder.

Why is black powder no longer used?

Black powder is sensitive to humidity; its residues can clog firearms; and it produces large amounts of smoke. It is also very dangerous to handle, since a very small amount of heat can set it off. For all these reasons, the mixture was abandoned in favor of pyroxyl or smokeless powder, which is still used today.

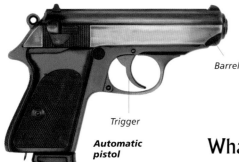

The automatic pistol has a removable magazine inside the handgrip.

Barrel

Trigger

Automatic pistol

Grip

What was black powder used for?

Black powder revolutionized the art of war by permitting the invention of the first modern weapons: cannons and firearms. The soldiers placed a small amount of black powder in the weapon, well tamped down, followed by a bullet. The charge was set off through a small hole. In time, these techniques improved and black powder was gradually replaced by less problematic powders.

Cannons were soon equipped with wheels. The extraordinary power that they gave to the attack revolutionized the art of war and necessitated the creation of new means of defense.

DID YOU KNOW?

PROJECTILES
These firearm projectiles, less than 20mm in caliber (diameter), are called bullets. Cylindrical in shape, they are often made of metal. The science that studies the motion of projectiles is called ballistics.

LIGHT ARMS
This is a group of weapons that can be carried and used by a single individual. The first ones were small-scale versions of artillery pieces such as the cannon.

A piece of light artillery

ARTILLERY
This word denotes large-caliber firearms and, by extension, the military units assigned to use them. There are four principal types of weapon: cannons, howitzers, mortars, and rocket launchers.

SAILING AROUND THE GLOBE

On September 20th, 1519, one Ferdinand Magellan set sail from a small Andalusian village. He was in command of 5 ships and 250 men, and had a single objective: to sail around the world. Unfortunately, the ambitious explorer was killed in an ambush in the Philippines. One of his companions took command and succeeded in carrying out Magellan's plan: he sailed around the world. This voyage, which was marked by other ambushes, opened the commercial route between America and the Orient and confirmed the theory that the earth was round.

When expeditions failed, it was often attributed to sea monsters or giant octopuses.

Ferdinand Magellan

What route did Magellan follow?

Magellan followed the African coast and then crossed the Atlantic to South America. He sailed along the eastern coast of the continent until he found a strait, which bears his name today, through which he passed to the other side. He sailed across an ocean which he named the Pacific for its calm waters. One and a half years after his departure, he dropped anchor at Guam, in the Mariana Islands, and then in the Philippines, where he lost his life.

The native population gave a friendly welcome to Magellan and his crew.

Who was the first to round the Cape of Good Hope?

Bartholomeu Dias was the first sailor to round the Cape of Good Hope. But the celebrated Portuguese navigator Vasco da Gama was the first to use this route to reach the East Indies.

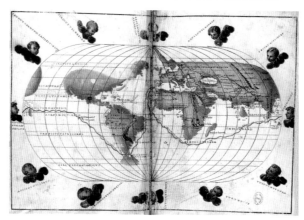

Magellan discovered the South-west Passage to Asia.

Who completed Magellan's voyage?

After Magellan was killed by natives on April 27th, 1521, the Spanish navigator Juan Sebastián Elcano took command of the Victoria. He completed the circumnavigation in 1522, when he passed the Cape of Good Hope. The spices he brought back were sufficient to pay the expense of the expedition.

Juan Sebastián Elcano

How did Tierra del Fuego gets its name?

As he was sailing through the strait that bears his name today, Magellan saw mysterious fires along the coast of South America. These fires were lighted by the native populations to protect themselves from the cold. This inspired the name "Land of Fire."

DID YOU KNOW?

THE STRAITS OF MAGELLAN
This is the most important natural passage between the Pacific and Atlantic Oceans; but because of its inhospitable climate and narrowness, it is rarely used.

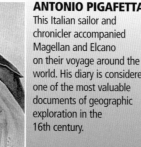

ANTONIO PIGAFETTA
This Italian sailor and chronicler accompanied Magellan and Elcano on their voyage around the world. His diary is considered one of the most valuable documents of geographic exploration in the 16th century.

THE SPICE ROUTE
This is the sea route, opened by Portuguese explorers in the 15th and 16th centuries, which connected Europe to the Spice Islands (the Moluccas); pepper, cloves, nutmeg, and cinnamon were of inestimable value.

DISCOVERY OF **THE SOURCES OF THE NILE**

Explorer's equipment

For centuries, the difficulty of penetrating central Africa prevented explorers from finding the origins of the Nile, the great river worshipped by the Egyptians. In the second half of the 19th century, some daring adventurers succeeded in piercing the mystery.

Who went in search of Livingstone?

Sir Henry Morton Stanley, a British journalist, went to Africa in 1869. His purpose was to find David Livingstone, of whom he had heard no news for some time. The phrase he spoke when he saw him – "Doctor Livingstone, I presume?" – is still famous.

At the time of the first explorations, Africa was under European colonial domination.

Who reached Lake Victoria?

In 1856, Richard Burton and John Speke, two British explorers, decided to follow a route left by Ptolemy, an Egyptian scientist of the 1st century AD: a map of the Nile showing that the river had its source in a great lake. But on the way, the two men contracted malaria. Burton was so ill that he interrupted his trip. Speke went on alone and discovered an immense lake which he named Lake Victoria. It was indeed the source of the Nile: Ptolemy had been right!

David Livingstone devoted part of his life to exploring the African continent.

Who were the pioneers of African exploration?

Up to the middle of the 19th century, most of the African continent was still a mystery to Europeans. Some English explorers then decided to go in search of the source of the Nile. The many tributaries of this river made this a difficult mission.

Dr. David Livingstone was the first man to cross Africa. Notably, he discovered Lake Ngami and a magnificent waterfall on the Zambezi which he named Victoria Falls in honor of the Queen of England. But he did not find the source of the Nile. When he died, his heart was buried in Africa and the rest of his body in England.

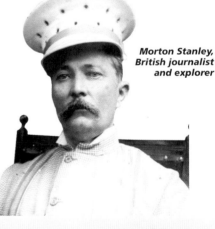

The English explorer Richard Burton

Morton Stanley, British journalist and explorer

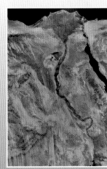

DID YOU KNOW?

NERO AND THE NILE
As early as the 1st century AD, the Roman emperor Nero sent an expedition of soldiers and scholars to find the legendary sources of the Nile. His explorers reached a high plateau in present-day Rwanda, but were so exhausted that they finally gave up.

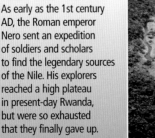

THE CONGO RIVER
This river in equatorial Africa, more than 2,670 miles long and the second African river after the Nile, forms a natural frontier between the Democratic Republic of the Congo and the Republic of the Congo. Its uppermost part was sometimes mistakenly thought to be the source of the Nile.

LAKE VICTORIA
Located in eastern Africa at an elevation of 3,720ft, this is Africa's largest freshwater lake and the second-largest on earth. Its principal tributary is the Kagera, the most distant source of the Nile. The lake is at the heart of a heavily populated region where fishing in the principal activity.

THE **EXPLORATION** OF THE **POLES**

The North and South Poles are the coldest and windiest regions in the world. In spite of this common point, they are very different from each other, contrary to what one might think. The North Pole is an enormous ice pack, i.e. a frozen part of the Arctic Ocean, that encircles the earth. The South Pole, on the other hand, is an immense continent, essentially covered with ice and surrounded by the Southern Ocean. The two regions' flora and fauna are very different. Their hostile climate made the first explorations, at the beginning of the 19th century, very difficult. Many men lost their lives in this exploit.

Between 1893 and 1909, Robert Edwin Peary led several expeditions to the Arctic.

Who reached the North Pole first?

It is not a historic certainty, but the American explorer Robert Edwin Peary is considered the first man to reach the North Pole, in 1909. He was accompanied by his assistant Matthew A. Henson, 4 Inuit, and many sled dogs.

In a cartoon from 1909, Peary and Cook fight over the conquest of the North Pole. Neither was successful, although they claimed the opposite!

On his expedition to the South Pole, Amundsen employed heavy wooden sleds pulled by dogs.

Who reached the South Pole first?

In 1911, two expeditions – one led by the Norwegian Roald Amundsen, and the other by the English officer Robert Scott – set out to conquer the South Pole. This race was won by Amundsen on December 14th, 1911. Fate was cruel to Scott and his men: they reached the Pole a month later, and all of them perished on their way back.

How did Amundsen and Nobile fly over the Pole?

On May 11th, 1926, Umberto Nobile and Roald Amundsen completed the first flight over the North Pole. They flew in the *Norge*, a airship designed by Nobile himself.

*The **Norge** flying over the North Pole*

DID YOU KNOW?

POLAR AURORAS

The polar auroras are strange luminous phenomena that appear in the night sky. Very spectacular, they have different forms and colours (with green predominating) and move around the sky. The one appearing in the Arctic is called the aurora borealis, and the one in the Antarctic, the aurora australis.

ICEBERGS

An iceberg is a piece of ice that has broken off an ice pack and floats on the ocean. It is composed of frozen fresh water. The visible part of the iceberg, the part that projects above the water, represents only one-tenth of its total size!

FRIENDSHIP AND RIVALRY

After their experience on the *Norge*, Nobile and Amundsen quarreled, each wanting to claim for himself the success of the enterprise. But when Nobile's airship was lost at the North Pole in 1928, Amundsen hurried to his aid and lost his life.

BOATS

Boats are structures that can float on water. They are employed mainly for transporting people and merchandise, but also for fishing and warfare. In ancient times, they were made of wood and were propelled by oars or sails; in the 19th century they came to be made of iron and used steam engines. The more modern ones are propelled by internal combustion engines, like cars.

How is a boat built?

Whatever its size, a boat always consists of the following elements: a flotation tank, which allows it not only to float but to remain watertight; a propulsion system (oars, a sail or an engine); and a directional system (a rudder). Various features are added depending on the vessel's purpose (bridges, keels, compartments and rooms of different kinds, machines, equipment etc.)

Where is the bow? Where is the stern?

It is not easy to steer a boat without knowing the proper language. The bow is the front end of the boat, and the stern is the rear end. In the same way, the left side of the boat, when you are facing the bow (forward), is called port, and the right side is starboard.

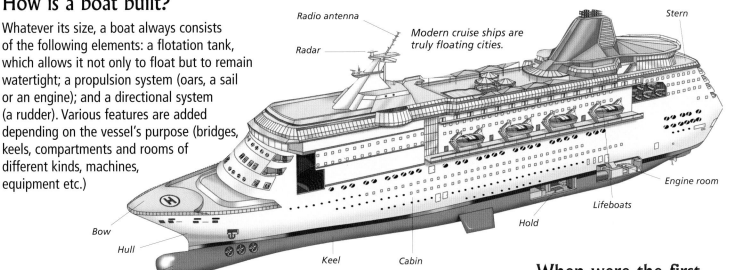

Radio antenna
Radar
Modern cruise ships are truly floating cities.
Stern
Engine room
Lifeboats
Hold
Cabin
Keel
Bulb
Hull
Bow

Why do boats float?

According to the theory called "Archimedes's Principle" (named for the Greek scholar who discovered it), in order for an object to float, it must weigh less than the volume of water it displaces. That is why a boat's interior, especially the part below the water line, consists of air. Thus, since it is lighter than the water it displaces, it can float!

Model of a galleon

The galleon, a warship with sails, was used in the 16th and 17th centuries.

When were the first boats launched?

The first frail boats were made of reeds or skins, or carved directly from tree trunks. Papyruses and pictures show that the ancient Egyptians were building ships as far back as 2,500 BC! These ships, which had both oars and sails, could transport people, cattle, or merchandise.

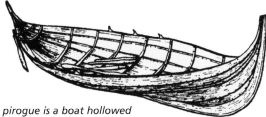

The pirogue is a boat hollowed out of a tree trunk.

DID YOU KNOW?

THE COMPASS
The compass is an instrument for finding direction. It has a magnetized needle which points toward the magnetic north pole. Be careful not to confuse the magnetic north with the geographic north!

THE LIGHTHOUSE
The lighthouse is a raised structure which, at night, shines a light to guide ships navigating near coasts. The lighthouse of Alexandria, built about 280 BC and destroyed by an earthquake in the 14th century, was one of the Seven Wonders of the World.

THE SEXTANT
Invented in 1730, this device allows one to calculate the angular distance between two objects. A sailor could also find his exact position (latitude and longitude) by calculating the angles of certain heavenly bodies, particularly the Sun.

STEAM ENGINES

A boiler creates steam, whose heat (thermal energy) is converted into mechanical energy. This energy makes it possible for a machine to function, such as a train. So we call it a steam engine. The very first one was invented in the 1st century AD by Hero of Alexandria! Although it was a true steam engine, called an aeolipyle, it was only a toy and not a source of energy.

A replica of the "Rocket" is on view in the Science Museum in London.

George Stephenson

A steam locomotive operates by burning coal or wood to produce the steam that provides energy.

How does a steam engine work?

A cylinder, with a piston inside it, is filled with steam. The steam presses against the piston, as in a pressure-cooker, and pushes it first in one direction and then the other. This creates a back-and-forth movement which, for example, can turn the wheels of a locomotive!

Who invented the locomotive?

The English engineer Robert Trevithick built the first locomotive in 1804, but this first steam vehicle was really quite crude. The modern locomotive did not come into existence until 1829; this was the famous "Rocket," built by George Stephenson. It was very successful, and brought about the development of the railway.

What revolution was made possible by the steam engine?

The invention of the steam engine played a considerable role in the industrial revolution, which took place in the 18th and 19th centuries. The countries involved passed from an economy based on agriculture to one based on the mechanized mass production of goods. Little by little, man was replaced by machine.

DID YOU KNOW?

THE PISTON ENGINE

Denis Papin, a 17th century French physicist, was one the first to try to make use of the energy produced by steam under pressure. He invented the first piston engine, which consisted of a cylinder in which water was boiled; its evaporation eventually raised the piston.

THOMAS NEWCOMEN

In 1705 he invented the atmospheric engine, an improvement on Papin's engine. It utilized steam and atmospheric pressure at the same time to raise and lower the piston in the cylinder. In spite of its ungainly appearance, it was used to pump water out of coal mines, and was even exported to North America!

JAMES WATT

This Scottish engineer (1736-1819) modernized Newcomen's machine mainly by adding a separate condensation chamber, which considerably reduced steam leakage in the cylinder. A brilliant scientist, he was the author of many other inventions, and gave his name to an electrical unit.

AIRCRAFT

An airplane is a vehicle that can move through the air. It is propelled by an engine, and its slightly curved wings keep it in balance. There are two kinds of airplanes, military, and civilian. Civilian aircraft include airliners, which are used for business trips, tourism, and transportation of goods.

The Wright brothers' Flyer 1

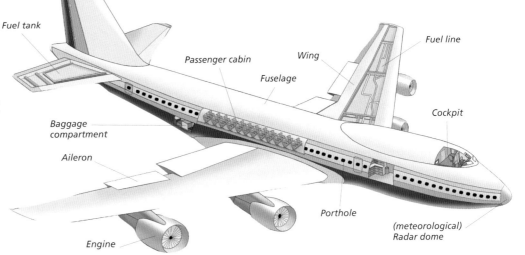

An airliner is a fixed-wing aircraft used for transporting passengers. The Boeing 707, the Boeing 747, the Concorde, and the Airbus 380 are airliners.

Rudder

Fuel tank

Passenger cabin

Wing

Fuselage

Fuel line

Cockpit

Baggage compartment

Aileron

Porthole

(meteorological) Radar dome

Engine

When did the first flight take place?

In 1903, in North Carolina, the Wright brothers succeeded in rising into the air for the first time aboard their airplane, the "Flyer," and stayed in the air for 12 seconds.

Who was the first pilot to fly across the Atlantic?

On May 20th, 1927, the American aviator Charles Lindbergh completed the first solo crossing of the Atlantic in his monoplane, "The Spirit of St. Louis." Having flown from New York, he arrived at Le Bourget, near Paris, after a flight of 33 hours, 32 minutes.

Charles Lindbergh

How is an airplane constructed?

An airplane has 5 principal sections: the central body, called the fuselage, which contains the cabin, the baggage compartment, and the cockpit; the engines; the wings; the rear section, called the empennage, which governs direction and altitude; and the wheels, or landing gear. An aircraft has to be long and smooth to be aerodynamic. In flight, its shape must offer the least possible resistance to the air.

DID YOU KNOW?

AIRSHIP
This machine consists of a balloon containing helium, a gas that is lighter than air. The most famous ones were the Zeppelins, named after their German inventor. They served most notably during the First World War, but their many accidents forced the army to stop using them.

HOT-AIR BALLOON
This is a balloon using hot air, invented by the Montgolfier brothers. It consists of 3 main elements: a gas-bag, a burner connected to a fuel system, and a gondola. It is used for sporting events and tourism.

HELICOPTER
The helicopter is an aircraft with revolving wings which can take off and land vertically, and hover at a given point in the air. The first true helicopter, the Gyroplane-Laboratoire, dates from 1936. It remained in the air for an hour and 20 minutes, and flew around a 27-miles closed course.

VACCINES

To vaccinate people means to inject them with a product that prevents them from catching an illness. The vaccine can be swallowed, or injected into the body with a needle or through a small scratch on the skin. Some vaccines only need to be taken once; others need to be administered a number of times in a person's lifetime, so they are called boosters. There are many vaccines, each for a specific disease. Unfortunately, researchers have not yet found vaccines for all diseases.

Edward Jenner, a country doctor, conquered smallpox.

Where does the word "vaccine" come from?

In the 18th century, a disease called smallpox claimed many victims. Then Edward Jenner, a British doctor, had an idea. He injected small amounts of vaccine into his patients. The vaccine was the bovine form of smallpox, which was less dangerous than the human form. The people who had been vaccinated thus became immune to the disease, in other words, protected against it.

Pasteur's research led to the development of a procedure for sterilising milk, called "pasteurization". Its purpose was to eliminate all micro-organisms dangerous to health.

Who was Louis Pasteur?

Louis Pasteur was a French scientist during the 19th century, a time of many essential discoveries. He developed a vaccine against rabies, and he proved the existence of the micro-organisms called bacteria and their responsibility for certain diseases. He found a way to destroy dangerous bacteria in food through a process called pasteurization, which is used everywhere today.

Viruses and bacteria are microbes, or micro-organisms, that are invisible to the naked eye. You need a microscope to see them.

Virus

What is in a vaccine?

A vaccine contains a very small amount of the virus or bacterium that causes the disease against which the patient is to be protected. This amount is too weak to make the patient sick, but it is sufficient to cause the creation of antibodies, i.e. means of defense. In this way, when he is exposed to the disease, the patient doesn't catch it because he is already protected! This protection is called immunity.

What is a virus?

A virus is a microbe that can cause disease. It is a parasite – in other words, it needs a "host" (the human body, for example) to be able to develop. Antibiotics are of no use at all in combating a virus. It is necessary either to be vaccinated or to take drugs called antivirals.

Eyepiece
Body Tube
Objectives
Glass slide
Stage
Light source

DID YOU KNOW?

PLAGUE
This is a serious and very contagious disease that strikes both humans and animals. It is caused by a bacterium that is normally present in rat fleas. The Black Death epidemic in 1348 killed a quarter of the population of Europe. Today, powerful antibiotics can fight this illness.

DIPHTHERIA
This contagious, infectious disease resembles a sore throat. It used to mainly affect children, with a high mortality rate. A drug was developed in 1894, and a vaccine in 1923.

TUBERCULOSIS
This is a contagious disease, caused by a bacterium, that principally attacks the lungs. The first antituberculin vaccine, called BCG, was developed in 1921. Although it can fight the most serious forms of the disease, it cannot eliminate the bacteria that cause it. Even today, tuberculosis claims many victims.

ELECTRICAL ENERGY

Electrical energy is obtained by means of mechanical energy from fossil fuels and nuclear and solar power. Today it is mainly used in developed countries, both for industrial and home purposes. It can be transported from generator to consumers in the form of electric current, through a network of wires. It can also be transformed into other types of energy, and can meet many needs.

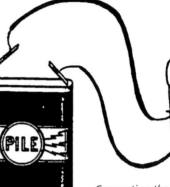

Connecting the two poles with an electrical wire creates a circuit. The battery generates current.

Who invented the light bulb?

The invention of the light bulb is attributed to Joseph Wilson Swan and Thomas Alva Edison. However, it is generally accepted that Heinrich Goebel, a German clockmaker, developed this technique in 1854, some 25 years earlier!

Inert gas

Filament

Base

In light bulbs, electric current is transformed into light. The fluorescent bulb is a more ecological type of light bulb.

What electrical units of measure have been given the names of famous scientists?

Many units of measure have taken the names of great physicists who studied electrical phenomena. The coulomb, the unit of charge, comes from the Frenchman Charles de Coulomb. The ampere (intensity of current) comes from the French mathematician André-Marie Ampère. The same is true for the watt, the unit of power, and the volt, the unit of electrical potential.

Where does the word "voltaic pile" come from?

The first electric battery was the voltaic pile. The word "pile" comes from the structure itself: a stack of small brass and zinc disks. The word "voltaic" comes from its inventor, Alessandro Volta, who also gave his name to the unit of electrical potential: the volt.

Voltaic pile

The current in a voltaic pile is generated by a chemical reaction between different elements.

What is a generator?

A generator is a device that can produce electrical energy from another form of energy. The dynamo, for instance, generates direct current.

Dynamo

DID YOU KNOW?

STATIC ELECTRICITY

When you rub certain non-conducting materials (such as glass or plastic), the electric charge this produces does not circulate but is trapped on the material's surface. This accumulation of charge causes what we call static electricity.

THE LIGHTNING ROD

Developed in 1752 by Benjamin Franklin, this device is intended to prevent lightning from striking a building. In its original version, a metal rod mounted on the roof was connected to the ground by a conductor which allowed the charge to dissipate.

CONDUCTORS

Unlike a non-conductor, a conductor is a material through which electric current can move easily. Metals are usually good conductors, including precious ones like gold and silver. But water and the human body can also conduct electricity.

RADIO AND TELEVISION

Radio and television are collective inventions. From the discovery of electromagnetic waves to the construction of wireless communication devices, they have made numerous strides. Radio and television are part of the daily life of a large part of the world's population. They laid the foundation of true mass communication.

In 1909, Guglielmo Marconi, barely 35 years old, was the first Italian to receive the Nobel Prize in physics.

What are radio waves?

Radio waves are electromagnetic waves with frequencies between 9 and 300 GHz, and wavelengths between 0.004 inch and 20 miles. They were discovered by Heinrich Hertz, and are therefore called "Hertzian waves." Also, the unit of measure of these waves' frequency is the hertz.

The first radio messages were sent by the military. Not long afterward, civilian broadcasting appeared.

Who sent the first radio message?

At the beginning of the 20th century, the Italian Guglielmo Marconi developed a system of wireless telegraphy that can be considered the ancestor of television, radio, and cellular phones. For the first time, electromagnetic waves could be used to transmit information.

LCD-screen television

Liquid-crystal screen (LCD)

How does a television work?

A television transmission uses radio waves which it transforms into electric signals. Some of these signals go to the loudspeakers as sound, and others go to the screen as images. The basic element of the television was the cathode-ray tube. This has gradually been replaced by liquid-crystal screens, which are flatter and more attractive.

The engineer John Baird, one of the pioneers of color television

DID YOU KNOW?

Morse telegraph

THE MORSE CODE
The Morse code or Morse alphabet is a system that allows transmission of text by means of short and long impulses. A unique combination of intermittent signals is assigned to each letter, number, and punctuation sign. It was developed by Alfred Vail and Samuel Morse in 1835.

RADIO BROADCASTING
The first public broadcast of voices and music occurred on December 24th, 1906. We owe this to the Canadian inventor Reginald Fessenden, who broadcast from Brant Rock, a town in Massachusetts.

TELEVISION STUDIOS
Modern television studios contain powerful lights, a variety of cameras, movable sets, and technicians with distinct functions (special effects, video, sound, etc.). A control and recording room coordinates all the operations.

COMPUTERS

The computer is a sophisticated electronic apparatus that can receive and execute instructions. It is used to perform calculations or to handle different kinds of information. There are computers for every need: large banking transactions, instruction, scientific research. They are also used for entertainment. Today, more and more households rely on a computer.

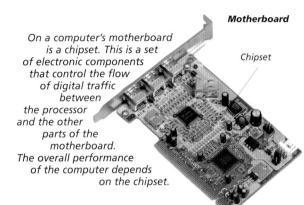

Motherboard

On a computer's motherboard is a chipset. This is a set of electronic components that control the flow of digital traffic between the processor and the other parts of the motherboard. The overall performance of the computer depends on the chipset.

Chipset

How does a computer work?

The operation of a computer may be summarized as a continual back-and-forth exchange of signals between a central unit (or tower) and other components (keyboard, CD player, etc.). The electrical signals move very rapidly around the circuits.
They activate or de-activate the lines of command that execute the instructions for carrying out an almost infinite number of operations.

The gigantic ENIAC, the first completely electronic computer (1946), which was programmed to solve all mathematical problems. Today, computers play a fundamental role in all areas of scientific research, especially in medicine.

What is a motherboard?

The motherboard is an electronic circuit that brings together all the elements of the computer. It is located in the main unit. Its principal components are: the processor (the computer's brain); the RAM (the memory); and the BIOS (which holds the information necessary for the computer to function). Also, graphics cards, audio cards, and network interface cards are connected to the motherboard.

Who invented the computer?

The principle of the computer was developed by the English. The first ones were calculators intended to aid scientists. During the Second World War, they made it possible to intercept and interpret the enemy's coded messages. Little by little, these machines have been perfected, offering much more than the ability to solve simple calculations. So the term "calculator" was dropped in favor of "computer."

The first portable computer was built in 1981. It weighed 24 lbs!

A mainframe is a computer designed for the highest performance.

DID YOU KNOW?

THE INTERNET
First conceived in the American Defense Department in the 1960s, the project of a universal network was finally applied to the civilian sphere in the 1990s. Today it connects hundreds of millions of computers.

ROBOTS
Robots are machines that can carry out precise tasks if they are correctly programmed. Some can disarm explosive devices, and others perform automated industrial functions.

BILL GATES
Bill Gates is the co-founder of Microsoft, the corporation that is the leading manufacturer of computer hardware and software. It is estimated that 90% of the software market is currently owned by this corporation.

SPACE OBSERVATION

The science of observing the heavens is called astronomy. This was probably one of the first natural sciences to appear, well before antiquity. At first, astronomy and astrology were connected, since the stars were considered gods. It was not until the 7th century BC, with the emergence of Greek civilization, that astronomy became a science in its own right.

How does a telescope work?

The optical telescope takes in visible light emitted by stars or reflected from the planets, by means of a system of lenses and mirrors. It makes the light converge on a point called the focus, where a viewing apparatus conveys the image to the observer.

Traditional reflecting telescopes are used to observe the planets in the solar system.

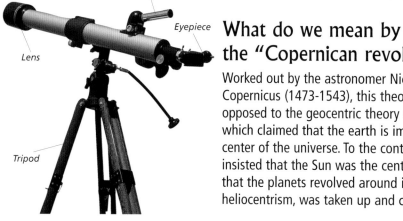

Observatory cupola · Principal mirror · Opening for observation

Telescope

Terrestrial telescope

Finder · Eyepiece · Lens · Tripod

Unlike the traditional telescopes, which capture visible light, the radiotelescope captures the radioelectric waves from heavenly bodies.

What is Hubble?

Hubble is a space telescope, the only true orbiting observatory in operation. It was placed in orbit in 1990 at 612km above the earth. It provides astronomers with valuable information and high-quality images.

Space telescope in operation

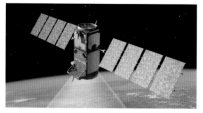

Space telescopes allow observations of the sky from above the earth's atmosphere, which distorts observations made from earth.

What do we mean by the "Copernican revolution"?

Worked out by the astronomer Nicolaus Copernicus (1473-1543), this theory was opposed to the geocentric theory of Ptolemy, which claimed that the earth is immobile and at the center of the universe. To the contrary, Copernicus insisted that the Sun was the center of the universe and that the planets revolved around it. This theory, called heliocentrism, was taken up and confirmed by Galileo.

DID YOU KNOW?

ARISTARCHOS OF SAMOS
Aristarchos of Samos, who lived in the 3rd century BC, was the first to develop the heliocentric theory. Unfortunately, his works were burned in the great fire at the library of Alexandria. We only know of his theories through other accounts.

JOHANNES KEPLER
Johannes Kepler (1571-1630) was a German astronomer famous for studying Copernicus's heliocentric theory. He discovered that the planets do not revolve around the Sun in perfect circles, but follow elliptical paths.

FIXED STARS
The expression "fixed stars" was formerly used to designate heavenly bodies that appeared to be motionless in the vault of the sky. It is not used today; it was invented to distinguish the stars from the planets, whose name came from the Greek "planetes" and meant "wandering stars."

THE CONQUEST OF SPACE

Man has always been fascinated by the idea of traveling in space. Since the end of the Second World War, space exploration has had an exceptional and very rapid development. From the first Soviet missions to probes and satellites to space shuttles, this exploration has gone through many stages. And it is not over yet!

Photograph of Yuri Gagarin in his helmet and space suit

What is the space shuttle?

The space shuttle is a vehicle that can make repeated trips into space. "Space shuttle" was also the name of the first such vehicle to travel into space. Built by the Americans, it was launched on April 12th, 1981. It is mainly used to put satellites into orbit, to repair them, and to bring back objects to earth. It was also involved in the construction of the International Space Station.

Exploded view of the space shuttle

Rudder
Vertical fin
Main engines
Remote-controlled manipulator arm
Scientific instruments
Tank
Wing
Control cabin
Nose
Stabilization motor

Who was the first astronaut to fly in space?

The first man to fly in space was the Soviet Yuri Gagarin. On April 12th, 1961, aboard the capsule *Vostok 1*, he made a complete orbit around the earth, flying at an altitude of 187 miles and a speed of 17,025 miles per hour. The flight lasted a total of 108 minutes.

What are space probes used for?

Space probes are unmanned vehicles sent by man into space to explore it. They travel for many years and are intended to send back to earth data, photographs, and measurements concerning the stars, planets, and other heavenly bodies.

Buzz Aldrin on the lunar surface

Who was the first man to walk on the Moon?

The first astronaut to walk on the Moon's surface was Neil Armstrong, commander of the American mission *Apollo 11*. He and his crew landed on the Moon on July 21st, 1969.

Picture taken from a space shuttle

DID YOU KNOW?

LAIKA, THE LITTLE DOG
Laika was the name of the little dog who, on November 3rd, 1957, left earth aboard the space capsule *Sputnik 2*. She was the first known living being to be put into orbit around the earth. Some countries have issued stamps in her honor.

THE COMPETITION BETWEEN THE USA AND THE USSR
The tensions of the Cold War produced a frantic race for the conquest of space. The first missions came from the Soviets: they launched the first man into space. The Americans responded with the Apollo missions.

ABSENCE OF GRAVITY
A vehicle in orbit has escaped the force of gravity. Being weightless, everything inside it – including astronauts – begins to float. Everyone goes into space has to get used to this strange environment!

THE HUMAN BODY

THE SKELETON

The skeleton is the solid structure that supports our body and allows us to stand upright. Many muscles are attached to the bones; this is how we are able to move, walk, and run. Also, the skeleton protects the most fragile organs: the brain, the heart, and the lungs.

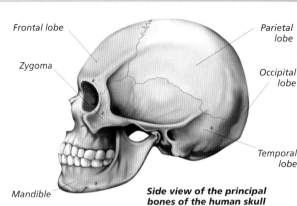

Side view of the principal bones of the human skull

Frontal lobe — Parietal lobe — Zygoma — Occipital lobe — Temporal lobe — Mandible

How many bones are there in our bodies?

When we are grown, there are 206, but when we are born, we have more than 300! In fact, the skeleton of a new-born baby is mostly made of rather soft cartilage; later on, as he grows, his bones harden and some of them grow together.

Internal structure of a bone

Periosteum — Spongy tissue — Marrow

What is bone composed of?

Made of calcium, a bone is composed of a solid, fibrous membrane called the periosteum. This is where the muscles, ligaments, and tendons are attached. Long bones are hollow and contain yellow marrow; flat bones are more spongy and contain red marrow, which manufactures blood cells.

Principal bones of the human body

Skull — Spinal column — Ribs — Pelvis — Humerus — Radius — Femur — Patella — Fibula — Tibia

What is the cranium?

This is the bony compartment that protects our brain, called the encephalon. It is made up of many bones, of which the occipital bone is joined to the first vertebra – the atlas – of our spinal column.

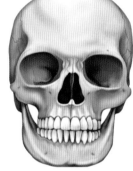

Skull, frontal view

Head of femur

The top of the femur is joined to the pelvis.

How large is a bone?

It varies a lot. The thigh-bone, or femur, is the longest bone in our body. By contrast, some other bones are quite small. This is why we have more than 200 altogether. The smallest bones are inside the ear: the stirrup (no bigger than a grain of rice), the anvil, and the hammer.

DID YOU KNOW?

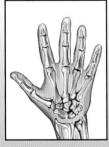

THE JOINTS
These are the connections between the bones that allow us to move (legs, arms, hands, head, etc.). For instance, the thumb is jointed in such a way that it can be bent in three different directions.

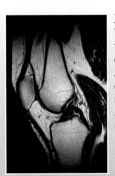

X-RAYS
These rays make it possible to take a "photograph" of the inside of the body. As they pass through our body, the X-rays are more or less absorbed, allowing us to take a picture of our bones and organs.

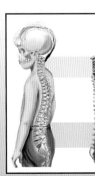

THE SPINAL COLUMN
Made of bone and cartilage, this is the structure which supports the human body and protects the spinal cord. It is made up of vertebrae, short bones stacked on top of each other and connected by ligaments. Between each pair of vertebrae is a cartilaginous disc.

MUSCLES AND JOINTS

The human body has about 650 muscles. Controlled by our nervous system, they contract and relax to let us move. Because of them, we can perform a great many movements.

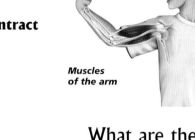

Muscles of the arm

How do the muscles work?

They are controlled by nerve impulses sent to them from the brain. All nerve impulses travel through the spinal column, which then distributes them to the muscles that we want to make work. We have three types of muscle: smooth, striated, and cardiac.

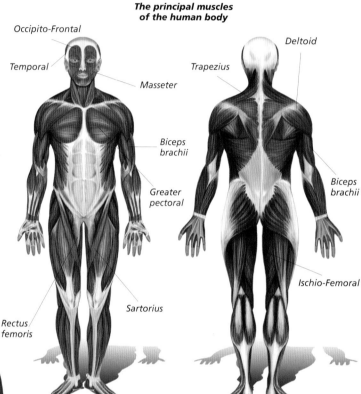

The principal muscles of the human body

Occipito-Frontal

Temporal

Masseter

Biceps brachii

Greater pectoral

Sartorius

Rectus femoris

Deltoid

Trapezius

Biceps brachii

Ischio-Femoral

What are the joints?

These are the parts that connect the ends of two bones, supported by ligaments. Some are more movable than others. For example, the joints in the skull hardly move at all; the joints of the spinal column have limited movement; and the joints of the elbow and knee have a very large range of movement.

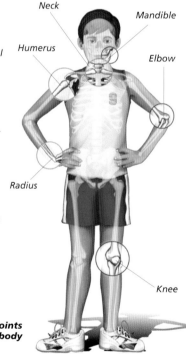

Neck

Mandible

Humerus

Elbow

Radius

Knee

Main joints of the human body

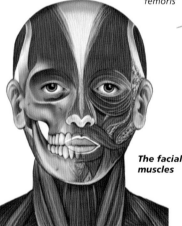

The facial muscles

Which are the muscles of the face?

There are two kinds. The facial muscles change our expressions, and the skeletal muscles are attached to the bones to allow them to move.

DID YOU KNOW?

THE DIFFERENT KINDS OF MUSCLES

Smooth muscle

Striated muscle

The striated or skeletal muscles are attached to the bones by tendons, making possible the movements of the body; they are controlled by our nervous system. The smooth muscles are located in the walls of our internal organs (intestines, stomach, etc.), and are called involuntary because we can't control their movements. Then there is the cardiac (heart) muscle, or myocardium, which is also an involuntary muscle although it is of the striated type!

TENDONS

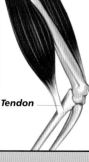

Tendon

These are fibrous tissues that join the muscles to the bones. White in color, they are covered by a protective sheath. The best-known tendon is the Achilles tendon, which connects the calf muscles to the ankle. It is very fragile, and if it breaks, you cannot walk anymore!

SPORTS

Taking care of your body is important, not just to look good, but because your muscles need it. Without physical exercise, the muscles atrophy (get smaller), and in the long run, every effort becomes difficult. By contracting and stretching our muscles on a regular basis, sports help us to stay in top form!

THE NERVOUS SYSTEM

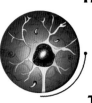

This consists of a network of nerve cells, the neurons, which carry information all over the body; the neurons send messages from one part of the body to another by means of electrical signals. The central nervous system consists of the brain and the spinal cord. The peripheral system is made up of nerves.

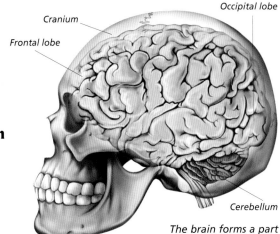

Cranium
Frontal lobe
Occipital lobe
Cerebellum

The brain forms a part of the central nervous system.

What is the cerebellum?

This is a part of the brain, located at the rear of the skull. With two lobes and a central part called the cerebellar vermis, the cerebellum lets us coordinate all the movements of our body!

Thanks to the cerebellum, we can keep our balance, i.e., walk without falling!

What is the spinal cord?

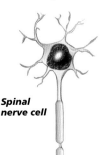

Spinal nerve cell

This is the means of communication between the brain and the peripheral nervous system. It passes through the 33 bones of the spinal column, which protect it. As they connect, the nerve cells transmit messages to perform movement that you have ordered in your brain!

Brain
Radial nerve
Medial nerve
Femoral nerve
Tibial nerve
Digital nerve

The nervous system

How does the brain function?

The brain is the most complex organ in the entire human body. It is located deep inside the cranium and is made up of about 100 billion neurons. Its function is to coordinate vital activities and to process our thoughts. The cerebral cortex manages everything, with three functions: sensory, motor, and associative. The sensory cortex receives signals brought to it by the nerves; the motor function orders the muscles to work; and the associative function coordinates different sensations and movements to place them in memory.

Nerve cell

The peripheral system passes along neural messages by way of the ligaments and tendons.

What does a nerve cell do?

It receives, and passes along to other cells, information about our body. For example, if you burn yourself, the nerve cells transmit a message of pain along the spinal cord to the brain. Then the brain – again, through the nervous system – orders you to pull your hand quickly away from the heat source.

DID YOU KNOW?

MEMORY
Memory is our ability to recall facts and experiences from the past. It is essential to our lives, since even the simplest actions, like riding a bicycle or preparing breakfast, require a certain kind of memory, called "procedural."

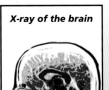

X-ray of the brain

THE CEREBRAL HEMISPHERES
The brain consists of two hemispheres. The right-hand one enables us to orient ourselves in space and to create (draw a picture, play music, etc.). The left-hand hemisphere is concerned with language, mathematics, and logic.

REFLEXES
These are rapid nervous reactions that we cannot control because they are mechanical. When you go to the doctor, your reflexes are tested to make certain your neurophysiologic system is operating correctly.

BLOOD CIRCULATION

It is fundamental for our bodies: our muscles, our organs, our skin, etc. have to be constantly irrigated by oxygenated blood coming from our lungs. It is estimated that the blood travels through the entire body in 30 seconds.

Arteries and veins

The heart pumps about 100 hl of blood every day.

Superior vena cava

Aorta

Pulmonary artery

What are the blood vessels?

These are the tube-shaped channels through with the blood travels. The ones leading away from the heart are called – depending on their size – arteries or arterioles; the ones leading toward the heart are called veins or veinules. The blood, oxygenated by the lungs, passes through the arteries to the heart and irrigates all organic tissues. Then the blood, loaded with toxins and carbon dioxide, makes a return trip through the veins and enters the lungs.
If you straightened out all the blood vessels in the body, they would measure about 62,137 miles long, or more than twice the circumference of the earth, and that is to carry an average of 5 litres of blood!

The blood's circulatory system, whose motor is the heart

Pulmonary artery

Carotid artery

Subclavial artery

Inferior vena cava

Femoral artery

▬▬▬ **Arteries**

▬▬▬ **Veins**

Plantar artery

Red blood cells

Is the heart a muscle?

Yes, it is an autonomous (or involuntary) muscle which does not need to receive orders from the brain. It acts as a pump. One side brings the blood, loaded with carbon dioxide, to the lungs; the other side receives the oxygenated blood through the arteries, and distributes it to all parts of our bodies.

Why is blood red?

Blood is composed of plasma, platelets, white cells, and red cells. The red cells contain hemoglobin, a protein with a large amount of iron, which has a red color; this is where the distinctive color of our blood comes from!

DID YOU KNOW?

THE CAPILLARIES
These are little arteries and veins, as thin as a hair. They make possible the exchange of oxygen and carbon dioxide between the blood and the cells.

THE AMOUNT OF BLOOD
In an adult in good health and of average height, the amount of blood is about 5L. The area of medicine devoted to blood diseases is called hematology.

Adult   *Child*

INJURIES
When you cut yourself, the blood coagulates and forms a clot, which allows the cut to form a scab. The lost blood cells are replaced by others, and a hard crust forms over the wound.

THE RESPIRATORY SYSTEM

Alveoli

In order to live, we need to breathe to supply our blood with oxygen. As soon as we have used it for our bodies, we breathe it out in the form of carbon dioxide. We can breathe because of our lungs.

Each lung is lined with a fine membrane (the pleura) and tiny alveoli.

The trachea is divided into two parts, called the bronchi.

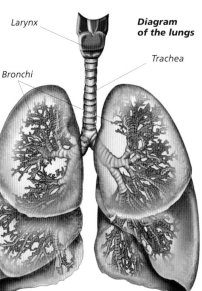

Larynx

Diagram of the lungs

Trachea

Bronchi

What is the respiratory apparatus for?

It allows our organism to oxygenate the blood and eliminate carbon dioxide. It consists of the lungs and the respiratory passages, but also the throat and the sinuses.

Air

Mouth

Route of air passing through our organism

Lung

How does the air travel when we breathe?

We breathe in air through the nose or the mouth. It passes down the trachea, and then into two powerful spongy organs in the interior of the thorax: the lungs. This is where the exchange of gases with the blood takes place. The blood distributes oxygen all throughout our bodies.

Diaphragm

When we breathe, the lungs contract and then expand.

Inspiration

Expiration

Illustration of the two phases of respiration

What are the stages of respiration?

Respiration occurs in two phases: inspiration (entry of air into the lungs) and expiration (expulsion of carbon dioxide). When you inhale, the diaphragm – a muscle inside the thorax – tightens to let air in. Then, during expiration, it relaxes in order to expel it.

What is a pulmonary alveolus?

Inside the lungs are the bronchi, which branch out into fine little tubes called the bronchioles. The bronchioles end in little sacs called alveoli. It is in the alveoli, which are supplied with a great many blood vessels, that the exchange of gases with the blood actually takes place.

DID YOU KNOW?

COUGHING AND SNEEZING

This involves rapidly expelling air from the lungs. You cough because of a reflex following irritation of the mucous membranes of your air passages. Coughing is above all a defense mechanism. When we sneeze, the speed of the air we expel through our nose and mouth can be as much as 95 to 125 mph!

HICCUPS

These are repeated involuntary contractions of the diaphragm. The sound "hic!" is caused by the rapid closing of the epiglottis – a sort of valve located in the larynx, that separates the trachea (the tube through which the air passes) from the oesophagus (the tube down which our food slides).

SNORING

This is noisy breathing caused by difficulty in air passing through the mouth: the vibration of the soft tissues creates the snoring. The relaxation of mouth and throat muscles during sleep makes the passage of air more difficult.

THE FIVE SENSES

These are the faculties that let us perceive the world around us. For instance, if we enjoy eating a fruit, or feel disgust when there is a bad smell, it is because of our senses. We have five of them: sight, hearing, smell, touch, and taste.

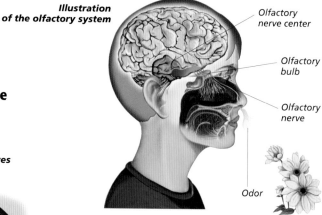

Illustration of the olfactory system

Olfactory nerve center

Olfactory bulb

Olfactory nerve

Odor

What are taste buds?

These are tiny rough receptors located on the tongue. Connected to the brain by nerves, they carry messages about the food and drink we ingest. Each part of the tongue picks up a particular taste: the tip senses sweetness; the bottom, bitterness; and the sides, salt and sour.

What is the sense of touch?

This is the sense that lets us feel heat, cold, or the textures of objects that touch our skin. The skin has nerve endings that act as receptors. So when you stroke an animal you can feel its softness, but when you bump yourself you feel pain.

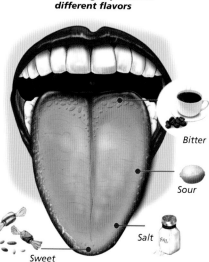

How the tongue perceives different flavors

Bitter

Sour

Salt

Sweet

How do you notice smells?

By means of the olfactory cells, located in the nasal sinuses. They play the part of receptors: molecules of scent circulating in the air attach themselves to the cells, and the information, transmitted by the olfactory nerve, is perceived by the brain as a smell. A human being can sense more than 10,000 different smells.

What is hearing?

This sense allows us to hear. Sounds are captured by the ear in the form of vibrations. Converted into nerve impulses, the vibrations are interpreted by the brain, which recognizes them as sounds.

Cross-section of eyeball

Iris

Pupil

Blood vessel

Retina

Vitreous body

Lens

Cornea

How do our eyes work?

A little like a camera. When you look at an object, its image is projected on your retinas in the form of signals. These signals are carried by the optic nerve to the brain, where the information is processed.

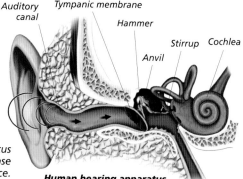

Auditory canal

Tympanic membrane

Hammer

Anvil

Stirrup

Cochlea

The hearing apparatus also controls our sense of balance.

Human hearing apparatus

DID YOU KNOW?

DECIBELS
These are the units (db) by which we measure the intensity of sound. Above 100 db, sound or noise can cause serious injury to the ear.

TEARS
This is a liquid continually produced by the lachrymal glands of the eye. It helps us to get rid of impurities and wet the cornea (the membrane that protects the eye).

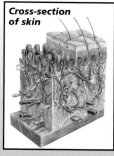

Cross-section of skin

THE SKIN
This is a protective envelope that covers the surface of our bodies. It has a great many nerve endings that give us our sense of touch. The skin also protects the internal tissues from physical attack, as well as attacks by chemicals and microbes.

NUTRITION

Every living being, humans included, has to eat and drink. Our organism needs vitamins, proteins, slow sugars (complex carbohydrates), and rapid sugars (simple carbohydrates). Humans are omnivores, meaning that we can eat both meat and vegetables; that is why our food is so varied.

Healthy eating and athletics allow our muscles and organs to function properly.

What does nutrition give us?

Energy! When you eat, the food is transformed into nutriments that make our cells and organs function properly. Good nutrition – eating a balanced diet – is important, because our good health depends on it.

Drinking water is also very important for our bodies!

Is water important for our bodies?

Yes! The human body consists almost 70% of liquid, and you lose more than 2.5 liters each day through sweating and urination. So it is important to drink water (rich in mineral salts) instead of over-sweetened soda; but it is not necessary to drink 2.5 liters to re-hydrate, since the vegetables we eat every day also contain water!

Foods have been classed in 7 main groups by nutritionists.

What is the nutritional pyramid?

It is a pyramid that many nutritionists use to show how to eat healthily. At the bottom are the body's most important foods, which we should eat every day. The higher up the pyramid you go, the more you should limit your consumption. Every day, you should eat grains, fruits, green vegetables, and dairy products. On the other hand, you should not eat fish, meat, or eggs more than once per day, especially if you are an adult. Fatty and sugary foods should be eaten in moderation.

How many nutritional groups are there?

There are seven (see illustration opposite), each of which supplies the body with specific nutriments: 1. meat, fish, eggs; 2. dairy products; 3. grains and complex carbohydrates; 4. simple carbohydrates; 5. fats; 6. green vegetables; 7. fruits.

DID YOU KNOW?

PROTEINS
Supplied mainly by fish, meat, eggs, and certain grains, proteins are essential to our bodies, especially children's. They make it possible for our cells to reproduce, and to multiply so that the body can grow.

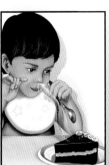

CARBOHYDRATES
These are the sugars that give us energy. At the same time, we should not consume too many of them because that can cause illnesses in the long run. There are different kinds: rapid or simple sugars (cake, soda, candy) and slow or complex sugars (pasta, rice, potatoes).

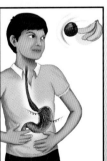

VITAMINS
Even though they are only present in our bodies in minute amounts, vitamins are indispensable to us because they protect us against viruses, bacteria, and toxins. Made up of simple molecules, they are easy to assimilate.

THE DIGESTIVE SYSTEM

This is the group of organs that carry out digestion. Through this process, the foods we eat are assimilated to nourish us in the form of proteins, carbohydrates, vitamins, etc. After these foods have passed through our digestive system, the residue is eliminated through the anus as excrement.

Intestinal folds (flexures)

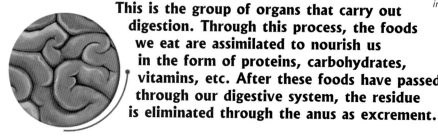

Ascending colon

Transverse colon

Small intestine

Descending colon

Rectum

Anus

The small intestine is a long flexible tube that could be more than 13 feet long if stretched out!

Where does digestion begin?

In the mouth. The very first stage in breaking down food is mastication: the teeth, the movements of the mouth, the tongue, and the saliva soften and grind it. A salivary enzyme, ptyalin, converts starches into maltose, a simple sugar. Then the food is swallowed, passing through the pharynx and down the oesophagus.

Buccal cavity

Pharynx

Oesophagus

Liver

Biliary duct

Stomach

Small intestine

Colon

The long tube from the mouth to the anus is called the digestive tract.

Anal canal

What is gastric digestion?

The stomach is an organ of the digestive tract, made of many muscular fibers that contract and expand to mix the food with the gastric juices. At the end of this process (which can last from a half-hour to seven hours, depending on what we have eaten), the food has been transformed into a whitish pulp called chyme. The chyme passes through the pylorus and arrives at the intestine.

What happens in the intestine?

In the small intestine (which is divided into the duodenum, the jejunum, and the ileum), bile and pancreatic juices convert the chyme into nutritive substances. The large intestine takes in the undigested waste materials, from which it absorbs water. The waste then accumulates in the rectum before it is expelled through the anus.

DID YOU KNOW?

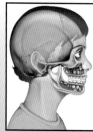

THE TEETH
As children, we have 20 baby teeth, but as the jaw grows, they are replaced by 32 permanent teeth. Each type of tooth has a specific function: the incisors and the canine teeth in the front of the mouth cut the food into small pieces so that the molars can grind it up.

THE EPIGLOTTIS
This is a thin, cartilaginous, elastic strip situated above the larynx. By closing when you swallow, it ensures that food and saliva go down the oesophagus and not down the trachea.

VOMITING
This is a natural reaction by which we eject noxious substances from the stomach. Vomiting can be caused by eating too much or by ingesting spoiled food.

CELLS AND DNA

The cell is the fundamental unit of all living things; it can function as an autonomous being. Inside it are chromosomes made of DNA (deoxyribonucleic acid), which provides information about every individual's genes.

Criminologists use DNA testing to catch people who have committed crimes.

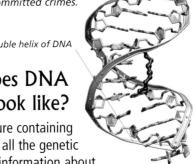

Double helix of DNA

What is a cell?

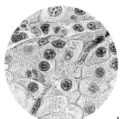

Group of cells

It is the structure underlying every living being. Cells are everywhere in our bodies: tissues, blood, organs, etc. The scientist Robert Hooke discovered them in 1665 while studying cork; he noted a regular structure consisting of tiny cells.

What does DNA look like?

It is a structure containing all the genetic information about an organism: what species it is, whether it is a mammal, whether it is human (for example), and whether it is male or female. The Englishman H.C. Crick and the American J.D. Watson discovered in 1953 that DNA was in the form of a double helix. Their work won them the Nobel Prize for physiology or medicine in 1962.

What is a vaccine?

It is a preparation of microbes (germs) that can cause disease. However, when it is injected into our bodies, it makes it possible for our cells to manufacture antibodies to fight the infection. So we run little risk of catching a disease if we have been inoculated with a strong enough vaccine.

The electron microscope was invented in 1931.

All the organs of the human body are composed of cells.

Why is genetics important?

Discovered in the 19th century as a result of experiments done on peas by the biologist Gregor Mendel, genetics plays a fundamental role in our lives. It has many applications: since genes are transmitted from parents to children, one can recognize and connect all the members of a family. A hair or drop of blood found at the scene of a crime can often make it possible to catch the criminal; but most important of all, much research can be done on genetic diseases. In recent years, geneticists have been doing research on the stamen cells of plants in order to find treatments for human diseases that at present are still incurable.

DID YOU KNOW?

BACTERIAL CELLS
Bacteria are microscopic organisms that are found everywhere: in the air, on the ground, in water, in ice, in thermal springs, and even in yogurt! Some of them are harmless and even useful to man, but others can cause serious diseases.

CHROMOSOMES
The chromosome is an element composed of DNA and proteins which can be found in the cells of every plant, mushroom, animal, and human! The chromosome carries the genetic information that is transmitted from one generation to another. The chromosomal chart of a living being is unique, like fingerprints.

Fingerprint

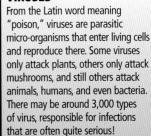

VIRUSES
From the Latin word meaning "poison," viruses are parasitic micro-organisms that enter living cells and reproduce there. Some viruses only attack plants, others only attack mushrooms, and still others attack animals, humans, and even bacteria. There may be around 3,000 types of virus, responsible for infections that are often quite serious!

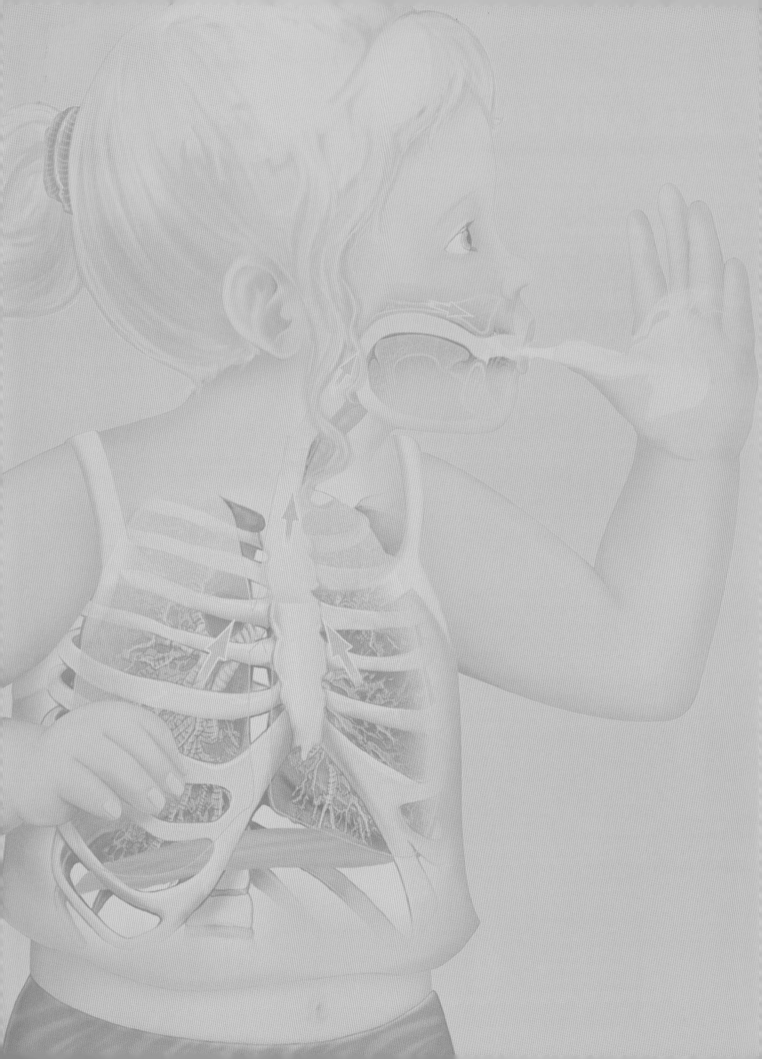

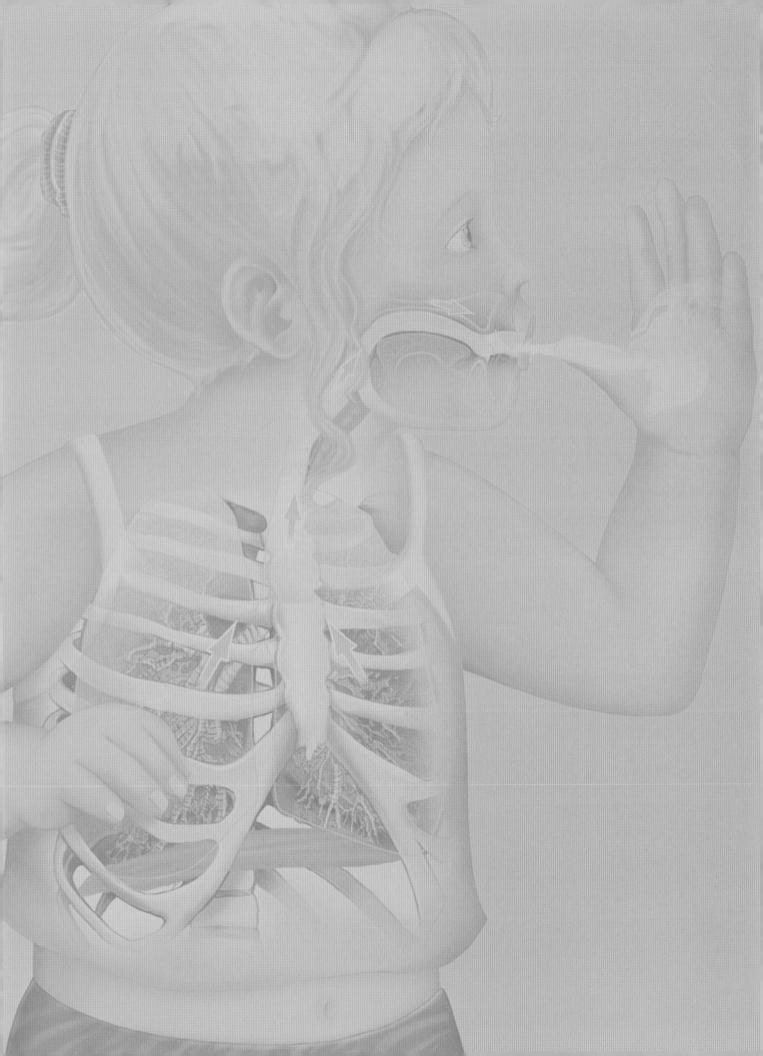

INDEX

INDEX